To: Scott , Sue
Happy New Yer 2021
from Dave +
Pauline

MORNINGS
with JESUS
2021

DAILY ENCOURAGEMENT *for Your* SOUL

 DEVOTIONS

SUSANNA FOTH AUGHTMON
JEANNIE BLACKMER
PAT BUTLER DYSON
GWEN FORD FAULKENBERRY
GRACE FOX
HEIDI GAUL
SHARON HINCK
PAMELA TOUSSAINT HOWARD
JEANETTE LEVELLIE
DIANNE NEAL MATTHEWS
CYNTHIA RUCHTI
ISABELLA YOSUICO

Guideposts
Danbury, Connecticut

ZONDERVAN
BOOKS

P9-DML-692

ZONDERVAN BOOKS

Mornings with Jesus 2021
Copyright © 2020 by Guideposts. All rights reserved.

Requests for information should be addressed to:
Zondervan, *3900 Sparks Dr. SE, Grand Rapids, Michigan 49546*

Zondervan titles may be purchased in bulk for educational, business, fundraising, or sales promotional use. For information, please email SpecialMarkets@Zondervan.com.

ISBN 978-0-310-35480-2 (softcover)
ISBN 978-0-310-35482-6 (ebook)

Acknowledgments: Every attempt has been made to credit the sources of copyrighted material used in this book. If any such acknowledgment has been inadvertently omitted or miscredited, receipt of such information would be appreciated.

Scripture quotations marked (AMP) are taken from the *Amplified Bible*. Copyright © 2015 by The Lockman Foundation, La Habra, California. All rights reserved. • Scripture quotations marked (CEB) are taken from the *Common English Bible*. Copyright © 2011 Common English Bible. • Scripture quotations marked (CEV) are taken from the *Contemporary English Version*. Copyright © 1991, 1992, 1995 by American Bible Society. Used by permission. • Scripture quotations marked (ERV) are taken from *Easy-to-Read Version Bible*. Copyright © 2006 by Bible League International. • Scripture quotations marked (ESV) are taken from the *Holy Bible, English Standard Version*. Copyright © 2001 by Crossway Bibles, a division of Good News Publishers. Used by permission. All rights reserved. • Scripture quotations marked (GNT) are taken from the *Holy Bible, Good News Translation*. Copyright © 1992 by American Bible Society. • Scripture quotations marked (GW) are taken from *GOD'S WORD Translation*. Copyright © 1995 by God's Word to the Nations. Used by permission of Baker Publishing Group. • Scripture quotations marked (HCSB) are taken from the *Holman Christian Standard Bible*. Copyright © 1999, 2000, 2002, 2003, 2009 by Holman Bible Publishers, Nashville, Tennessee. All rights reserved. • Scripture quotations marked (ICB) are taken from *The Holy Bible, International Children's Bible®*. Copyright © 1986, 1988, 1999, 2015 by Tommy Nelson™, a division of Thomas Nelson. Used by permission. • Scripture quotations marked (ISV) are taken from *The International Standard Version of the Bible*. Copyright © 1995-2014 by ISV Foundation. All rights reserved internationally. Used by permission of Davidson Press, LLC. • Scripture quotations marked (KJV) are taken from the *King James Version of the Bible*. • Scripture quotations marked (MSG) are taken from *The Message*. Copyright © 1993, 1994, 1995, 1996, 2000, 2001, 2002 by Eugene H. Peterson. • Scripture quotations marked (NASB) are taken from the *New American Standard Bible*. Copyright © 1960, 1962, 1963, 1968, 1971, 1972, 1973, 1975, 1977, 1995 by the Lockman Foundation. Used by permission. www.Lockman.org • Scripture quotations marked (NCV) are taken from *The Holy Bible, New Century Version*. Copyright © 2005 by Thomas Nelson. • Scripture quotations marked (NIV) are taken from *The Holy Bible, New International Version*. Copyright © 1973, 1978, 1984, 2011 by Biblica, Inc. Used by permission of Zondervan. All rights reserved worldwide. www.Zondervan.com • Scripture quotations marked (NKJV) are taken from *The Holy Bible, New King James Version*. Copyright © 1982 by Thomas Nelson. • Scripture quotations marked (NLT) are from the *Holy Bible, New Living Translation*. Copyright © 1996, 2004, 2007 by Tyndale House Foundation. Used by permission of Tyndale House Publishers Inc., Carol Stream, Illinois. All rights reserved. • Scripture quotations marked (NRSV) are taken from the *New Revised Standard Version Bible*. Copyright © 1989 by the Division of Christian Education of the National Council of the Churches of Christ in the United States of America. Used by permission. All rights reserved. • Scripture quotations marked (RSV) are taken from the *Revised Standard Version of the Bible*. Copyright © 1946, 1952, 1971 by the Division of Christian Education of the National Council of the Churches of Christ in the United States of America. Used by permission. • Scripture quotations marked (TLB) are taken from *The Living Bible*. Copyright © 1971 by Tyndale House Publishers, Inc., Carol Stream, Illinois. All rights reserved. • Scripture quotations marked (TPT) are taken from *The Passion Translation®*. Copyright © 2017 by BroadStreet Publishing® Group, LLC. Used by permission. All rights reversed.

Any internet addresses (websites, blogs, etc.) and telephone numbers in this book are offered as a resource. They are not intended to be or imply an endorsement by Zondervan, nor does Zondervan vouch for the content of these sites and numbers for the life of this book.

Cover and interior design by Müllerhaus
Cover photo by Shutterstock
Monthly page opener photos by Pixabay
Indexed by Kelly White
Typeset by Aptara, Inc.

Printed in the United States of America

20 21 22 23 24 25 26 27 28 29 30 31 32 /LSC/ 20 19 18 17 16 15 14 13 12 11 10 9 8 7 6 5 4 3 2 1

Dear Friends,

Welcome to *Mornings with Jesus 2021*! In 365 new devotions, twelve women of faith share stories and experiences from their daily walks with Jesus. In John 15:11, Jesus said, "These things I have spoken to you, that My joy may remain in you, and that your joy may be full" (NKJV). As you read the daily Scripture and narrative and contemplate the "Faith Step," we pray that you will be filled with the love and joy that comes from spending time with Him.

Each new morning presents a fresh opportunity to spend time with Jesus by reading His Word and discovering His joy—not just any joy but the "full joy" that is found only in Him. In life, we face challenges, sorrows, and hardships, but as we move forward day by day, we can find joy in a myriad of ways as we open our hearts and follow Jesus.

Many cherished *Mornings with Jesus* writers return in 2021's edition. Grace Fox updates us on life at home in the marina and kicks off the New Year by sharing what happens when she gives Jesus control of her calendar. Susanna Foth Aughtmon points out the "joy stealers" in her life (and maybe yours too) and spreads holiday cheer in Advent and Christmas devotions. Gwen Ford Faulkenberry guides us through Holy Week. Heidi Gaul continues to delight us with her childlike wonder. Sharon Hinck, who finds herself now in a caregiving role, inspires us to look at life through the eyes of the Savior, making each moment precious. Isabella Yosuico reflects on the benefits and blessings of resting in Jesus. Dianne Neal Matthews recounts treasured family memories, reminding us there are always reasons to rejoice in the Lord. Cynthia Ruchti writes with her signature gusto, determined to find the joy of Jesus, whether it is in the midst of a blackout, a spiritual reckoning, or a home renovation! Four new writers, Jeannie Blackmer, Pat Butler Dyson, Jeanette Levellie, and Pamela Toussaint Howard join the fold and invite us into their hearts and homes as they journey with Jesus.

It is our hope that *Mornings with Jesus 2021* will comfort and inspire you and provide a daily measure of joy as you draw closer to Jesus.

Faithfully yours,
Editors of Guideposts

P.S. We love hearing from you! Let us know what *Mornings with Jesus 2021* means to you by emailing BookEditors@guideposts .org or writing to Guideposts Books & Inspirational Media, 100 Reserve Road, Suite E200, Danbury 06810-5212. You can also keep up with your *Mornings with Jesus* friends on facebook.com /MorningswithJesus.

Especially for You!

Enjoy the daily encouragement of *Mornings with Jesus 2021* wherever you are! Receive each day's devotion on your computer, tablet, or smartphone. Visit MorningswithJesus.org/MWJ2021 and enter this code: joy. Sign up for the online newsletter *Mornings with Jesus* at Guideposts.org/newsletter-sign-up. Each week, you'll receive an inspiring devotion or personal thoughts from one of the writers about her own devotional time and prayer life and how focusing on Jesus influenced her relationship with Him!

New Year's Day, Friday, January 1

Your eyes saw my unformed body; all the days ordained for me were written in your book before one of them came to be. Psalm 139:16 (NIV)

AT THE START OF EACH year, I ask Jesus to take control of my calendar. I also ask Him to fill in the blank dates to mesh with His purposes for me. This practice keeps me mindful of my role: I'm His servant, here to do His bidding. He alone knows what that looks like on a day-to-day basis. This also reduces my stress when the unexpected happens. If He's in charge, then there's no need to fret when plans change, right?

On one occasion, I'd experienced three difficult months due to medical reasons. Everything climaxed when I broke into shingles ten days before I was to speak at a women's retreat. Determined to fulfill my commitment despite the pain, I didn't mention my situation to the event planners. Five days before the retreat, they phoned me and canceled due to circumstances beyond their control. I've spoken at women's events for nearly two decades, and only two groups have canceled. This was one of those instances. When our call ended, I sensed Jesus remind me that I'd invited Him to rule my calendar, and He had ruled in favor of rest (Psalm 23:2).

On another occasion, I had a month with no scheduled commitments, which made me available to travel to Alberta to visit my mother and lend a hand for a week. A few days later, another family member experienced an emergency and needed me. The timing was perfect.

Inviting Jesus to take control of my calendar is one of the best practices I've begun doing. I can't imagine a better way to start the year. —GRACE FOX

FAITH STEP: *Invite Jesus to fulfill His purposes for your life every day this year.*

SATURDAY, JANUARY 2

*See, I am doing a new thing! Now it springs up; do you not perceive it?
I am making a way in the wilderness and streams in the wasteland.*
Isaiah 43:19 (NIV)

YEARS AGO, I SAW A pastoral counselor for some painful, persistent issues. One day, she—a passionate Christian—announced excitedly, "Jesus gave me this verse for you," and recited the verse above. I was hungry for a new life but paralyzed by my past and unable to see the new possibilities unfolding before me. I promptly wrote down the verse to remind me that God is the Author of new things!

I've made many New Year's resolutions. Along with the familiar "lose a few pounds" or "stick to a budget," I've had many ambitious, worthy goals. I gleefully attained some big and small goals, though more often my goals were shelved shamefully by March or sooner.

I recently heard the expression, "Whatever we create in our own strength, we sustain in our own strength." It struck a chord. I've labored very hard for some goals, fighting against a strong current, and wondering if God was present in my struggles.

The Bible is full of ordinary people with God-given goals far beyond their human capacity, achievable only by God Himself: Nehemiah rebuilding the wall, Joshua and Gideon fighting formidable foes, and the apostles sharing the Gospel worldwide.

Now, as I seek Jesus's peaceful, gentle way, I look for the new thing He is already doing and aim to align myself with Him, the true Stream in the desert, and then behold with wonder what He does. Jesus makes all things new and His resolutions never fail.
—ISABELLA YOSUICO

FAITH STEP: *This New Year, resolve to draw near to Jesus and the newness He offers. Behold what He does!*

SUNDAY, JANUARY 3

But Jesus called the children to him and said, "Let the little children come to me, and do not hinder them, for the kingdom of God belongs to such as these. Truly I tell you, anyone who will not receive the kingdom of God like a little child will never enter it." Luke 18:16–17 (NIV)

I LOVE GAMES AND PUZZLES, so this morning I decided to complete a crossword. I hadn't done one in years. I poured some coffee and settled at the kitchen table to fill in the empty squares. Hmm…a four-letter word meaning "endnotes." I'd come back to that one. A ten-letter word describing "dinner-bell sequence." I couldn't even guess. At my house, I just say, "It's ready," and step aside. For an hour I deciphered definitions, even going through the alphabet letter by letter until I found the correct words. By the time all the squares were filled, the coffee pot was empty.

Sometimes my life seems like a puzzle, packed with senseless bits and pieces that don't appear to fit together. Solutions can shift from simple to complicated in an instant, leaving me confused and frustrated as I think, *Why has Jesus allowed this to happen to me?*

But I don't need to understand the "why" behind His choices—that's not what He's teaching me. Instead, I'm here to learn trust, with a capital T. My daily, childlike dependence on Jesus pleases Him. When things go well, I can offer thanks, and when they don't, I'll cling to Him in faith. I know He'll guide me until I finish this puzzle called Life.

But for now, what's a five-letter word for peace? *Jesus.* —HEIDI GAUL

FAITH STEP: *Find a word puzzle. As you work on the confusing parts, remember that when life confounds you, you can trust Jesus to guide you through. He's got you!*

MONDAY, JANUARY 4

---

*He replied, "Because you have so little faith. Truly I tell you,
if you have faith as small as a mustard seed, you can say to
this mountain, 'Move from here to there,' and it will move.
Nothing will be impossible for you." Matthew 17:20 (NIV)*

AFTER A STRESSFUL YEAR, MY husband and I planned for some time to regroup, pray, and seek Jesus for where to serve next. I envisioned several peaceful months of settling back into a routine. The very next week a family member was diagnosed with Alzheimer's.

As many people before us have discovered, this is a journey that is painful and is paved with appointments, research, and decisions. Most of all, my heart breaks as I see my loved one slipping away. Her confusion and frustration make me ache. I answer her same question a dozen times in a row, then hang up the phone and cry. It's been physically, mentally, and spiritually exhausting.

Today I was pondering the overwhelming obstacles that this diagnosis presents. Then I remembered that Jesus encourages us to pray for mountains to be moved. The mountain of phone calls, paperwork, and doctor appointments. A mountain of grief and sadness. For some of us, it is a mountain of illness, financial strain, broken relationships, loneliness, addiction, or a lack of direction. Whatever needs we have, Jesus can provide answers. When we remember how much bigger He is than those mountains, they begin to shrink before our eyes.

There are a thousand things that are hard about these mountains. But Jesus is the Lord of millions of blessings. He will outnumber the problems with His overwhelming grace and mercy.
—SHARON HINCK

FAITH STEP: *If you're facing a mountain, imagine it shrinking before our Savior.*

TUESDAY, JANUARY 5

This is the day the LORD has made; We will rejoice and be glad in it.
Psalm 118:24 (NKJV)

MY FRIEND CAROLE HAS EXPERIENCED significant losses. She and her husband went bankrupt. Then one of her daughters was killed by a drunk driver. A hurricane destroyed her home, and later cancer claimed her husband *and* son-in-law within a year.

Carole acknowledges these events and the pain they've caused her, but she refuses to cling to that pain. She realizes that doing so would only steep her in discouragement, and that's no way to live.

Carole is one of the most upbeat women I know. Her love for Jesus radiates from her face, and her words reflect the depth of her relationship with Him. She truly knows what it means to practice living in His presence.

When I visited her recently, Carole told me that her mother had always been an upbeat person too. "I learned it from her," Carole said. "Every morning when she woke up, she'd say, 'Good morning, Lord. What wonderful things do You have planned for us today?' That invited His presence and set the tone for her entire day. No matter what happened, she knew that He was sovereign."

Since my conversation with Carole, I've sought to practice the same ritual. I find that it sets my mind and heart in a place of eager anticipation. No matter what the day holds, Jesus holds me. I will rejoice and be glad in His presence, His power, and His promises.

What's the first thought that enters your mind when you wake up? If it's anxiety about the day, then retrain your thoughts to focus on Jesus through the simple prayer in today's Scripture verse.
—GRACE FOX

FAITH STEP: *Memorize Psalm 118:24. Thank Jesus for the gift of today.*

WEDNESDAY, JANUARY 6

Trust in him at all times, you people; pour out your hearts to him, for God is our refuge. Psalm 62:8 (NIV)

I OFTEN SAY THAT I'M about as transparent as plastic food wrap, and it's true—much to the dismay of my husband, who is reserved. But lately it seems that I've developed a tendency to hold back during prayer time. The heaviest burdens on my heart seem to be ones that I sometimes skirt around, lightly touch on, or even ignore. These are requests I've been praying about for years with no visible answer yet, or situations that seem so messy I just don't know where to start. I'm afraid my attitude reveals a cynicism and lack of faith.

I'm always touched by 1 Samuel 1 where Hannah was so caught up in her prayer about her childlessness that the priest accused her of being drunk. Hannah explained that she wasn't inebriated but was pouring out her heart to the Lord. In the New Testament, we see people pour out their hearts to Jesus about their blindness or infirmity or on behalf of their suffering child.

The Bible makes it clear that Jesus knows us better than we know ourselves. He knows our inner thoughts and motivations and what we will do and say. He also knows our need to unburden our hearts before Him. His Word encourages us to confess our sins, confide our deepest longings, and share what is troubling our minds. Jesus wants us to open up to Him, not because He needs to know what's going on but because *we* need the reminder that He is with us through it all. —DIANNE NEAL MATTHEWS

FAITH STEP: *Examine your prayer life to see if there's a problem troubling your spirit that you've been reluctant to discuss with Jesus. Demonstrate your trust in Him by pouring out your heart.*

THURSDAY, JANUARY 7

Come to me, all you who are weary and burdened, and I will give you rest. Matthew 11:28 (NIV)

LADIES FROM MY BIBLE STUDY introduced me to picking a theme word for the year. The subject came up several weeks into the year, but when I heard it, I knew right away what my word was. Before I could open my mouth, a wise and older mentor who knows me, said the word: *rest*. Yes! I knew the word was for me.

Jesus had been hammering that theme for a long time, but I just couldn't hear Him. Or maybe I heard Him, but I was *working* to rest. As in, I was reading everything I could about rest. I was making sure to rest. I was chastising myself when I failed to rest—and growing weary of trying so hard. Because that's what I do. But that's not what this verse has in mind.

Was it a coincidence that the theme word appeared just as I was pressed into rest by exhaustion? I was so tired I'd thrown up my hands in defeat and said emphatically, "I can't, Lord!"

Now, I'm enjoying a lot of genuine rest. Later in this passage, Jesus describes His rest: easy, light, gentle, humble. I'd add peaceful. It's not lazy rest but an internal sense of peaceful ease—going with the flow, so to speak.

I am sleeping in more, but I'm just really a lot more restful in my mind and actions. The results are amazing. Some of the things I'd been mentally and physically toiling over are falling into place and unfolding with ease. *I could really get used to resting in You, Jesus. Is this what you meant all along about giving us rest?* —ISABELLA YOSUICO

FAITH STEP: *Pick a problem you've been working on and apply this verse by stopping whatever you're doing. Let Jesus have it while you rest.*

FRIDAY, JANUARY 8

Many are the woes of the wicked, but the LORD's unfailing love surrounds the one who trusts in him. Psalm 32:10 (NIV)

I HAVE A THING FOR quilts. I love their cottony softness against my skin. My mom's avid quilting birthed this love in me. She has made each of her grandchildren a quilt of their own, from twenty-eight-year-old Alyson to three-year-old Lily. My youngest son, Addison, received his quilt this last year. He sat down with my mom earlier in the year, leafing through pattern books, and landed on a simple geometric design. He gave her a range of muted colors to work with, and three months later, the quilt was tucked around the foot of his bed. She made my sixteen-year-old son Will a quilt with bright beach colors—aqua, navy, and coral—reflecting his exuberant personality. Our cat, Toby, often snuggles among its folds. When I asked my eldest son, eighteen-year-old Jack, if he wanted to take his quilt to college, he said, "No, Mom. I don't want to take any chances of it getting ruined." Those quilts are precious, tactile symbols of my mom's painstaking care. My boys sleep sheltered in the knowledge that they are as unique and precious as the quilts that enfold them. Nestled beneath their colorful weight, my boys know they are deeply loved.

Jesus's compassion for us is even more precious than my boys' quilts. He weaves a tapestry of joy and hope around us as we are sheltered in His care. In the depths of our spirits, we can know that Jesus sees us as we are: unique, beautiful, and precious in His sight. He loves us completely. In His all-encompassing love, we find safety, peace, and rest. —SUSANNA FOTH AUGHTMON

FAITH STEP: *Do you believe that Jesus's love surrounds you completely? Take time to meditate on Psalm 32:10. Ask Jesus to reveal His great love for you.*

SATURDAY, JANUARY 9

*The King will reply, "Truly I tell you, whatever you did
for one of the least of these brothers and sisters of mine,
you did for me." Matthew 25:40 (NIV)*

THE WORDS "Mailed from a Correctional Institution" were stamped
boldly across the letter that read, "Dear Pat, Kitchenettes, Church,
and Pastor." The writer, a man I'll call Trevor, had enjoyed a
Guideposts article I'd written about women who call themselves the
Kitchenettes at Calder Baptist Church who prepare lunches for our
Lenten noonday services.

In three pages of meticulously handwritten words, Trevor told me
about himself—his family, the jobs he'd held, the courses he was
taking in prison, and his love for Jesus. References to Scripture were
generously sprinkled throughout, including my favorite, Jeremiah
29:11, which Trevor was holding onto because he believes God still
has a plan for his life. He spoke of regret for his mistakes, loneliness,
and a desire to receive mail from fellow believers outside the walls.

My heart went out to Trevor, but I hesitated about writing him.
He was a stranger. I had no idea what crime he'd committed. Would
he ask me for money? I heard Jesus whisper softly, *The least of these,
Pat.* Rereading Trevor's letter, I wondered how many of us reside in
our own prisons of loneliness and regret? Trevor's last line cinched
my decision: "Please, please, please, don't forget or judge me." He
signed it, "Love in Christ, Trevor."

Corresponding with Trevor would be an act of love, not only
toward Trevor but to Jesus. I'm planning to correspond with Trevor
and recruit others to do so too. —PAT BUTLER DYSON

FAITH STEP: *Write a letter to someone in prison and show Jesus's love.*

SUNDAY, JANUARY 10

For the joy set before him he endured the cross . . . Hebrews 12:2 (NIV)

IT WAS A TYPICAL SUNDAY morning at our church—except for one thing: two spaces down sat a man I hadn't seen in a long time. It's not that he hadn't wanted to worship with our church family, but he'd been incarcerated for seven years. This was his first Sunday of freedom.

I saw everything that morning through his eyes. The smiles and hugs and tears that greeted him, grateful of his return. The new prayers for him as he moved from serving Jesus behind bars to serving "at large." The way every lyric of the worship songs and every Scripture passage seemed divinely orchestrated to remind us of freedom in Christ and the power of the Holy Spirit to help us live day to day.

The joy on his face reflected what must have felt like finally drawing a deep breath after so long in the "grave" of his circumstances, and I couldn't help but consider the inexpressible joy of the moment when Jesus drew His first breath after His resurrection.

Suffocated by the weight of our sins, Jesus conquered death to breathe and worship anew. What was the reason for the joy on His face? Us. He'd successfully purchased our freedom and future. Within a short time, He'd return to the right hand of His Father. But before then, He had another assignment—showing Himself to His followers, even those who let doubts creep in.

He knew we earth dwellers would find our joy in His very presence. The plan worked. He gave up His life for ours and then breathed again. Imagine how loudly He sang on His first Sunday of freedom! —CYNTHIA RUCHTI

FAITH STEP: *What's your favorite "freedom" worship song? Sing it from your heart, as if you've been liberated just moments ago. That's the kind of joy worth maintaining every day.*

MONDAY, JANUARY 11

You know when I sit and when I rise; you perceive my thoughts from afar. You discern my going out and my lying down; you are familiar with all my ways. Psalm 139:2–3 (NIV)

OUR ONLY DAUGHTER, MARIE, DECIDED four years was long enough to work in retail. She enrolled in a program that helps women find new jobs. In her initial interview, she told the director, "I'd be happy to sit in a cubicle all day and enter data." Marie finds satisfaction in a job well done, even with little interaction with others.

I could never thrive in such a setting. I'd be standing by my cubicle wall fifteen times a day, chatting with my coworkers. If I go too long without talking to people, I become depressed. Give me a hectic store over a quiet cubicle any day.

When Jesus planned our personalities, He wired each of us uniquely. He made us all different, special, and precious. It must delight Him that no one—even identical twins—thinks and acts exactly alike.

Jesus relates personally to each of us. He rebuked His disciple Peter for His lack of faith, gently taught Martha, whose brother Lazarus had died, and forgave and corrected the woman caught in adultery. Every encounter was as unique as the individual to whom Jesus talked.

When I have a problem that seems unfixable, it comforts me to know my Lord has a custom-made solution. He never gives His children cookie-cutter answers. We each hold an exclusive place in His heart, and He loves us as individuals. We can be confident that when we pray, He will respond in the way we most need.
—JEANETTE LEVELLIE

FAITH STEP: *Ask Jesus to show you three unique qualities you possess and then thank Him for loving you just as you are.*

TUESDAY, JANUARY 12

Though you have not seen him, you love him; and even though you do not see him now, you believe in him and are filled with an inexpressible and glorious joy. 1 Peter 1:8 (NIV)

WE'RE WATCHING OUR YOUNGEST SON and his wife prepare for the arrival of their first child, our sixth grandchild. It's been eleven years since we've had a newborn in the family. Most days, I manage my exuberance fairly well. Somedays I can't. Like today. I found an infographic that listed more than a dozen ways to affirm and build confidence in your child without inadvertently building cockiness. One click, and the information was sent to my son and daughter-in-law.

As of this writing, I haven't seen their little girl yet, except in a grainy sonogram image. At this moment, my son and his wife are counting down the days until their baby's due to appear. But that doesn't stop me from staying just shy of giddy over the idea of holding that little one to my heart and whisper-singing "Jesus Loves Me" into her tiny little ears. The sight of newborn-sized sleepers makes me swoon, and when I pass the baby section in the store, I have to resist the urge to pop open the baby lotion and draw a deep whiff. *I love you, little girl. And I haven't even seen you yet.*

The joy is inexpressible. So, I have no trouble understanding the verse (1 Peter 1:8) saying that even though we haven't seen Jesus face to face yet, we feel inexpressible joy at the thought of Him, His nearness, the "movement" of His Spirit within, the certainty of His love, and the promise that we'll see Him face to face one day.

Even as an expectant Grammie, I can say there's no joy like Jesus.
—CYNTHIA RUCHTI

FAITH STEP: *Write a love letter to the Jesus whom you have yet to see. Express your current joy and your anticipation for what's ahead.*

WEDNESDAY, JANUARY 13

Remember His marvelous works which He has done, His wonders, and the judgments of His mouth. 1 Chronicles 16:12 (NKJV)

THERE ARE MANY ASPECTS OF technology that I enjoy: my laptop, smartphone, and DVR and the ability to stream music and FaceTime loved ones. But in some ways I'm old school. I have friends who have almost completely replaced paper with apps, calendars, and alerts on their phone or computer. Not me—I still use paper. I have a wall calendar hanging in the kitchen and a day planner sitting on my desk. My drawers contain small notebooks for jotting down products to research, DIY recipes that were successful, and other info, such as the last time I fertilized the houseplants. Periodically, I update my list of birthdays and addresses of family and friends. A magnetic pad on the memo board keeps a running grocery list. Each day I divide my to-do list into three parts: phone calls to make, emails to write, and tasks to get done. If I want to remember something, I write it down—on actual paper with a pen or pencil.

One day a thought struck me: *Why not write down things I want to remember about Jesus?* The Bible shares wonderful truths about Jesus and our relationship with Him. But sometimes I forget the exact truth I need to remember during trials, periods of loneliness, times of crisis, or just in the pressures of day-to-day living. So now I've started a to-remember list: Jesus loves me unconditionally. His Spirit lives inside me. He's promised to never leave me. He will work out every circumstance in my life for good. He's prepared a perfect, eternal home for me.

Simply reading the first few items is enough to brighten my day. —DIANNE NEAL MATTHEWS

FAITH STEP: *Keep a small notepad tucked inside your Bible. Each time you read a truth about Jesus that you need to remember, jot it down on your notepad.*

THURSDAY, JANUARY 14

Being found in appearance as a man, he humbled himself
by becoming obedient to death—even death on a cross!
Therefore God exalted him to the highest place and gave
him the name that is above every name. Philippians 2:8—9 (NIV)

MY FEATURES RESEMBLE MY LATE father, just as my daughter is my mini-me. Our full lips, smiles, and artistic natures mimic Dad's. I'm fascinated by how each of us, deep within our DNA, carry reflections of our forefathers. As I gather facts and photos of my family tree, I search for hints of bravery and humor in my ancestors' faces and hands and the way they stand or sit.

As I study Jesus's lineage, I again and again notice foretastes of His holy character. Don't Tamar's boldness and Rahab's cleverness point to their future descendant? There is David, alone in the fields, gathering his sheep. As he watched over them, he captured God's heart. Consider Jesus's closest physical tie to humanity: Mary, whose spirit defines humility and obedience. We see all those attributes in our Lord.

Researching my past has helped me understand who I am through who I was. It strengthens my sense of identity. But when I shut my laptop, none of those ancestors mean as much as the one whose name is above every other—Jesus. He represents my past, my present, and my future. Every attribute I glean from Him transforms me into something else, someone better.

It's Jesus I want to mirror. Can my words help heal a broken soul? Am I willing to serve others with obedience and humility?

When others look at me, I hope they see an unmistakable resemblance. Above all, I am of the family of God. —HEIDI GAUL

FAITH STEP: *Trace your family tree back a few generations. Do you see likenesses? Now find ways you resemble the individuals in Jesus's lineage.*

FRIDAY, JANUARY 15

Be sure of this: I am with you always, even to the end of the age.
Matthew 28:20 (NLT)

RECENTLY I BEGAN READING A funny novel about an awkward young female character, and early in the story, she mentions she had gone an entire weekend without speaking to a single human being. She asks herself, "I exist, don't I?" This was supposed to be funny, but it hit too close to home.

For the past few months, I've been fighting loneliness. As a writer, I spend a lot of time isolated. Because my husband travels and our children no longer live at home, the empty rooms, tidy floors, and squeaky-clean bathrooms make our home feel deserted. Also, many close friends have drifted in different directions. So, when I read those words, I panicked and thought, *That could be me.*

I used to look forward to solitary time, but now that I have lots of it, I dread it. I've found the ache of loneliness so intense that sometimes I'm immobilized and can even sink into self-pity. I know this is not Jesus's desire for me. He doesn't want me to stay stuck in a slump, feeling forgotten or believing no one cares.

So, during this season of isolation, I'm making a daily choice to spend time with Jesus and also reach out to friends. I put that novel back on the shelf to read in a less lonely season. I picked up my phone and made plans to meet a friend for lunch, then grabbed my Bible to spend time with Jesus because He is always there for me.
—JEANNIE BLACKMER

FAITH STEP: *Write Matthew 28:20 on a piece of paper and tape it on your mirror to remind you of His caring presence.*

SATURDAY, JANUARY 16

---

*If we are faithless, He remains faithful; He cannot deny
Himself. 2 Timothy 2:13 (NKJV)*

WITH THE PUBLICATION OF MY first book, I was invited to join an online group of professional women authors and speakers. Joining required a promise to work on developing the speaking side of my ministry. I attended one conference and met many wonderful women, but I soon stopped actively participating in the group. In 2015, my speaking went from little to none and my husband unexpectedly lost his job. It made sense to drop my membership. When I notified Linda, the group's founder, she responded that the speaking requirement had been lightened and reminded me that members don't have to requalify each year. She ended with saying, "I want to offer you a scholarship instead of accepting your resignation, okay?"

Over the next four years, I skipped paying the annual dues. I hardly ever thought about reading the group's email digest because I could only access that email account on my phone. Yet, the website still listed me as a member, along with my books and bio. Sometimes I felt guilty. I contributed nothing and never communicated with the group members. Then one day the thought hit me—*Linda has refused to let me go!* Within days, I paid my dues, had the group's digest switched to my primary email account, and felt excited about the potential fellowship and the blessing of belonging.

Once we belong to Jesus, we never need to requalify. He understands our weaknesses; He knows we will sometimes struggle with doubts, be rebellious or complacent, and even sin. During such times, we may hide and miss blessings and fellowship with Him, but Jesus always stays faithful to us. He simply will not let us go.
—DIANNE NEAL MATTHEWS

FAITH STEP: *What can you do today to renew your joy in belonging to Jesus?*

SUNDAY, JANUARY 17

The scribes of the Pharisees, when they saw that he was eating with sinners and tax collectors, said to his disciples, "Why does he eat with tax collectors and sinners?" And when Jesus heard it, he said to them, "Those who are well have no need of a physician, but those who are sick. I came not to call the righteous, but sinners." Mark 2:16–17 (ESV)

AFTER YEARS OF MIDWESTERN WINTERS, my husband and I invested in a gas fireplace. With the press of a switch, a cozy fire flared to life, sending out warmth and light. All winter, I pulled my chair close and worked near the hearth. As icy winds rocked the house and snow piled up outside, I adored that fireplace.

Eventually, summer arrived. Temperatures soared and the sun blazed. I no longer settled by the fireplace. I didn't need more warmth.

I'm no fan of blizzards, but the frigid weather deepened my appreciation for the fireplace. I'm also no fan of the cold and bitter trials of life, but they remind me of my need for Jesus.

When my life is in a summer place, unclouded and still, I often forget to rely on Christ. The Pharisees also didn't see their need for Him. They even scorned those who had obvious spiritual struggles. Yet Jesus invites us to acknowledge how cold and empty our lives are without Him. Confessing that we are among those "tax collectors and sinners" doesn't disqualify us from His grace. In fact, we are the men and women He came to save.

Is your life in a winter season that wracks you with shivers? Jesus knows, and He cares. He invites us to draw near to the warmth and comfort of His love. —SHARON HINCK

FAITH STEP: *Sit by a fireplace (or heating vent) and ponder the warmth and grace that Jesus offers.*

MARTIN LUTHER KING JR. DAY,
MONDAY, JANUARY 18

But I say to you, love your enemies, bless those who curse you, do good to those who hate you, and pray for those who spitefully use you and persecute you. Matthew 5:44 (NKJV)

TODAY WE CELEBRATE THE PURPOSEFUL and impactful life of Reverend Doctor Martin Luther King. As a Baptist minister, Dr. King was no doubt inspired by this verse when he said, "Love is the only force capable of transforming an enemy into a friend." Men have feet of clay, but Dr. King modeled Christ and exemplified the principle of this verse. He did so in a way most of us will never have a chance to—or could we?

A recent news item led me to a Twitter string I wish I'd never read: people were making hateful comments about a celebrity, whom they didn't know personally. Admirably, the celebrity responded with humor and kindness, and love won because she took the high ground. The vitriol lost its power.

The anonymity and reach of social media have made it possible for anyone to spread hatred without having to face their victim. People post impulsive insults, setting off an outpouring of like-minded enmity. Scathing tweets, bigoted Facebook posts, and the bitter commentaries that follow have stoked the culture of hatred and misunderstanding that Dr. King gave his life to mend.

Dr. King tried to live out Jesus's commandment to love one's neighbor and showed us what one person could achieve with a courageously loving response. Let's all be inspired by Jesus Himself to love our enemies, real or perceived! —ISABELLA YOSUICO

FAITH STEP: *Next time you see a hateful post, contribute a loving response—a Scripture verse or an encouraging quote—and see what happens.*

TUESDAY, JANUARY 19

Humble yourselves before the Lord, and he will lift you up.
James 4:10 (NIV)

I JUST FINISHED REREADING THE children's classic *Millions of Cats* by Wanda Ga'g. This sweet book about an older couple in search of a new pet has captured my heart for decades.

In the story, the old man finds a hill covered with millions of cats. How can he pick just one when all of them are exquisite? He decides to let the cats choose among themselves which is prettiest. But each one believes he is, and a huge squabble ensues. When the dust settles, they've all disappeared, save for a single scrawny kitten. The reason? He didn't consider himself special, so the others left him alone. Through the love the old couple share with him, this little kitty truly becomes the most beautiful cat in the world.

I shut the book with a satisfied snap.

Like those trillions of cats, I've wasted time competing to be the best, the most creative, the fastest. I've discovered that sort of contest is impossible—and pointless—to win.

Then I remember Jesus's humility and see beauty as it's meant to be.

As with the scraggly kitten in my storybook, there is nothing outstanding about me. When people look at me, they don't see a celebrity, a genius, or anyone special. But Jesus does. He seeks the treasure within me. To Him, I'm beautiful—the most beautiful me in the entire universe. And that's enough. Because like that little kitten in the book, I've found worth in His eyes, and my spirit flourishes under His care. —HEIDI GAUL

FAITH STEP: *Make a list of the ways Jesus has lifted you up and made you feel special. Give thanks for His nurturing love.*

WEDNESDAY, JANUARY 20

Until now you have not asked for anything in my name. Ask and you will receive, and your joy will be complete. John 16:24 (NIV)

RATHER THAN CHOOSING BETWEEN THE two, I've been both a coffee and a tea drinker, depending on the time of day and my mood. For years, I considered myself a purist—black coffee only. Why would anyone want to mar the wonder of deep, rich, bracing black coffee? Then I discovered froth. Living in a rural area near no large cities, I usually only have access to "fancy" coffee when I travel. Some cities have a well-known chain coffee shop every few blocks, but our nearest town has only one for the whole town, plus a couple of independent coffee shops, all of which I usually buzz past when I'm running errands.

So when I discovered that I could purchase a small, handheld, cute-as-a-bug's-ear mini milk frother, I couldn't wait to begin adding frothy foam to my traditional morning cup of coffee. But after three unsuccessful tries, I complained to my coffee-expert daughter that the frother didn't work. She asked, "Did you heat the milk first?"

I had skipped a step. An important step, it turns out.

Too many times, I confess, I have expected an outcome from the kind hand of Jesus but have skipped an important step. I may have complained, whined, tried to manufacture a homegrown solution, but neglected to *ask* in His name. Many theologians agree that we're to ask not only in the power of Jesus's name but in alignment with His will. When I ask that way, complete joy is the ultimate end product. —CYNTHIA RUCHTI

FAITH STEP: *What Jesus-honoring answer have you been longing to see? Take the first step—ask!*

THURSDAY, JANUARY 21

Be alert, be present. I'm about to do something brand-new.
It's bursting out! Don't you see it? . . . Isaiah 43:19 (MSG)

ONE MORNING, I WAS FEELING glum because I wondered if the best part of my life was behind me. I had no meaningful work or adventures in my near future. I put on my glasses so I could read the small print and opened my Bible to Isaiah 43:19, "I'm about to do something brand-new. It's bursting out! Don't you see it?" (MSG). *No, I don't see it,* I thought, realizing how ironic it was that my eyesight is gradually getting worse. I can hardly see the words on the page of my Bible, much less see Jesus doing something new.

But then I read those words again. Jesus was speaking directly to me in my present situation through His word. I looked up verses about hope and came across Hebrews 11:1, "Now faith is confidence in what we hope for and assurance about what we do not see" (NIV). I could be blind and still have hope. I made a list of what I was hoping for, what would make my life feel purposeful. I wrote down a writing project, community, meaningful activities that foster friendships, and more. I prayed over this list and asked Jesus to help me see with new eyes. Just doing this revived my hope as I anticipated what the future holds rather than feeling sorry for myself or clinging to my past.

Now, when I feel anxious or discouraged about my future, I "put on" my glasses with lenses that see with hope. I look to my future with anticipation, believing something new is about to burst out.
—JEANNIE BLACKMER

FAITH STEP: *Make a list of what you're hoping for in your future that you don't yet see. Pray over each item. Put your list away and set a reminder on your phone to reread it a month from today.*

FRIDAY, JANUARY 22

Jesus said to all of them, "If people want to follow me, they must give up the things they want. They must be willing to give up their lives daily to follow me." Luke 9:23 (NCV)

THE GOSPEL OF JESUS IS simple, but that doesn't mean it's easy. As Luke records, Jesus said we must be willing to give up our lives daily to follow Him. There's no other plan. No step-by-step directions to follow, no self-help book, no stairway to heaven. It's just the dying, the grave, and the rising. Day after day after day.

Once when I was grousing about something that annoyed me, my mentor Roy said, "It's just another thing to die to." We laughed but then talked seriously about how that's really the attitude faith in Jesus requires. Once I started using Roy's mantra, I found myself saying it several times a day. Turns out there are plenty of opportunities. Everywhere we look there's another thing to die to: another hurt or frustration, another door in the face, another bout of anger or pride, another pang of jealousy. All things must be put to death in me that Christ may live.

The beautiful irony is that it's in those very deaths that life is found. It's where true power lies—true joy. Because the same God who brought Jesus out of the grave reaches down into the tombs where I reside and delivers me from the clutches of my own darkness and fear, my own bad choices, my own laziness, prejudice, and pain. Each time I am buried with Christ, He raises me to walk in resurrected life. Old things have passed away; He is doing something new! —GWEN FORD FAULKENBERRY

FAITH STEP: *When faced with moments in which you must surrender your will today, say it with me: "Just another thing to die to." Then wait for the rising.*

SATURDAY, JANUARY 23

*Accept one another, then, just as Christ accepted you,
in order to bring praise to God. Romans 15:7 (NIV)*

CATS. I LOVE THEM. SO, when a nearby farmer needed a home for a barn cat's female kitten, I volunteered. The thought of that tiny bundle snuggling on my lap drew me in like a cat to yarn.

But Ivy, an independent calico, soon let me know there would be none of that nonsense. She had a job to do and intended to do it. Even at six weeks, she hunted her prey—the unsuspecting earthworms. Daily, I'd find them wiggling on the floor and return them to the soil, sprinkled with my apologies. As she grew, her hunt continued. Mice, voles, and the odd gopher met their match—and their Maker—at her acquaintance.

It's been five years, and she's yet to cuddle with me. I doubt she ever will. Ivy isn't the purring companion I'd expected. Instead, Jesus gave me a half-pint teacher. And the lessons I'm learning are heavier than her seven pounds.

Ivy doesn't live according to my whims but lives according to the way Jesus made her. She knows who she is and lives her life to that purpose. Whether I approve or not. As I glance out the window, I spot her chasing a leaf, the embodiment of joyful well-being.

And then I understand. In the same way I've accepted her, Jesus loves me—just as I am. I don't have to be anything but true to Him and myself. As with Ivy, my purpose and worth aren't dependent on pleasing others. I've found myself in Christ, and that's enough. I'm enough. And like my small but fierce cat, I'm complete. —HEIDI GAUL

FAITH STEP: *Watch the behavior of your pet (or a friend's pet) for a few days. What can you learn from their simple acceptance to life and self? How can that knowledge bring you closer to God?*

SUNDAY, JANUARY 24

He called, "Any fish, boys?" "No," we replied. Then he said, "Throw out your net on the right-hand side of the boat, and you'll get plenty of them!" So, we did, and couldn't draw in the net because of the weight of the fish, there were so many! John 21:5–6 (TLB)

EVER NOTICE JESUS'S HABIT OF overdoing it when it came to meeting people's needs? He was extravagant. From His first-ever miracle, turning water into wine at a wedding, He made way more than the guests could consume. Then He fed four thousand and five thousand folks and had baskets full of food leftover. In today's passage, a weary apostle Peter returned to the comfort of his once-successful fishing business. When Jesus entered his dilemma, there was no condemnation, only love, acceptance, direction, and so much provision that the net—and Peter's heart—were about to burst. Jesus provided more than enough, again.

While planning my wedding, I had just the opposite attitude. I was focused on spending "just enough." I haggled with the venue and the host hotel, secretly hoped people wouldn't eat too much at the rehearsal dinner, and showed up frazzled and late for my own big day to avoid paying extra for hair and makeup! One of my bridesmaids emailed, "Of course you did that, Pam. You are Frugal Franny!" When I read that I felt like the crying-smiley-face emoji she put after it: smiling because "just enough" was a deeply held value and crying because of how out of step that was with Jesus's "more than enough" attitude. My Heavenly Father promised He would supply, and I needed to let go and trust Him to do it extravagantly—and He did! —PAMELA TOUSSAINT HOWARD

FAITH STEP: *Stretch today when giving anything to others—push past your comfort zone—with money, a listening ear, or your time. Practice being extravagant.*

MONDAY, JANUARY 25

In your relationships with one another, have the same mindset as Christ Jesus: Who, being in very nature God, did not consider equality with God something to be used to his own advantage; rather, he made himself nothing by taking the very nature of a servant, being made in human likeness. Philippians 2:5–7 (NIV)

IN OUR FAMILY OF THREE teenage boys, there is no greater battle than that war of who gets to ride in the passenger seat of the car. We have gone so far as to assign whose week it is to avoid conflict. The person in the passenger seat reigns supreme, commandeering both the music selections for the ride and the temperature inside the car. Riding shotgun means you are king of the car. Everyone else is beneath you.

We are not so different from my boys. We all want to ride shotgun in life. We shape our days around these selfish questions: What do *I* want? What is best for *me*? What can *I* get out of this? While we feel that being king of our lives will lead to happiness, selfishness often snowballs into impatience, discontentedness, and jealousy, giving us less of a life than we had hoped for. We can never get enough, be enough, or have enough on our own.

We weren't made to serve ourselves. We were made in the image of Jesus, the ultimate Servant. When we give up "riding shotgun" and invite Jesus to order our thoughts, our desires, and our actions, we start to become like Him: selfless, empathetic, caring, loving, thoughtful, generous. This is just the kind of snowball effect that fills the heart with joy. —SUSANNA FOTH AUGHTMON

FAITH STEP: *Shape your day with a selfless attitude. Invite Jesus to order your day, going out of your way to care for those around you. Get ready for some joy!*

TUESDAY, JANUARY 26

Once when we were going to the place of prayer, we were met by a female slave who had a spirit by which she predicted the future. She earned a great deal of money for her owners by fortune-telling. She followed Paul and the rest of us, shouting, "These men are servants of the Most High God, who are telling you the way to be saved." Acts 16:16—17 (NIV)

WHEN PAUL AND SILAS TOLD the people of Philippi about Jesus, they had a strange encounter with a woman who followed them and shouted affirmations. At first, it sounds like a little fan club of one. Yes, it may have been disruptive, but her intentions were good, right? When we look closer, we see a woman who was enslaved, not just by her human owners but by a demon. She said the right words, but she was eaten up inside. Paul responded with compassion, and in Jesus's name, he cast the demon from her. She was freed to live in truth.

Today a friend asked how I was doing. Instead of sharing my needs, I smiled. I deflected, and spoke about the weather, and affirmed many blessings in my life. With too much pride to admit my need for help and encouragement, I said what sounded like all the right things. Yet, deep inside I was hurting about a relationship and exhausted by a conflict.

Like Paul with the woman, Jesus sees beyond our pretty words. He sees our bondage and looks at us with compassion. Jesus invites us to get real. Whether our bondage is fear, doubt, anger, or greed, at times we are all enslaved and eaten up inside. Only Jesus's power can free us. Today, let's focus not just on saying the right things, but on letting Him make everything truly right. —SHARON HINCK

FAITH STEP: *Talk to Jesus and a trusted friend about your struggles so they can support you.*

WEDNESDAY, JANUARY 27

Don't hide your light! Let it shine for all; let your good deeds glow for all to see, so that they will praise your heavenly Father. Matthew 5:15–16 (TLB)

IT'S EASY TO GO TO work or shop or do other activities and never let anyone know you are a Christian. Usually, folks will think you're a nice person or a good employee, and you can just peacefully coexist through life that way. But that is not what Jesus Himself is calling us to in today's Scripture passage. He depends on us to be salt and light (Matthew 5:13–14) in a dark world, showing people there is a better way and pointing them to Him. When we share our treasure with others, we truly shine as Christians.

I developed a friendship with a coworker who wasn't a Christian. We talked and laughed and went to lunch and worked well together for several months. One day she shared how she had lost a beloved grandparent to cancer a few years before and told me what a devout Christian this person had been. I could tell that the grandparent's death had hurt her and challenged whatever faith she had that God existed. How could I stay silent? The compassion of the Holy Spirit welled up in me as I listened, and I shared my faith with her at the appropriate moment. Since then, she has begun listening to the Bible on CD in her car on the way to work, and she tells me what she is learning and asks me questions! I know that Jesus will continue the work He began in her heart. And I'm going to continue to let my little light shine. —PAMELA TOUSSAINT HOWARD

FAITH STEP: *Is there someone in your life with whom you can share your light? Be prayerful and shine for Him.*

THURSDAY, JANUARY 28

Jesus Christ is the same yesterday and today and forever. Hebrews 13:8 (ESV)

MY MOM WAS RIGHT WHEN she said, "You never stop mothering." Even as a mother of adult sons, I'm tempted to manage them, but I know I need to let them figure out their own lives. Especially as they struggle with adult issues such as heartbreak, career choices, and financial needs.

As I let go of interfering, which can stunt their growth, I focus my energy on prayer. One morning when they were teens and I was discouraged, I discovered a new way to pray for them. I searched the Psalms in hopes of finding something inspirational. That morning, praying the Psalms felt as if I was praying only for myself: I know God is *my* refuge, and He holds *my* right hand. I cried out, "I don't care about *me* right now. I care about my kids. Show me how to pray for them." I feel the same today.

Then I thought, *If I believe Jesus is who He says He is, then can't He do for me what He did for others when He walked on earth?* I searched for encounters in the Bible of parents who approached Jesus for help. I found several, including a ruler, two mothers, and a father. Their prayers expressed my own feelings. I immersed myself in these stories and imagined myself face to face with Jesus, making requests on behalf of my children.

I experienced His healing words and comfort in a new way. Today I'm still praying this way for my sons as they struggle through hard times. Jesus is the same yesterday, today, and forever, so I know He's able to handle all of my concerns. And thankfully, He hears my prayers. —JEANNIE BLACKMER

FAITH STEP: *Imagine yourself face to face with Jesus. Talk with Him about specific concerns for your own children or a friend's child.*

FRIDAY, JANUARY 29

*I want you to understand what really matters, so that you may live
pure and blameless lives until the day of Christ's return. May you
always be filled with the fruit of your salvation—the righteous character
produced in your life by Jesus Christ—for this will bring much glory
and praise to God. Philippians 1:10–11 (NLT)*

MATURING IN MY RELATIONSHIP WITH Jesus has helped me identify
inaccurate thoughts I've had regarding my faith. For instance, take
the matter of living a pure and blameless life—I believed it mattered
solely because God expected it. Failing to meet His expectations
would either disappoint or anger Him. My attitudes and behaviors
would either receive His reward or result in consequences. End of
story.

Now I understand things differently. The apostle Paul's prayer for
the believers in Philippi helps me see that living a blameless life matters
but for reasons other than avoiding punishment. It matters because
I represent Jesus to a watching world. Representing Jesus places a
responsibility on me to behave with integrity. Unbelievers expect that
from me and rightfully so, but sometimes I fall short. My old nature
wrestles with the new and wins. When that happens, it's my responsibility to try to things right.

My behavior can either make Jesus attractive to those who don't
know Him, or it can turn them away. Thankfully He's all about
helping me succeed. As I surrender my will to Him, He transforms
me through the power of His Spirit living in me. I become more
like Him and my life creates a curiosity in others to know the One
who changes me and gives me hope.—GRACE FOX

FAITH STEP: *Ask Jesus to make your life like salt, creating a thirst in others for
the Living Water.*

SATURDAY, JANUARY 30

He ran ahead and climbed a sycamore-fig tree to see him, since Jesus was coming that way. When Jesus reached the spot, he looked up and said to him, "Zacchaeus, come down immediately. I must stay at your house today." —Luke 19:4–5 (NIV)

I LOVE THE STORY OF Zacchaeus the tax collector, whose very occupation was associated with sin. Yet, when he heard Jesus was coming to town, he ran to meet Him. Crowds blocked his view, until he spotted a tree. There the story took a radical turn.

Jesus sees everything, so I doubt He was surprised to find the tax man straddling a branch overhead. But in this story, it's not Jesus or Zacchaeus that captures my attention—it's the tree. Because God had planted it years earlier for that specific purpose: to grow until one day a short man in need of salvation would climb it to see His Son. God's wisdom astounds me. That He cares so much about one small sinner leaves me in awe.

It's time I recognize the "trees" in my life—the people and things Jesus has planted in the path of my salvation.

Years ago, before I knew Christ, a friend invited me to an intensive international Bible study. I attended, and over time I grew to love Jesus and gave my life to Him. Thirty years later, I lead a group in that very same Bible study. Who was the "tree" here? My friend? The study itself? Being in the Word daily? I think Jesus planted an entire forest for my short, scrawny soul.

Now it's my turn to be a "tree." Who can I pull up out of the world's cares and help him or her see the Savior? —HEIDI GAUL

FAITH STEP: *On a paper, list the "trees" God planted in your life to help you see Him better. Give thanks for each one. Think of people for whom you can be a "tree."*

SUNDAY, JANUARY 31

Finally, all of you be of one mind, having compassion for one another; love as brothers, be tenderhearted, be courteous. 1 Peter 3:8 (NKJV)

I DASHED OUT OF THE house, having overscheduled as usual. My daughter Melissa, who wasn't feeling well, texted me, asking what she could eat to settle her stomach. I suggested yogurt, but since she didn't have any, I told her I'd run to the store and get some for her. Nothing I had to do was more important than helping my child.

Puzzling over yogurt flavors at the dairy counter, I heard a voice behind me say, "What can I get to help my baby gain weight?"

Oh, Lord, I don't have time for this! I thought. But I faced the worried-looking woman in a coral sweater and asked, "How old is your baby?"

"Twenty-two," she replied. She told me her daughter had undergone surgery several weeks before and now had no appetite and had lost ten pounds. I could relate to the fear I saw on this mother's face. *I really don't have time for this, Jesus.* But how could I not help?

"How about an ice cream shake?" I asked. "Mix in some protein powder." I suggested a loaded baked potato, macaroni and cheese, pizza, and yogurt. "I'm getting yogurt for my daughter, who's been sick," I told her.

"Thanks so much," said the other mother, who looked a little less worried now that she had a plan. "I'm going to get the things you suggested, go home, and make my girl a shake. I'll pray for your daughter."

"And I'll pray for yours," I promised. *Oh, Jesus, you knew all along I DID have time for this.* —PAT BUTLER DYSON

FAITH STEP: *Today omit completing two items at the bottom of your to-do list. Use the extra time to extend kindness to someone Jesus places in your path.*

MONDAY, FEBRUARY 1

You have turned my mourning into joyful dancing. You have taken away my clothes of mourning and clothed me with joy, that I might sing praises to you and not be silent. O LORD my God, I will give you thanks forever! Psalm 30:11–12 (NLT)

THERE IS A DEEP JOY—THE sort of meaningful, overwhelming, heart-swelling sort of joy—that can't be expressed in words alone. Because I was a dancer and choreographer in my younger days, my eyes light up when I come across a Bible verse that mentions dancing. I understand that impulse to worship with my whole being. During my private devotions, as I ponder the love of Jesus and all He has done for us, I still sometimes raise my arms or spin across the room in an expression of praise.

Whether we use song or dance or whispers from a timid heart, there are many ways to rejoice in the presence of our Savior. But today, I looked at the first part of the verse. David's psalm is not speaking of a carefree happiness; his praise comes out of heavy mourning. What a strange concept! It seems that the deepest and most heartfelt joy is born through what we learn from Jesus in times of loss, grief, and pain.

Each year I spend on this earth, my list of loved ones who have gone ahead to heaven grows longer. Yet daily, Jesus brings joy into the sadness. All that He has done for me means that one day my joy will be complete. Mourning will be over for good. He will ultimately clothe me in joy, and in the meantime, He daily invites me to a dance of celebration—anticipating in faith what is to come.
—SHARON HINCK

FAITH STEP: *Lift your arms in praise to Jesus this morning. If you are mourning, meditate on today's verse and believe that He will transform that pain into joy.*

TUESDAY, FEBRUARY 2

*For I am not ashamed of the gospel, because it is the power of
God that brings salvation to everyone who believes: first to
the Jew, then to the Gentile. Romans 1:16 (NIV)*

I WORK AS A CHURCH administrative assistant. My first day on the
job, I asked the pastor how often people stopped in to request
financial help. "Not that often" he said. I sighed in relief. I knew
there would be times when I'd have to say no to a request, which
would grieve my heart.

That first year, once or twice a month, we helped people with
gas, groceries, and bus tickets. As word got out that the redhead
in the church office on Court Street was sympathetic, the requests
poured in. A few months ago, the deacon board decided to limit the
number of times an individual could receive help from us.

Although I understood the reason behind that decision (the
church's funds are not limitless), I still hated to turn away needy
people. What would I tell them? An idea straight from heaven sailed
into my heart: *Tell them about Jesus.* Of course. Whether I was able
to give people monetary help or not, I could always share the good
news of the gospel.

Now whenever someone pops into my office needing assistance, I
briefly tell him or her how I became a child of God through placing
my trust in Jesus. I give them a story I wrote about God's forgiveness and love. Sometimes I pray with them to find work or receive
healing. Even if they don't leave with a gas card or a sack of groceries, they receive the best gift I have to offer: the joy they can experience through knowing Jesus. —JEANETTE LEVELLIE

FAITH STEP: *Write a brief account of how you came to faith in Jesus. Print it out
and share it with someone who needs joy in his or her life.*

WEDNESDAY, FEBRUARY 3

---

*I will give you a new heart, and I will put a new spirit in you.
I will take out your stony, stubborn heart and give you a tender,
responsive heart. Ezekiel 36:26 (NLT)*

WHEN MY HEART PALPITATIONS INCREASED in frequency, my doctor had me wear a heart monitor taped to my abdomen, which continually recorded data. After that, he scheduled a stress test. I walked on the treadmill, watching my heart function in real time on the monitor in front of me. Suddenly, a palpitation struck, and the monitor showed my heart beating at 190 beats per minute. It was not a pretty sight. I lay on my side as a cardiologist massaged my carotid artery until my heart returned to normal rhythm.

A medical stress test helps diagnose problems with our physical heart (nothing serious in my case). In life, an emotional stress test often pinpoints problems with our spiritual heart. It might be easy to put on a good front when things go smoothly, but under the pressures of trials, hurts, and disappointments, what's really in our heart usually comes out. Sometimes it's not a pretty sight. How we respond to stressful situations mirrors how we respond to Jesus as Lord. Do we trust Him to work out the circumstances of our lives? Are we willing to submit to His plans and obey His commands? Do we really believe He is always good and has our best interests in mind?

Even if we fail a spiritual stress test, there's good news. Jesus is ready to align our hearts with His so that we can respond to negative situations with a Christlike attitude that honors Him. The process begins when we ask for His healing touch. —DIANNE NEAL MATTHEWS

FAITH STEP: *Think of the last time you faced a highly stressful situation. How did you respond? Ask Jesus to make your heart more responsive to Him, regardless of your circumstances.*

THURSDAY, FEBRUARY 4

He will rejoice over you with gladness; he will quiet you by his love; he will exult over you with loud singing. Zephaniah 3:17 (ESV)

I ADMIT I AM PERFORMANCE oriented. The familiar urge to achieve was triggered recently when I met with a friend about her work. I listened to her talk about her job, her busy schedule, and the interesting people she meets. "How about you? What are you up to these days?" she asked. I didn't have much to say other than "I'm trying to figure that out."

I've been an achiever since a young age. I got in trouble rarely, played competitive tennis, and received good grades. I went to college, then got my master's. I worked. I married, had kids, and wrote some books. I volunteered. I learned to cook, sort of. I did everything I thought I should do. Life zoomed ahead, and now with my adult children launched, I recently started to ask myself again, What should I do? What's my purpose?

Then I came across this quote by Brennan Manning in his book *Abba's Child*, "Define yourself as one radically loved by God. This is the true self. Every other identity is illusion." That was just the reminder I needed to hear—I am radically loved. In fact, Jesus loved me so much He died for me.

I can't undo my past, but I can move forward with confidence because I am loved, not because of what I do. I don't have to strive to impress anyone because Jesus rejoices over me with gladness, quiets me with His love, and exults over me with loud singing. When I find myself struggling with my identity, I look at today's Scripture verse, now posted above my desk, and my spirit is quieted and content because of His love. —JEANNIE BLACKMER

FAITH STEP: *Write three ways your life would be different if you lived truly believing that Jesus radically loves you.*

FRIDAY, FEBRUARY 5

God of Heaven's Armies, you find so much beauty in your people!
They're like lovely sanctuaries of your presence. Psalm 84:1 (TPT)

MY HUSBAND AND I WERE eating a continental breakfast at an out-of-town motel. As we ate, I noticed a woman three tables away from us. She ate alone. Every time I glanced her way, she was smiling at me. Was this a red flag warning? No. I had a sense stranger danger was the opposite of what was happening.

When friends of ours staying at the same motel arrived for breakfast minutes later, I temporarily forgot about the woman's stares and interacted with our friends—a man and his mid-twenties son who is significantly disabled from a brain injury.

Eventually, I got up to refill my coffee. The woman who'd been watching me followed. "Excuse me," she said, her soft voice mellowed with age and what sounded like wisdom. "I couldn't help notice that when that young man greeted you, his face lit up. I've worked with special needs young people my whole life. You've obviously made an impact on him." I explained we weren't related, but that I felt I'd become part of his family, and then thanked her for her kind words. In moments, a familiar and special bond formed, and I suspected I knew the source. She revealed she was in town to celebrate the life of her sister. I expressed my condolences for her loss. The woman said, "My sister's last words were, 'I love Jesus. And Jesus loves me.' That's what made her funeral a celebration."

That bond. A Jesus bond had knit us together in a random hotel breakfast room. It's because His people are lovely sanctuaries of His presence and joy magnets. What a gift! —CYNTHIA RUCHTI

FAITH STEP: *Watch for moments of unexpected Jesus bonds today. Celebrate each one as a joyful gift.*

SATURDAY, FEBRUARY 6

But Moses pleaded, "O Lord, I'm just not a good speaker.
I never have been, and I'm not now, even after you have spoken to me,
for I have a speech impediment." "Who makes mouths?" Jehovah asked
him. "Isn't it I, the Lord? . . . " Exodus 4:10–11 (TLB)

My HUSBAND, ANDREW, HAS ALWAYS shied away from public speaking. He often has valuable insights on things, yet his comfort zone is to sit back and observe. It didn't help that he stuttered as a child and was sometimes teased by his classmates. Recently, he had to give an oral report at work in front of twenty-five colleagues. We prayed the night before, and he came home the next day beaming—he was commended by his supervisor for how well he spoke! What had happened? When he stood up to speak, he remembered who had made his mouth and allowed the Lord to talk through him instead of focusing on his past failures or the fear of men's faces—the same things Moses struggled with in today's passage.

I on the other hand had no problem talking (several nuns in my old grammar school can attest to this), but I was always hesitant to share my faith, especially with strangers. I never thought I had the right words or the right approach, and I greatly feared rejection. I preferred writing, with time to prepare, mull over, rehash, and rewrite. But when I have only a few seconds to encourage or pray with a waitress, delivery person, cab driver, or coworker in need, there isn't time for editing! I've learned that Jesus is the maker of my mouth—so I forget myself and trust Him to guide my tongue.
—PAMELA TOUSSAINT HOWARD

FAITH STEP: *Commit to listening to the Lord's prompts in your spirit today as you go out into the world. Say what He tells you to say and trust that He will be with your mouth.*

SUNDAY, FEBRUARY 7

We have this treasure in jars of clay to show that this all-surpassing power is from God and not from us. 2 Corinthians 4:7 *(NIV)*

MY PARENTS OFTEN STRUGGLED TO make ends meet, so everything they acquired carried extra value. When I hold items they cherished, I remember their hard work and their rare wisdom in valuing beauty as highly as practicality. Damaged, discarded items often ended up at our home, from scraps of carpeting to cracked flowerpots and scratched silver. Dad repaired with nails and glue, and Mom cleaned and scrubbed until each treasure shone as if it was new. Our home reflected culture and class on a repurposed shoestring.

While searching a cabinet for a serving platter, I stumbled across my mother's favorite bowl. The pressed glass could almost pass for crystal, and the chipped edges hardly showed. What's important is that it's able to hold the salad, for which it was intended, and do it with grace. Like many of Mom's heirlooms, its imperfections don't matter.

Like the bowl, I'm a vessel. Not for lettuce, but for Jesus. When the joy and love and life that Christ placed in me spills over my edges and slips through my cracks, that's good. And as I glance at friends during church this week, I see scratched silver trays ready to serve others and mugs without handles eager to warm hearts and hands. I see candle stubs still glowing with faith and wobbly chairs offering rest to the weary. We're like the components of a cozy home, working in harmony despite our broken parts. Jesus has taken our cracks and shards, the parts life broke loose, and mended them so they're stronger than ever. And He cherishes us. That's very, very good. —HEIDI GAUL

FAITH STEP: *Make a point to use one of the damaged items in your home. As you do, think about how much Jesus loves you, cracks and all.*

MONDAY, FEBRUARY 8

"Do not think that I came to destroy the Law or the Prophets. I did not come to destroy but to fulfill. For assuredly, I say to you, till heaven and earth pass away, one jot or one tittle will by no means pass from the law till all is fulfilled. Matthew 5:17–18 (NKJV)

LAST WINTER I DECIDED TO attempt transcription and captioning work from home. The work was more challenging than I imagined. I would select a project, and the audio would be faint and crackly. The various people speaking would be difficult to identify. Often the discussion was packed with technical terminology that I had to research to be sure to get everything correct. In the captioning projects, the words had to be inserted with precise timing into the video and with specific symbols.

Projects were randomly evaluated. Although I was painstaking in my efforts, every once in a while, I was docked for being a fraction of a second off or for leaving out one tiny symbol. The experience reminded me of Jesus's words in today's passage about the tiniest dot above a letter, or the smallest symbol.

When it comes to God's law, it's easy to look at broad strokes and decide I'm not doing so badly. But the truth is, my smallest sinful attitude or weak moment shows that I can't fulfill the law. Instead of frustration and despair, that realization floods me with new gratitude for Jesus's grace and what He has done. Because He fulfilled every requirement, I am forgiven and free, no longer under the weight of chasing each jot and tittle. Instead, His love can grow in me, so that my actions align more and more with Jesus's ways, and I can respond joyfully to His grace rather than trying to earn it. —SHARON HINCK

FAITH STEP: *Notice all the dots, commas, and other tiny markings on this page. Thank Jesus for fulfilling each detail of the law for our sakes.*

TUESDAY, FEBRUARY 9

The LORD is my strength and my shield; my heart trusts in him, and he helps me. My heart leaps for joy, and with my song I praise him. Psalm 28:7 (NIV)

THE FIRST WINTER LIVING ON a sailboat tested my grit. More than once I felt like my coping skills had been overstretched. Then circumstances stretched them more.

The first challenge came when snow fell and turned the dock into a slippery, slushy mess. I'd fallen on the dock a couple of months prior, so I found myself in a state of heightened alert whenever I left the boat, especially when it was still dark outside.

Then ice formed on the river. It flowed past us, thumping and scraping our hull. My imagination entertained thoughts of the Titanic.

The tipping point came when our diesel furnace died. We layered clothes, wore jackets, and wrapped in blankets to stay warm. For two weeks, the repair man promised to come several times but kept canceling at the last minute.

Expressing gratitude changes one's perspective. More importantly, it's a matter of obedience. I truly wanted to obey the Word, so I thanked Jesus for being my strength when I felt weak. I thanked Him for helping me stay upright on the dock and for keeping our hull safe. I thanked Him for jackets and blankets and hot tea.

Giving thanks changed my thoughts from *I can't handle this* to *I can't handle this on my own, but I can with Jesus's strength*. Adversity turned to adventure.

Winter will come again next year. No doubt it will bring challenges. No doubt it will test my grit. But I'll make Psalm 28:7 a staple for my thoughts, and I know anxiety will turn to joy. —GRACE FOX

FAITH STEP: *What characteristic about Jesus makes your heart leap for joy?*

WEDNESDAY, FEBRUARY 10

Behold, there arose a great storm on the sea, so that the boat was being swamped by the waves; but he was asleep. And they went and woke him, saying, "Save us, Lord; we are perishing." Matthew 8:24–25 (ESV)

DRIVING HOME FROM THE MOUNTAINS, I was caught in a major snowstorm. I clutched my steering wheel so tightly my hands ached. Cars and trucks surrounded me as we drove on a traffic-filled highway. Suddenly, I hit black ice, and my car started sliding. I tried to steer, but I had no control of the direction I was headed. A big cargo truck was on my left but, thankfully, I was slipping to the right. "Jesus, help!" I cried—it was all I could muster. Miraculously, no vehicles smashed into me. When I finally drove out of the worst of the storm, relief washed over me.

In crisis situations sometimes all we can manage is a desperate plea for help. The disciples had a life-threatening experience on the Sea of Galilee one day. They were in the middle of the lake, with Jesus sound asleep, when a massive storm rolled in. The huge waves tossed their little wooden boat like driftwood, and water gushed into it. They cried out to Jesus, "Help, we are perishing!" He awoke, spoke, and the winds calmed immediately. The storm I drove through didn't instantly dissipate, but I drove through it, asking Jesus for help the entire trip. He kept me safe.

In the midst of a crisis and chaos, many of us today would not use the words "Help me; I'm perishing," but we would simply cry "Help." Whatever words you use to pray urgently, things happen in heaven and earth when you call on Jesus. He will calm your storm. Don't hesitate to ask Him for help. —JEANNIE BLACKMER

FAITH STEP: *Are you in a storm? Write your version of a "Jesus, help me," prayer and trust in the calm to come.*

THURSDAY, FEBRUARY 11

Rejoice always, pray continually, give thanks in all circumstances; for this is God's will for you in Christ Jesus. 1 Thessalonians 5:16–18 (NIV)

"REALLY, GOD?" I'VE WANTED TO ask. "Rejoice *always*?" Yet that's what it says. Over years of desperately seeking Jesus, I've learned to pray a lot, if not continually, and to find reasons to be grateful in even the most abysmal circumstances. Rejoicing was the last stronghold. How can I "feel joy or great delight" (as Merriam-Webster puts it) in the face of the assorted mundane or massive trials we all face this side of heaven? Yet I persist—not in seeking joy but in seeking God. I think that's the key to everything, really (Matthew 6:33).

I can hardly believe it myself, but as I'm writing this, I'm close to "rejoicing always," something I was pretty sure was impossible. Right now, I'm in the midst of marital woes, financial straits, vocational uncertainty, and a long-dreaded business bankruptcy after a long and scary ordeal, yet I'm truly full of joy and peace.

Yes, my joy is fueled partly by the hope promised in Romans 8:28 and my own experience of Jesus making lemonade out of lemons. Mostly, I'm experiencing that inexplicable joy that defies explanation and is disconnected from circumstances. I wonder if this is a tiny taste of the joy we sense in Paul's letters, which were written in jail or other hard places. Whatever it is, I really like it and pray Jesus's grace will let me linger here no matter what comes.
—ISABELLA YOSUICO

FAITH STEP: *Suspend your disbelief and set aside your resistance and vocally praise Jesus for the very thing that's bothering you, rejoicing intentionally rather than waiting for the elusive feeling.*

Friday, February 12

---

*...Trust steadily in God, hope unswervingly, love extravagantly.
And the best of the three is love. 1 Corinthians 13:13 (MSG)*

I CAN'T REMEMBER WHEN I first realized that Jesus expects us to love as He does—unconditionally, extravagantly, audaciously. It was probably a thought floating somewhere within the pool of information I'd been introduced to in Sunday school and then further developed through Bible studies and sermons in my early adult years. In my journey to understand Jesus better, I stopped imagining Him as simply really, really skilled at loving people and instead realized His brand of love was in a class by itself.

Part of that dawning on the subject of Jesus's love happened just the other day.

After years of court-appointed exile from society, a family member and friend returned to us. I told him, "I love you," and meant it.

"Thank you," he said.

His response startled me, so I said, "You don't have to thank me for loving you."

He was silent for a moment, then said, "Some wouldn't." The words came out as a whisper laced with experience.

I didn't *have* to love him. But loving comes easily because of the way I've been loved by Jesus—lavishly, in spite of my failures. Reading about Jesus's limitless love—for those who came to Him with nothing but their brokenness, their pain, and their unsavory past—has convinced me that defaulting to love is heaven's expectation and my best option. —CYNTHIA RUCHTI

FAITH STEP: *Someone in your circle of friends and family or even a stranger needs to know he or she is loved outrageously and extravagantly. Are you the carrier Jesus wants to use to deliver that message?*

SATURDAY, FEBRUARY 13

As he neared Damascus on his journey, suddenly a light from heaven flashed around him. He fell to the ground and heard a voice say to him, "Saul, Saul, why do you persecute me?" Acts 9:3–4 (NIV)

MY HUSBAND DAVID AND I love flowers—*all* flowers. While touring Hawaii many years ago, we visited an orchid nursery and brought home several of those exotic plants. But ten years later, and despite all my nurturing, not one of them flowered. I became discouraged and resigned myself to tending just the green leaves.

Then, for no reason I could understand, the plants began to blossom. Not just one plant but three, each of which sprouted a delicate green stem crowded with buds. Every morning when I entered the kitchen, another delight surprised me. *What if I'd thrown them out?* Too often I'd entertained that thought.

A Pharisee named Saul had built his life around persecuting our Lord and His followers. Empathy for Christians and producing fruit for the kingdom weren't even on his radar. Spiritually, he was as barren as my island flowers. But Jesus saw the potential and power hidden in Saul's heart—the intense devotion that would grow inside him. He waited, and when the time was right, Jesus transformed this man into Paul, one of His strongest apostles. The faith that grew in this once cruel man was beautiful, even shocking, and it fuels believers' needs to this day.

Jesus does the same for us, feeding and cultivating our souls. Whether we take a day or most of our lives to give our hearts to Him, He will never forsake us. He's done His part.

Now it's time for us to bloom right where we are. —HEIDI GAUL

FAITH STEP: *Buy an orchid or other slow-to-bloom plant to remind you of those you know who are "slow to bloom." Never give up on them. Jesus won't.*

VALENTINE'S DAY, SUNDAY, FEBRUARY 14

You have been born again, not of perishable seed, but of imperishable, through the living and enduring word of God. 1 Peter 1:23 (NIV)

WHEN MY HUSBAND, SCOTT, AND I were first married, we lived in a cute fourplex. Some of our neighbors discovered an antique steamer trunk while cleaning out their garage. Inside was a large packet of early 1900s love letters with Norwegian and Californian postmarks between a couple whose names were Bertha and Henry. No one in our complex knew Bertha and Henry. I researched their names online but hit a wall. The letters remained tucked away for safe keeping for the last twenty years. This spring, my tech savvy sixth-grade class began to research the letters as treasured artifacts. *Who in the world were Bertha and Henry? Did they marry and have a family? Where was their family now?* Each history class was like a treasure hunt. My students archived the letters in chronological order. They researched ship manifests. They mapped the towns the letters hailed from. With their bright minds, they poured over the letters. There was a sense of excitement in the air. We were solving a mystery no one had ever solved before. Each letter was a treasure to be dug into. Henry and Bertha's words were echoing through history.

Letters are powerful messages, connecting hearts across miles, sharing truth, hopes, and dreams. Jesus's words in Scripture are just that—powerful messages to our hearts. Each time we read the Bible, we are unravelling the great mystery of His love for us. With our bright minds pouring over His words, our hearts are linked to His across eternity. His Living Word, a sixty-six book love letter to humanity, endures forever and is a treasure worth searching out. —SUSANNA FOTH AUGHTMON

FAITH STEP: *Read John 17:6–26. Jesus's heart for us is revealed in His prayer to His Father. Hear His enduring words of love echoing through eternity.*

MONDAY, FEBRUARY 15

I will be a Father to you, and you will be my sons and daughters, says the Lord Almighty. 2 Corinthians 6:18 (NIV)

LOVE IS A BEAUTIFUL THING. But the mystery of Henry and Bertha's love letters wasn't just a love story; it was a family story. When you marry love with family, it is powerful. My sixth-grade history class could not wait to reunite the letters with Bertha and Henry's family. They spent hours researching possible leads. They hit dead end after dead end, until one of my students used her own mother's genealogy account to access a larger database. In a great moment of excitement, she shouted, "We found them!" The whole class cheered. Our joy grew as the class mapped out Bertha and Henry's entire family tree: generation after generation, layer upon layer of love and history. Weeks later, coming full circle, we connected with Adam, Bertha and Henry's great-grandson, via a video call. The students couldn't wait to share all they knew about his family. Adam couldn't believe we had found him, and his excitement was invigorating. With a huge grin, he said, "I cannot wait to share these with the rest of my family." We grinned back. We felt like we were a part of his family reunion, getting in on the love.

Family is a powerful thing. Connected by blood and spirit, we all want to know our history and where we came from. When we follow Jesus, we are adopted by our heavenly Father. His story of grace becomes a part of our history. Connected by the blood of Jesus and His Holy Spirit, we are grafted into a new family tree, rich in mercy and rooted in love. We are sons and daughters of the Most High.
—SUSANNA FOTH AUGHTMON

FAITH STEP: *Map out your spiritual family tree. How did you become a part of Jesus's family? Know that you are rooted and grounded in His love and care.*

TUESDAY, FEBRUARY 16

Finally, brothers and sisters, whatever is true, whatever is noble, whatever is right, whatever is pure, whatever is lovely, whatever is admirable—if anything is excellent or praiseworthy—think about such things. Philippians 4:8 (NIV)

MY HUSBAND, ZANE, AND I participated in a small group to test content for a leadership book written by Christian neuroscientists about developing habits for increasing trust, joy, and engagement in the people you lead. Every week we met, we walked away with "aha" moments and habits to employ in our lives.

One habit I learned is to return my thoughts to something joyful when I feel conflict brewing. Science shows this helps my brain stay in a relational mode rather than jumping to an enemy mode. In marriage we all experience conflict—sometimes it's a tiny thing and other times it's a big blowup. The practice of pausing when I sense conflict and returning my thoughts to a joyful experience, such as remembering the fun bike ride we shared, helps me to stay relational. If I'm having difficulty thinking of a positive mutual experience because I'm angry, then I can turn my mind toward my relationship with Jesus. I remind myself who He says I am and His unwavering love for me. When I remember to value the relationship with my husband—more than my desire to be right—then I know the conflict will have a healthier outcome. When I train my mind to stay relational, then I can experience joy even in the midst of conflict.

Paul encourages us in Philippians to think on what is true, noble, right, pure, lovely, admirable, excellent, or praiseworthy. This helps us stay in a constant relational mode, which ultimately results in life-giving relationships. Isn't that what we all want? —JEANNIE BLACKMER

FAITH STEP: *Meditate daily on Philippians 4:8. Joy will follow.*

ASH WEDNESDAY, FEBRUARY 17

Do not cast me off in the time of old age; forsake me not
when my strength is spent. Psalm 71:9 (ESV)

MY MOTHER AND STEPFATHER RECENTLY moved into a senior living home. On Ash Wednesday, a guest pastor hosted a service in the event center, so I arrived early to walk them upstairs. We found chairs in the back of a room that was soon crowded with white hair, walkers, and wheelchairs.

Other than a few aides, I was the youngest by several decades. The pace of the readings and liturgy was much slower than I was used to. A guest pianist played show tunes in the downstairs lobby, and because of the vaulted design of the building, his music wafted up and filled the room where we had gathered. At first, I felt restless and distracted as aides helped patients and "Moon River" played from downstairs. But before long, my eyes stung with tears. I saw the room for what it was—a holy place where Jesus met with His beloved children. Those around me had lived long lives of service to Him and had endless stories of His faithfulness and a deep love for Him. Each person also knew that, within a few years or even months, they would meet Jesus face to face. Their expressions reflected no fear, only joy and faith.

Their example strengthened my heart. Witnessing a room full of people about to hear Jesus tell them, "Well done, good and faithful servant," took my breath away. My petty problems faded into the background. I prayed He would help me prepare for the day when I would be near my eternal home, as these seniors were, and I also rejoiced that Jesus walks with us at any age. —SHARON HINCK

FAITH STEP: *Spend time with someone older than you and ask them about their experiences of following Jesus.*

THURSDAY, FEBRUARY 18

Create in me a pure heart, O God, and renew a steadfast spirit within me. . . . Restore to me the joy of your salvation and grant me a willing spirit, to sustain me. Psalm 51:10, 12 (NIV)

NO ONE TOLD ME THAT living on a boat in British Columbia in winter would be so damp. I first clued in when our bedding began to smell musty. We stripped the sheets and pulled up the mattress. I could scarcely believe my eyes.

Mildew spotted the mattress, and water—enough to soak up with a sponge—covered the wooden base on which it rested. Thankfully, we made this discovery on a sunny day, so we pulled the mattress outside where we cleaned and dried it. Gene, my husband, scrubbed the base and treated it with chemicals that prevent mildew from growing. Then he installed a special fabric designed to allow airflow between the mattress and the base.

We did the same for the guest bed. Then I checked every cupboard for mildew. Sure enough—there it was. I scrubbed and treated the walls with the same chemicals. But that wasn't enough. We also ran a dehumidifier every day until spring arrived.

Do we, as believers, work as intentionally to ensure our hearts are clean from sin? We might be tempted to deny what's hidden in our hearts or we might be too embarrassed or proud to uncover it, but that won't work well for us.

Rather than letting sin exist and grow to our detriment, let's invite the Holy Spirit to inspect us. When He exposes sin, let's ask Jesus to wash us clean. Then let's take preventive measures to ensure we don't fall into the same trap again.

The effort is worth it, for a clean heart is a joyful heart. —GRACE FOX

FAITH STEP: *Read Psalm 51:10 and make this your prayer every day.*

FRIDAY, FEBRUARY 19

Let us stop passing judgment on one another. Instead, make up your mind not to put any stumbling block or obstacle in the way of a brother or sister. I am convinced, being fully persuaded in the Lord Jesus, that nothing is unclean in itself. But if anyone regards something as unclean, then for that person it is unclean. Romans 14:13–14 (NIV)

WHEN I BECAME A CHRISTIAN, I stopped listening to certain music to avoid unhelpful temptations. I stopped wearing certain clothes to avoid attention I no longer wanted. I quit drinking. I stopped going certain places and socializing with certain people. My new behavior was partly a new believer's zeal, partly wisdom, and partly genuine spiritual conviction. My early religious zeal also led me to judge others who didn't behave as I did.

I've continued to learn about intimacy with Christ and the conviction of the Holy Spirit, which Paul alludes to in today's Scripture passage and elsewhere. As I've matured spiritually, I've become more relaxed about certain things and stricter about others. All this aligns nicely (and relies heavily) on our *personal*, ongoing, and growing relationship with Jesus.

There are some clear guidelines in Scripture about how I'm to live, but ultimately I'm called to respond to the Holy Spirit's conviction as I'm transformed from the inside out. This process of sanctification is as unique as I am. Jesus knows my personal vulnerabilities, my level of spiritual understanding, and the forces working against me. Drawing close to Christ enables me to tune into what He's doing in me, which also keeps me humble even as I grow.
—ISABELLA YOSUICO

FAITH STEP: *Are you letting others be your Holy Spirit or are you casting yourself in that role? Return to Jesus, who knows just what you need.*

SATURDAY, FEBRUARY 20

He got up, rebuked the wind and said to the waves, "Quiet! Be still!"
Then the wind died down and it was completely calm. Mark 4:39 (NIV)

I LOVE OREGON'S WILD COAST. Though it's stunning during the summer, I'm a storm watcher, so every winter I travel to a historic inn at a tiny seaside town. Rain pelts the windows and sneaks in under the doorjambs at this oceanfront place. Trees twisted by unrelenting wind stretch out their branches, as if warning visitors to stay clear of the shore. And as the sea wages battle against the rugged cliffs, each wave lashes skyward in untamed fury.

Witnessing nature's drama unfold in these squalls reminds me of the terror the disciples experienced as they struggled to stay afloat during a storm. All the while Jesus, in perfect peace, slept. Upon waking, He spoke but three words—"Quiet! Be still!"—to calm the waters, the very same waters He'd created. Settling the seas was no challenge for Him. But like those men, how many times have I forgotten Jesus, in His limitless power, is right beside me?

Today, I sit at my room's window seat, a cup of hot tea cradled in my hands, flames crackling in the fireplace. As I watch the turbulence outside, I sense His peace. Though storms rage all around me, I am safe and warm and dry. Secure. I know Jesus could calm these seas if He chose to, just as He did so long ago.

Jesus can calm the daily chaos that fills our lives as well. And He's there to quiet our souls when tempests brew inside us. When troubles overwhelm, He stills our thoughts and calms our fears. We need simply remember we aren't sailing solo. —HEIDI GAUL

FAITH STEP: *Next time a rain- or snowstorm approaches, grab a cup of tea or coffee and watch. Think of the storms of life Jesus has calmed for you and thank Him.*

SUNDAY, FEBRUARY 21

God is able to bless you abundantly, so that in all things at all times,
having all that you need, you will abound in every good work.
2 Corinthians 9:8 (NIV)

WE USED TO CHAT WITH our three out-of-state grandkids every Sunday. "I liked the package you sent us this month," said twelve-year-old Grace, shortly before her family moved near us. I told her that soon we wouldn't need to send packages anymore. We could give her stuff all the time, in person. Her response surprised me. "I don't think you need to give us presents all the time, Gramma. I don't want to get spoiled."

My eyebrows shot up in amazement as I looked across the table at my husband. What an impressive attitude for a preteen. Still, I see no danger that Grace may become spoiled, but as her grandma, of course I would say that. I don't worry about this because she's always grateful for things we give her. Grace readily shares her possessions with others. I pray she always keeps that generous, thankful attitude.

I believe Jesus feels the same way toward us. He enjoys sharing His blessings, from a new friendship to a new job or house. My closet is full of clothes. My fridge is full of food. My car's gas tank is full. Does that mean I'm spoiled? Only if I refuse to acknowledge that Jesus is the one who gave me all I have.

As long as we don't take His generosity for granted and as long as we are willing to share, we won't become spoiled. We realize that Jesus is far more interested in what His Spirit is doing *in* us than what He does *for* us. Knowing Him is the best gift. —JEANETTE LEVELLIE

FAITH STEP: *Think of ten blessings Jesus has given you. Thank Him by sharing one of them today.*

MONDAY, FEBRUARY 22

Trust in the LORD with all your heart and lean not on your own understanding. Proverbs 3:5 (NIV)

THE EMERGENCY ROOM DOCTOR REFERRED me to an orthopedist after I fell down a staircase. An MRI of my rotator cuff showed no tears, and I felt fine, but the doctor recommended a few weeks of rehab so I could gain range-of-motion strength. When I walked into the rehab facility—a room filled with people on crutches and walkers—I was convinced: *Jesus, I don't belong here!* But the therapist ordered stretching exercises and ultrasound treatments, and I reluctantly got started.

I hurried through my exercises and left. *I really didn't belong. I felt just fine!* As I hustled out, I ran into Sue, my old tennis coach. She was there for shoulder rehab but mentioned her recent bout with breast cancer, so I promised to pray for her. The next day, while icing my shoulder, I sat next to Edmond, who was recovering from knee replacement. We had taught at the same high school years before and enjoyed reminiscing.

Later in the week, I exercised near Carol, a woman whose friend was in hospice. She was caring for her friend's two cats and knew nothing about cats, but I did. I gave her advice about food and cat care. During my ultrasound treatment, my technician Beth kept wiping her eyes. I asked whether her allergies were bothering her, but she said, "No, today is the one-year anniversary of my son's death. I should be over it by now." Having lost a son myself, I was able to reassure her that when grieving the loss of a child, a year was no time at all. We hugged and cried. Thank You, Jesus. Maybe I *did* belong here after all. —PAT BUTLER DYSON

FAITH STEP: *Trust Jesus to place you right where you need to be.*

TUESDAY, FEBRUARY 23

Now I want you to know, brothers and sisters, that what has happened to me has actually served to advance the gospel. As a result, it has become clear throughout the whole palace guard and to everyone else that I am in chains for Christ. Philippians 1:12–13 (NIV)

THERE ARE MANY EVENTS THAT we we'd prefer would never touch us. I'm sure Paul felt that way about being chained in prison. After all, Paul had work to do, places to visit, and churches to encourage. Yet even in these frustrating and painful circumstances, he watched for ways to serve Christ with joy in the midst of it.

Our chains may look different than Paul's. We may be held back by injustice in the workplace so we can't accomplish our vocation— or at least can't fully enjoy the work. Or injury and illness may keep our body chained to a hospital or to our home, when we long to be serving elsewhere. Depression or anxiety can chain our hearts, holding us captive and separating us from others.

Paul knew what it was like to live in chains. Yet he knew the purpose: He was in chains for Christ. Even with frustrating limitations, he saw ways that Jesus was using those very circumstances to give him new ways to serve, new ways to advance the gospel.

I will never enjoy the chains in my life. Where I have choices, I will fight to improve my circumstances. When problems intrude that are beyond my control, I will find ways Jesus is at work—even in the hardship. Ultimately, Jesus will free us from all pain. But while we live in this troubled world, we can trust Him to use our situation—even the chafe of shackles—to bring freedom to others. —SHARON HINCK

FAITH STEP: *What painful situation is holding you back? Ask Jesus to free you from those chains and in the meantime give you ways to advance the gospel because of them.*

WEDNESDAY, FEBRUARY 24

His Son is the reflection of God's glory and the exact likeness of God's being. He holds everything together through his powerful words. Hebrews 1:3 (GW)

WHEN MY MIDDLE GRANDDAUGHTER WAS a toddler, it seemed as though she spoke a language we'd never heard before. During FaceTime calls, Lilah would grab the phone and jabber away. Occasionally she would throw in a real word. Those few words along with her facial expressions allowed us to understand her meaning—most of the time. But one day when she was two-and-a-half years old, she came through loud and clear. I walked into the room to find her nibbling on her Easter bunny. As I pulled it away and rewrapped it, I reminded her that her mom had told her not to eat any more candy that afternoon. She spoke four words: "Don't touch my chocolate!"

Often a few carefully chosen words can convey the clearest message. The Word of God is so powerful that even the shortest phrase can hold a world of meaning. When I'm lonely, I remember Jesus's promise: "I am with you always" (Matthew 28:20, NIV). If I'm worried, I imagine Him saying, "Let not your hearts be troubled" (John 14:1, ESV). When I'm facing a tough or confusing decision, I can pray, "Not my will, but yours" (Luke 22:42, NIV). When I'm becoming complacent about spiritual matters, I need His reminder—"Abide in me" (John 15:4, ESV).

I admire people who memorize whole passages or chapters; I know I need to work on that. But I'm grateful for these stripped-down messages that mean so much at just the right time. Hebrews says that Jesus holds everything together through His powerful words. On some days, just a few of His words are enough to hold me together. —DIANNE NEAL MATTHEWS

FAITH STEP: *Think of brief Bible verses or phrases that are especially meaningful to you. Which one do you need to hear Jesus speaking to you today?*

THURSDAY, FEBRUARY 25

Though your riches increase, do not set your heart on them.
Psalm 62:10 (NIV)

WHEN MY HUSBAND, KEVIN, CALLED to say the insurance company totaled our Cadillac after a deer rammed it, I sighed. (Okay, I cried.) We'd only had that cherry-red beauty for ten weeks. It was a gift from Jesus—through friends who'd recently purchased a new car. The prettiest, fanciest vehicle we'd ever owned. And I loved it.

Every time someone complimented the Caddy, I'd say, "Jesus gave us that car" or "It was a gift." I didn't want anyone to think we were getting rich from Kevin's salary as a pastor or my writing royalties. Even so, my heart filled with pride whenever I drove it.

I was not happy when we had to go car shopping. I knew we'd never find another vehicle I loved as much with our insurance money. We settled on a boring blue SUV that seemed able to withstand future deer collisions. But it was only a car, not my adored Cadillac.

While praying a few days after purchasing our SUV, I finally admitted that the luxury car had made me feel important, special, and significant. Jesus's voice in my heart gently reminded me, *You were important and special before you owned the Caddy and after you lost it. Your possessions don't define you. I do—and I love you dearly.*

I'm certain Jesus didn't cause that deer to crunch our Cadillac to prove His point. He has nothing against us owning pretty things, as long as we don't love them—like I did. I thanked Him for not rebuking me for my prideful attitude. He simply loved me and brought me back to where I belong: with my eyes on Him. —JEANETTE LEVELLIE

FAITH STEP: *Ask Jesus if you own any possessions you might care too much for. If He brings one to mind, simply repent. Then thank Him for defining you by His love.*

FRIDAY, FEBRUARY 26

And he arose, and rebuked the wind, and said unto the sea, Peace, be still.
And the wind ceased, and there was a great calm. Mark 4:39 (KJV)

PEACE, BE STILL. I'VE THOUGHT about tattooing this on my fore-head. But then, helpful as it might be to others, I wouldn't see it. And I need to see it—one hundred times a day.

Although I've got this body that doesn't care much for movement, my mind never rests. I could sit on the couch and watch Outlander all day. (In theory, of course.) But ask me to be still—as in not spinning thoughts around in my head like a whirlpool—and I can't do it without an enormous amount of effort.

This year I've discovered a less strenuous stillness inducer that also produces something good to eat. It's a win-win! But it's not really an "it." It's a he—Herman. Herman the sourdough bread starter. Herman requires my absolute devotion. I must refrigerate him, feed him, and once a week, I must mix him with flour, water, and salt and knead him. Then he rises. Then I knead again. Then he rises again. Bread day means I have a five-hour period of time in which I must be still, paying attention to directions and time and textures. It has become this therapeutic ritual that fills my home with the delicious smell of carbs. But it also fills me—with peace.

Herman has taught me new meaning of the concept of Jesus as the Bread of Life. Besides the obvious metaphor of food, there's stillness—the great calm—that comes from paying attention to His presence, listening to His voice, and placing my will under His authority. —GWEN FORD FAULKENBERRY

FAITH STEP: *Create a ritual that helps you be still. Let me know if you need some bread starter—Herman has many children.*

SATURDAY, FEBRUARY 27

God added, "Regarding Sarai your wife—her name is no longer 'Sarai' but 'Sarah' ('Princess'). And I will bless her and give you a son from her! Yes, I will bless her richly, and make her the mother of nations! Many kings shall be among your posterity." Genesis 17:15—16 (TLB)

A PEDIATRICIAN AND I COAUTHORED a book about birth and a baby's first year. In my research, I found a little paperback titled, *What's In a Name?* It was full of baby names and their meanings. The preface urged future parents to be prayerful about selecting a name instead of just picking something cute from a "Names Trending Now" list. In the passage above, the Lord shows us with Sarah that He attaches great significance to names. After He spoke to her husband, Abram ("exalted father"), he changed his name to Abraham ("father of nations"). He changed Sarai's name ("my princess") to Sarah ("princess of many"). The Lord changed their *identities* and helped them own it by giving them new names. He enlarged their vision of themselves.

Do you see yourself making more of an impact for Jesus in your family, your neighborhood, your city, or the world? Perhaps it's time for a name change! A missionary friend who now serves orphans in rural Russia never saw herself as more than the bored-but-stable paralegal she was before accepting God's call. It began with an assignment she hated—writing a vision for herself on a blank piece of paper. As she let the Holy Spirit inspire her, she wrote one word: *love*. Then another word: *people*. After that assignment, she knew exactly what she was supposed to do! Today, she receives hundreds of letters of thanks, all because she allowed Jesus to show her a new identity. —PAMELA TOUSSAINT HOWARD

FAITH STEP: *Try the same blank-paper exercise my friend did. Trust God to show you a new purpose.*

SUNDAY, FEBRUARY 28

Come with me by yourselves to a quiet place and get some rest.
Mark 6:31 (NIV)

TOMMY IS MY LONG-HAIRED MARMALADE cat. He just showed up one day years ago and elected to stay. I was determined not to feed him, lest we end up with yet another cat. But after a month of his curling around my feet and sleeping on the porch, I realized the decision wasn't mine.

I don't know this little fellow's history, but I've learned he doesn't like being indoors and he loathes being carried and only tolerates our other pets. He is, indeed, a cat unto himself.

Today, as I headed for the mailbox, Tommy appeared. He raced up the stairs to meet me, meowing. I couldn't resist him. I never can. He hopped up almost before I'd settled into the rocker. As he purred, I stared into his green-gold eyes, fascinated.

Why did Jesus drop this cat onto my lap—my life?

I take a deep breath. Tension slips free from my shoulders and neck. I scratch this orange ball of fluff under his chin, and he rolls onto his back. He looks ridiculous, all four chunky paws pointing skyward. I hear gentle laughter and realize it's mine.

Minutes pass, and Tommy decides he's had enough. He jumps to the floor and scurries out of sight. I close my eyes. The breeze is soft on my face, and the deep resonance of our wind chimes stills my thoughts. I rock more slowly.

This ten-pound cat—the one Jesus picked—has led me to this quiet place. Jesus is resting with me. This is peace. —HEIDI GAUL

FAITH STEP: *Take a few minutes today to steal away to a quiet place with Jesus. Rest in His peace.*

MONDAY, MARCH 1

Fear not, for I have redeemed you; I have called you by name,
you are mine. Isaiah 43:1 (ESV)

I ARRIVED BRIGHT AND EARLY at the DMV with a stack of papers, ready to renew my driver's license. Because of new regulations, I needed my passport, my old license, a property tax statement, and my social security card. My turn to approach the counter finally arrived, and I handed all the information to the clerk.

She frowned at my passport. "This doesn't use both of your middle names. They shouldn't have done it this way, so now I can't use it. And the property tax statement uses initials, so that won't qualify. You'll need to come back with a birth certificate and marriage license and utility bills."

I trudged back outside, wondering if I'd ever be able to get enough documents to prove who I am.

I'm grateful that even if the government doesn't know my name, Jesus does. It's one thing to know He came to save the world. It's another thing to realize He knows me intimately and individually and calls me by name, as it promises in Isaiah 43.

In our modern life, it's easy to feel invisible, unknown, misunderstood. And if we seek to find our identity in the things of the world, we'll often be as disappointed as I was at the DMV counter. But when we know that Jesus identifies us as His, we can move through life with joy and confidence. Today's Scripture verse is a source of comfort. We are redeemed. We are cherished. We are known by name. —SHARON HINCK

FAITH STEP: *Write your name on a slip of paper and tuck it in your Bible as a reminder that Jesus calls you by name.*

TUESDAY, MARCH 2

Since we are his children, we are his heirs. In fact, together with Christ we are heirs of God's glory. But if we are to share his glory, we must also share his suffering. Yet what we suffer now is nothing compared to the glory he will reveal to us later. Romans 8:17–18 (NLT)

WHILE IN THE MIDDLE EAST, I met a man who'd been tortured by ISIS for studying social justice and human rights. One night in prison, he prayed, *God, if You exist, then save me.* A short time later, bombs fell on the prison. The attack enabled my new friend to escape to a neighboring country, and that's where believers introduced him to Jesus.

Now he's in a dilemma. He can't return home because his father and brothers have vowed to kill him for converting to Christianity, and the political situation in his country of residence makes it impossible for him to get the necessary paperwork to remain there legally.

My friend suffers from posttraumatic stress disorder, and he lives under constant threat of being deported to certain death, but he will not turn his back on Jesus. He knows that Jesus suffered for his sake, and he counts it a privilege to suffer for Jesus in return.

Love for Jesus and others compels him to daily seek out other refugees who speak his language, even though doing so puts his life at risk. When he finds them, he shares the gospel with them. He disciples those who respond, so their spiritual roots go deep. The reality of hope amid a present hopeless situation and the promise of heaven's future glories motivate him.

This man humbles me. Sharing Jesus's suffering is something I know little about in my secure surroundings. I have much to learn, and I'm thankful for his example. —GRACE FOX

FAITH STEP: *Pray that persecuted believers will remain steadfast in their faith.*

WEDNESDAY, MARCH 3

"Even the dogs eat the crumbs that fall from their master's table." Then Jesus said to her, "Woman, you have great faith! Your request is granted." And her daughter was healed at that moment. Matthew 15:27–28 (NIV)

I FEED MY CAT TOMMY on the porch. He considers a half-full bowl unacceptable and scorns it, so I was surprised to find it empty one night. Not a crumb remained. I thought through possibilities—*raccoons, skunks, a loose dog?* But there was no evidence to support those ideas.

The next evening, I heard strange noises on the porch. I hurried to peek outside.

Surrounding the bowl on skinny stick legs stood a mother bird and her three babies. As they squawked, the mama went from chick to chick, distributing bits of cat chow to them. Our bird feeder hung nearby, but this family preferred a seafood mix. Who was I to question? I left them to their meal, but I couldn't stop thinking about them. Were they outcasts in the feathered community?

It reminded me of the Canaanite woman whom Jesus encountered who begged His mercy on her demon-possessed daughter. When she persisted, eager even for a crumb of His healing, He relented.

This winged family bravely dines from the same bowl as their natural enemy. Like them, I've experienced rejection, shame, and the courage born from the will to survive. I've also tasted the sweetness of Jesus's mercy as He meets my needs. He cares for everyone who faces Him in faith and says, *Please, Lord.*

Today, I'm hanging another feeder. I want that mama and her babies comfortable and happy. Just like me. —HEIDI GAUL

FAITH STEP: *Remember when you've experienced rejection. Have you turned away from someone? Find a way you can help that someone, as the Lord has helped you.*

THURSDAY, MARCH 4

Share each other's burdens, and in this way obey the law of Christ.
Galatians 6:2 (NLT)

SOMETIMES LOVE MEANS SHAVING YOUR head. At age eight, my grandson Roman faced a serious surgery. When he learned that a strip of his hair from one ear to the other would have to be shaved, Roman said, "Nope, it's got to be all my hair or none." His dad agreed and promised to shave his own head as well. His mom offered to join in, but Roman vetoed that.

The day before the surgery, the family gathered on the patio for a head-shaving party. Roman's three-year-old sister begged to have hers done but wasn't allowed to. When I look at photos from that day, I'm always struck by the smile on Roman's face. Despite his age, he understood the nature of the surgery. I think he was able to have that big smile because each time he looked at his dad's bald head, he knew he was not going through the scary time alone. His family had made their love for him obvious.

John 3:16 tells us that, for God, love meant giving up His one and only Son so that people who choose to believe in Him can have eternal life. First John 3:16 explains that the appropriate response to such great love is to imitate Jesus and be willing to lay down our lives for others. We probably won't be called to literally die for another person, but meditating on Jesus's sacrifice makes us want to help share someone else's burden. That might mean practical help, such as childcare, food prep, or chauffeuring. It might mean offering our presence, prayers, and a listening ear. Sometimes, it might even mean shaving our head. —DIANNE NEAL MATTHEWS

FAITH STEP: *Think of someone you know who is facing a heavy burden right now. Ask Jesus to show you ways you can help share their load.*

FRIDAY, MARCH 5

Do not worry about tomorrow, for tomorrow will worry about itself.
Each day has enough trouble of its own. Matthew 6:34 (NIV)

MY HUSBAND, KEVIN, AND I exchanged heated words twice this week. Wait, I may as well tell it straight—we argued. Although we've enjoyed a happy marriage for decades, our different outlooks on everything from taking risks to treating a cold sometimes get us in trouble. *We haven't fought like this in months,* I thought. *I wonder what's going on.* I don't function well when we argue—strife smothers my joy.

I wept as I prayed this morning, distracted by troubled thoughts. With His gentle voice in my heart, Jesus reminded me of our schedule: moving our daughter and her three teenagers to live near us; Kevin starring in a drama on the west coast; my teaching four workshops and sharing a morning message at a writing conference three states away; and caring for my ninety-two-year-old mom who suffers from hearing loss, macular degeneration, and dementia. No wonder we'd fought. We'd let the pressures around us cause tension inside us, upsetting our usual calm relationship.

But what can I do, Lord? We just don't agree on how to manage everything.

Then I heard God's voice: *Is your job to manage everything or to trust Me for the help and wisdom you need?*

Aha. I realized Kevin and I were trying too hard to make sure every detail of our lives—and those we love—worked out perfectly. I'd forgotten that Jesus gave us His Spirit to show us how to live with joy and serenity one day—sometimes one minute—at a time.

I dried my tears, told Jesus thanks, and went to find Kevin. We both needed a hug. —JEANETTE LEVELLIE

FAITH STEP: *Picture Jesus cradling you in His enormous hands, pouring out His wisdom for the day—or perhaps the season—ahead of you.*

SATURDAY, MARCH 6

Confess your sins to one another and pray for one another, that you may be healed. James 5:16 (ESV)

I REGULARLY ATTEND AL-ANON FAMILY meetings, a group dedicated to helping family members of alcoholics. At a recent meeting the topic was step 7, "Humbly ask Him to remove our shortcomings." My "Him" is Jesus who died, not only to take away my shortcomings but to take away the sin of the world (John 1:29). The woman leading the group read a passage out of an Al-Anon book called *Courage to Change* that struck me. "Sometimes the sign that I have actually gotten humble enough to ask my Higher Power to remove a shortcoming is that I can laugh about it." Then the meeting was opened up to sharing.

The man who rides his bike and brings his knitting shared his shortcoming about conflict avoidance. He grew up in a home with alcoholic parents and avoided conflict at all costs because it created chaos. This resonated with a young woman who shared her terror of an upcoming trip home because of her dysfunctional family. Then another woman said something that cracked us up: "I just came back from an Al Anon field trip." She had spent time with her alcoholic sister and two nephews. Renaming her dreaded family gathering as a "field trip" made it sound a lot more fun. What started out as a heavy topic was lightened with a sense of humor.

When we reach a point where we can laugh about our shortcomings, perhaps we're closer to overcoming them. Saying our sins out loud lessens the power of that sin over us, and thankfully, because of Jesus our sins are forgiven. We may struggle with them, but confessing them begins the healing. —JEANNIE BLACKMER

FAITH STEP: *What is a shortcoming in your life? Ask Jesus to help you, then call a trusted friend and share with her your struggle.*

SUNDAY, MARCH 7

For it is by grace you have been saved, through faith—and this is not from yourselves, it is the gift of God—not by works, so that no one can boast.
Ephesians 2:8–9 (NIV)

I CRADLED THE BREAD CUBE and tiny cup of juice in my hands and bowed my head. Due to travel and illness, it seemed a long while since I'd been at my church on a Communion Sunday. I wanted to heed Paul's warning in 1 Corinthians 11:27 not to partake in "an unworthy manner" (NIV). I did not want to take the symbols of Christ's costly sacrifice lightly. So I began to search my heart, and I felt unworthy.

I remembered how many days I'd recently let slip by without time in prayer and Bible reading. The days spent focused on my personal interests rather than on seeking His will. Moments when I did not act like a Christ follower. Then He reminded me that salvation is not something I've earned but a gift of grace. I don't have to "perform" in order to keep it. Communion, or the Lord's Supper, is not about me, but about Jesus and the unconditional love that compelled Him to lay down His life. The love that prompted Him to offer the bread and wine to His disciples during that last Passover meal even though He knew how they would fail Him during the next few days.

Hebrews 7:25 says that Jesus "is able to save completely those who come to God through him" (NIV). He's accomplished it once and for all. Even if I never pray, attend church, or read the Bible again, I will still belong to Him. I will still be cleansed by His blood.
—DIANNE NEAL MATTHEWS

FAITH STEP: *Memorize Ephesians 2:8–9 so you can quote it next time you're tempted to evaluate your performance.*

MONDAY, MARCH 8

Let each of you look not only to his own interests, but also to the interests of others. Philippians 2:4 (ESV)

MY KIDS HAVE HINTED I'M a bit compulsive. No way! I just thrive on my routine. Every weekday morning after devotions with my husband and a power breakfast of boiled eggs and wheat toast, I don my riding gear and hop on my bike. I ride for thirty minutes, seven miles—the same route daily.

One Monday morning, I was late getting started. *I'll ride fast and make up the time,* I thought, and off I zoomed. I sped along, ignoring the man in the black car who signaled me to stop. Lowering his window, he hollered, "Have you seen an elderly lady on the street? My wife's mother has Alzheimer's and she's wandered off." And just like that, my plan for the morning flew out the window.

I asked, "How long has she been gone? What street does she live on? What was she wearing?"

Slowly I cruised down every street in my neighborhood, my eyes peeled for a small figure in a pink robe. *Jesus,* I prayed, *please keep this dear woman safe.* It could have easily been my own mother, who'd suffered from dementia.

Finally, I saw the black car again. The man inside was grinning as he yelled, "We found her! She'd fallen in a ditch, but she's okay. She's in the ambulance now. Thanks for caring!"

Thank you, Jesus. I headed home, and it dawned on me that I hadn't gotten my normal aerobic exercise—but so what? Someone's mother was safe. The lost sheep had been found. How much more important was that than sticking to my routine? —PAT BUTLER DYSON

FAITH STEP: *Today, pay attention to how Jesus wants to use you. When He calls or you see a need, don't hesitate to help.*

TUESDAY, MARCH 9

There remains, then, a Sabbath-rest for the people of God; for anyone who enters God's rest also rests from their works, just as God did from his. Let us, therefore, make every effort to enter that rest... Hebrews 4:9–11 (NIV)

A HIGH ENERGY TYPE A person, most of my life I've been very disciplined, structured, and motivated. Like all virtues, it has a flipside. While I've enjoyed (and shared) tangible benefits from my manic methods, it's also cost me and others peace and pleasure. I've been so driven that I've sometimes made hasty mistakes, been insensitive to others, and missed God's quiet leading. I have a very hard time being in the moment and simply enjoying life. As they say, I am sometimes a "human doing" instead of a human being.

After encountering Jesus, I confess my zealousness became religious—and maybe not the kind of zeal we celebrate. My heavenly Daddy kindly sent me messengers to help: First, my son Pierce, since all kids have a way of reordering our priorities. And then, more pointedly, my son Isaac, who has Down syndrome. Isaac lives life on a leisurely pace, relishing every minute. He has taught me so much about slowing down and smelling the roses.

Moving from suburban Baltimore to West Virginia and then Florida has also taught me a lot about enjoying everyday life, valuing people over productivity, and simply being present. The rest of the world wasn't rushing along at my pace. Eventually, I had no choice but to slow down.

Jesus promises an abundant, peaceful, and love-filled life. Living in rhythm with His Spirit is gentle, unhurried, and full.
—ISABELLA YOSUICO

FAITH STEP: *Is there any area of life where you see yourself rushing and rigid and anything but restful? Make an intentional effort to experiment with doing the opposite. Ask Jesus for help.*

WEDNESDAY, MARCH 10

You make known to me the path of life; in your presence there is fullness of joy . . . Psalm 16:11 (ESV)

AFTER WAITING NINE YEARS TO use my passport—for more than just a hop across the border into Canada—I took great joy presenting it to the customs agent in Copenhagen, Denmark. My daughter's training for her job kept us in Denmark for more than a month. It was the trip of a lifetime.

Unlike a typical tourist visit, we lived in a neighborhood. Like the locals, we walked to the market and did other errands. My daughter and I appreciated the immersion into a new culture. The people we met were polite, kind, and caring. They knew enough English to cover for our lack of knowledge of the difficult Danish language. We kept fresh flowers on the table, because flower stands abounded on the streets, as if the Danish people understand the importance of feeding joy.

But one stark absence stood out. I only once heard or saw the name of Jesus in public. His name came up often in our apartment but not beyond its walls, though I may not have been looking or listening in the right places. But I noted that absence with a heavy sadness. I also regret not spreading the joy of Jesus while I was there.

I'd return to Denmark in a heartbeat. And I have a new prayer burden for those who follow Christ in the community in which we lived but have little public voice and those who have yet to discover that nothing is as important to individuals and communities as the presence of Jesus. —CYNTHIA RUCHTI

FAITH STEP: *Wherever you go, make it a practice to whisper a prayer or declare the name of Jesus.*

THURSDAY, MARCH 11

And they said to Him, "We have here only five loaves and two fish."
He said, "Bring them here to Me." Matthew 14:16–18 (NKJV)

MARRYING LATER IN LIFE, I was thrust into a new role—stepmom
to two tall, lovely teenagers. When we first met years before, the
question in my heart was, *Will they like me?* Once I married their
dad, it became, *Do they* still *like me? Can I do this?* Although I had
written loads on the subject of parenting, it was mainly as an inter-
viewer, editor, or ghostwriter—I relied on another person's wisdom,
then came alongside and made their experiences sound pretty. That
method doesn't work so well when you're the parent. I'm blessed
that things have been great with my bonus kids so far, but there
are times when I feel like the disciples in the passage above, overwhelmed and underfunded. This is when I need Jesus's direction:
"Bring them here to Me." I found I have more loaves and fish than
I thought!

Perhaps you have decades of experience parenting or just a few
years on the job like me. Either way, don't rely so much on what
you know, nor be so moved by what you see (which can sometimes
be scary!). In everything—what to say when, and how and when
to hold back and pray for an answer—bring Him your loaves and
set them down. It's okay to tell Jesus, "This is all I have for this
situation." It shows honor to Him as our Parent. Then what we
get from our heavenly Dad, we pass down and watch it multiply.
—PAMELA TOUSSAINT HOWARD

FAITH STEP: *In your next worrisome situation, turn to Him as soon as possible
instead of the Google search bar. Relax your heart. Be still and listen. He will
make a feast out of a famine.*

FRIDAY, MARCH 12

When the Chief Shepherd appears, you will receive the crown of glory that will never fade away. 1 Peter 5:4 *(NIV)*

"I HOPE BILL FROM THE Optimists Club invites me to judge their youth speech contest again this year," I told my husband, Kevin. He smiled. I'm sure he remembered how much I enjoyed the experience. I told him, a little embarrassed, how associating with English and speech teachers made me feel important. Taking notes while the young people delivered their speeches, conferring with fellow judges, and even receiving an Olive Garden gift card as a thank you bolstered my self-esteem.

I know my worth isn't based on whom I associate with. In fact, the contest director was desperate for a judge, and someone gave him my name. This honor had more to do with my availability than my credentials as a writer and public speaker.

An ancient Roman custom ensured that their generals remained humble. When a conquering general returned from battle, Roman citizens cheered and threw flowers as the general paraded by in his chariot, his children at his side. Behind him stood a slave who whispered in his ear, "All glory is fleeting. All glory is fleeting. All glory is fleeting."

Everyone likes to feel important. God created us with the need for affirmation and respect. But we must balance that need with the constant reminder that glory from people fades more quickly than flowers in the street the day after a parade. Only the glory Jesus gives never fades. His praise comes to those who say yes to His grace and whose hearts belong to Him. His glory is the only glory that lasts forever. —JEANETTE LEVELLIE

FAITH STEP: *Think of something you've done that others have praised you for. Give that applause back to Jesus. Ask Him to show you something He admires about you, and pray for grace to please only Him.*

SATURDAY, MARCH 13

Let us run with perseverance the race marked out for us, fixing our eyes on Jesus, the pioneer and perfecter of faith. For the joy set before him he endured the cross, scorning its shame, and sat down at the right hand of the throne of God. Hebrews 12:1–2 (NIV)

IT'S BEEN A PARTICULARLY DIFFICULT week. I have some tough decisions looming, and even though I've prayed and sought direction, I haven't found any peace yet. On top of that, I'm experiencing stress at home that can be described in one word: *teenagers*. And, of course, there is always a mountain of laundry to do and a pile of papers to grade. I know everyone has weeks like this, but the question is, How do we keep difficulties from stealing our joy?

There's a verse in an old hymn that says, "Turn your eyes upon Jesus." It's akin to the verse above, which tells us to fix our eyes on Him. Study what He does and Jesus's example: "For the joy set before him he endured the cross." I think that means that He knew He could make it through anything, even death on a cross, because He kept His eyes on the prize. Jesus's prize was to be seated at the right hand of God.

What's our prize? Some might say it's heaven, and I think that's true. But before that—our prize here on earth is Jesus. Spending time with Him. Being in His presence. The joy set before us is Jesus. He's where we find our joy in the midst of trouble; He's the One we trust to see us through to the other side. —GWEN FORD FAULKENBERRY

FAITH STEP: *Think about where you look for joy. Is it acquiring things? Gaining the approval of people? Set your mind on Jesus today and find your joy in knowing that wherever you go, He goes with you.*

SUNDAY, MARCH 14

My God will meet all your needs according to the riches of his glory in Christ Jesus. Philippians 4:19 (NIV)

LAST SUNDAY, AS I HEADED across the parking lot after church, a woman I hadn't seen for a while walked ahead of me. I caught up and asked the too-traditional question, "How are you doing?"

She answered, "Great... okay, there's more behind that response." Her smile didn't fade, but her voice had dropped by several decibels. She explained that life was great only because Jesus is good, not because her circumstances were. She'd been betrayed, made bad relationship choices when she thought that Jesus wasn't enough, and she was still recovering from recently distancing herself from her bad choices, still choking on the fallout. But her confidence in the goodness of Jesus had been strengthened in the process. She could say with conviction that He'd proved Himself more than enough, even when everyone else—and her own decisions— disappointed her.

Many of us can point to a time when life around us crumbled— financially, physically, relationally—but during that season we learned with greater clarity to embrace the wonder that Jesus is the only truth that never lets us down, abandons or disappoints us.

In some ways, my church friend represents thrill seekers everywhere—those convinced the things that thrill the human heart are worldly experiences, possessions, or other human beings. By holding us tightly while we discover the truth—sometimes at great cost—Jesus proves again and again that He is not just more than enough but all we will ever need. —CYNTHIA RUCHTI

FAITH STEP: *The next time someone asks how you're doing, respond with "Great!" to match your conviction—because of Jesus.*

MONDAY, MARCH 15

*Go therefore and make disciples of all the nations, baptizing them
in the name of the Father and of the Son and of the Holy Spirit.*
Matthew 28:19 (NKJV)

I REMEMBER MY FIRST TRY at evangelizing. It was at a church event
held near a local park. We were told to approach strangers in pairs,
tell them the Good News, and invite them to church. As a new
believer, this was very tough for me. I was tongue tied and embarrassed to walk up to people in New York City that I didn't know.
New Yorkers definitely didn't want to be distracted, I reasoned. But
the truth is I was ashamed and ashamed of being ashamed. How
would I make disciples of "all the nations" when I couldn't even
approach someone in the park up the street?

After years of going around the mountain, I settled the evangelism
issue in my heart: I would share my faith naturally, in whatever way
I could, with whomever I could, whenever I saw an opportunity. I
would be mindful, willing, and available. Resolving this dilemma
has freed me to have many wonderful "Jesus encounters" with wait-
resses, neighbors, HVAC repairmen, extended family members,
folks in nursing homes, and grocery-store clerks. Even small gestures
like writing "Jesus cares about you" on the envelope with a hotel staff
tip or on a dinner check, is evangelism. As a result of being available
this way, I've prayed with many and even seen some healed in Jesus's
name. Don't get me wrong, evangelistic events and overseas mission
trips are awesome experiences. But the main way I fulfill the Great
Commission is by simply sharing my faith with people I encounter
as I walk along life's way. —PAMELA TOUSSAINT HOWARD

FAITH STEP: *Commit to being mindful of Him, willing, and available to speak
for Him as you go about your daily activities.*

TUESDAY, MARCH 16

God made him who had no sin to be sin for us, so that in him we might become the righteousness of God. 2 Corinthians 5:21 (NIV)

ON THE TELEVISION SHOW *LET'S Make a Deal*, the host invites audience members to make transactions. For instance, he hands someone a thousand dollars and then presents her with a choice: "Do you want to keep it or trade it for what's hidden behind the curtain?"

Making a trade means taking a risk. The contestant stands to either win a prize, such as a dream vacation, a car, or furniture, or she'll walk away with an item worth little or nothing. Some participants hesitate and weigh their options. Others immediately accept or reject the offer.

God invites us to make a transaction too, but it's not a game. "Come now, let us reason together, says the LORD: though your sins are like scarlet, they shall be as white as snow; though they are red like crimson, they shall become like wool" (Isaiah 1:18, ESV). It's as if He's saying, "Do you want to keep your sin stains or trade them for a clean slate?" Some folks hesitate and weigh their options. Others immediately accept or reject the offer.

Making that spiritual transaction seems an obvious choice. We give Jesus our sin and the death penalty attached to it, in exchange for His spotless record and the reward that goes with it—eternal life (Romans 8:1–4). Put another way, we give Jesus our guilty verdict for breaking God's law, and He gives us a full pardon. But He takes it a step further. He also fulfills our sentence to satisfy justice.

We trade our rags for heaven's riches. The transaction is a sweet deal for everyone who makes it, and everyone who makes it wins. —GRACE FOX

FAITH STEP: *Thank Jesus for His role in the transaction that made you a winner in this life and the next.*

WEDNESDAY, MARCH 17

You will not have to fight this battle. Take up your positions; stand firm and see the deliverance the LORD will give you, Judah and Jerusalem. Do not be afraid; do not be discouraged. Go out to face them tomorrow, and the LORD will be with you. 2 Chronicles 20:17 (NIV)

WHEN A LOVED ONE WAS diagnosed with a serious illness, I jumped into action: appointments with social workers, doctors, palliative care nurses; arranging help; making lists of all the recommendations, medications, and plans from the various specialists.

I arranged delivered meals, but my relative didn't like them. I scheduled home care, but she wouldn't allow them to help her clean or cook. Every step felt like a battle. I was running in circles, and nothing was working. My efforts only stressed out my loved one who didn't want help.

At one point, a home care nurse said, "I know you're worried about her, but is it worth fighting all these battles? Even if you do everything right, it won't cure the illness. Perhaps for now it would be wise to focus on other things instead of forcing her to accept help she doesn't want."

The next time I visited, I determined not to drive the agenda, not to scold, not to make suggestions. Instead I listened and validated her feelings and needs. Soon she was sharing childhood stories, and we were laughing together. I was reminded that sometimes I waste energy fighting for control over things that aren't in my control. There are battles I can't win. Yet Jesus will fight for me. He wins all the ultimate battles. Healing comes—in heaven, if not on earth. Sins are forgiven. Relationships are restored. Not because of my efforts, but because He is with me. —SHARON HINCK

FAITH STEP: *Is there a battle He is calling you to relinquish? Stand firm and watch for His salvation.*

THURSDAY, MARCH 18

For everyone who asks receives, and he who seeks finds, and to him who knocks it will be opened. Luke 11:10 (NKJV)

THE THING I DO BEST is multitasking. One afternoon, I decided to combine my exercise bike ride with a trip to the mailbox. As luck would have it, I'd gotten a package—a long but lightweight box. No problem! I'd center the package across my handlebars, drop it off at the house and resume my ride. But the patch of mud from a recent rain, right in front of my driveway, took me by surprise. Riding too fast and braking hard with my one free hand sent me airborne, hurtling over the handlebars and landing with a splat on the slimy concrete.

Sprawled in the cul-de-sac, humiliated, I prayed, *Dear Jesus, please don't let anyone see me!* I was bleeding and my shoulder hurt. I knew my daughter Brooke was in the house. Surely she would see me and come to my aid. About five minutes later, I modified my prayer: *Dear Jesus, please let someone see me!* Time passed with no apparent hope of rescue, so I gingerly moved to my hands and knees, finally rising to my feet. All body parts seemed to be working, so I gathered the package and the muddy mail, righted my bike and went into the house.

"What happened to you?" Brooke exclaimed. I told her I'd just taken a little tumble but was okay. I washed as much of the mud and blood off as I could and went back out to resume my ride. As I rode, I had a revelation: even if you send Jesus mixed messages, He sends you an answer. Mine was *Help yourself!* —PAT BUTLER DYSON

FAITH STEP: *Ask Jesus to help you trust Him to lead you, no matter what your situation.*

FRIDAY, MARCH 19

Happy are those who are merciful to others . . . Matthew 5:7 (GNT)

I'M IN AWE OF THE talented people who take a concept or business and create a fitting logo. With simple art, design, and lettering, a logo becomes a symbol of the company or idea. The public is reminded what the business represents when it sees the logo, without an explanation from sales or marketing.

My logo for my writing business is a pen shaped like a threaded needle, which accompanies the tagline "I can't unravel. I'm hemmed in Hope." Even if no one else recognizes the connection, I do. It informs how I write, reminding me that hope lies at the core of it all.

Haven't we too often assumed that joy's logo must be a smiley face? The bright yellow sunlike image with two eyes and a single curved line or toothy grin has somehow come to represent "I'm smiling" or "I'm happy" or "That gives me joy."

But according to words Jesus said—His marketing copy—the truly happy and joy-filled aren't represented by a smiley-face logo. How do you create a fitting and recognizable logo for "the poor in spirit . . . those who mourn . . . those who hunger . . . the merciful . . . those who are persecuted [for Jesus's sake]" (Matthew 5:3–12, NIV)? What symbol encapsulates all that Jesus said about authentic joy?

The fish symbol? No. That was born out of a coded method of letting others know of one's authentic faith in Christ. The cross? That's a priceless, iconic symbol of authentic sacrifice and authentic love. The empty tomb? Authentic victory and hope. If only a graphic designer could capture a representation—an iconic image—of the depth of joy a soul knows when at peace, when fully trusting in Jesus. —CYNTHIA RUCHTI

FAITH STEP: *You'll come across many company logos throughout the day. Let them serve as a reminder of what Jesus offers you—authentic soul peace.*

SATURDAY, MARCH 20

In My Father's house are many mansions; if it were not so, I would have told you. I go to prepare a place for you. John 14:2 (NKJV)

I WILL DO ALMOST ANYTHING to avoid cleaning my house. Watch reruns of stupid TV shows. Alphabetize my spices. Even peruse online sites that sell super-duper cleaning gadgets. My dust never settles into bunnies but rather into elephants.

Yet I'm always willing to clean someone else's mess. If Mom leaves dirty clothes on her bathroom floor or letters on her coffee table, I pick them up without a thought. If friends invite us to dinner, I cheerfully help clear the table and wash dishes. When our daughter's new home needed cleaning before she moved in, I made a party of it. Two friends and I packed up all our cleaning supplies, and I called ahead for a large pizza. I didn't complain once as I scrubbed counters, washed windows, and swept away cobwebs.

Why do I enjoy helping others clean, yet neglect my own house? Because I love those precious people more than I love my own comfort.

When Jesus left His glorious home in God's presence, He knew He was coming to a life of suffering, persecution, and eventual death. But He loved each one of us more than He loved the comfort of heaven. Although separation from the Father grieved Him, He embraced the sacrifice with joy, because it meant giving us a place in His family.

I believe Jesus also delights in preparing our heavenly dwelling places. Building our homes—mansions—isn't a chore for Him because He loves us with abandon.

And I'm looking forward to a clean house in heaven with no dust elephants. —JEANETTE LEVELLIE

FAITH STEP: *As you clean your home today, listen to praise music and thank Jesus for the sacrifice He willingly made for you.*

SUNDAY, MARCH 21

By faith Sarah herself also received strength to conceive seed, and she bore a child when she was past the age, because she judged Him faithful who had promised. Hebrews 11:11 (NKJV)

IS THERE ANYTHING YOU'VE BEEN trying to birth? A personal goal, a ministry, a business, a baby? Whatever that burning desire is, if it lines up with the Word of God, be assured that Jesus gave you the strength to conceive it and will see you through to the joyful birth!

It can be challenging to nurture something that others say is not possible: it's too big, too small, too much, or too late. Sometimes just through a frown, gesture, or negative attitude, a person can communicate, "It won't happen." The outside world can also rain on your dream. Your internet browser pulls up reasons why you cannot and should not do it and reminds you that there's only a 1 percent chance of success. Whose report will you believe? Let's believe the report of the Lord.

I have a dear friend who is the closest thing I've seen to the apostle Paul in the twenty-first century. She ministers wherever and whenever there is a need. One thing she told me years ago is when God says yes and people say no, just stand. She meant spiritually but also literally. When I step forward to receive that dream, I might have to go to a bank, a passport office, a doctor, or to someone who has the resources to help me. And they may say no. But by the grace of God, a no can become a yes when I stand and receive what I know He has conceived inside me! —PAMELA TOUSSAINT HOWARD

FAITH STEP: *Take a step today toward accomplishing your vision. If people say no, don't argue—just stand up on the inside and outside, and watch what happens.*

MONDAY, MARCH 22

I have told you this so that my joy may be in you and that your joy may be complete. John 15:11 (NIV)

"DESCRIBE YOURSELF IN ONE WORD," the keynote speaker suggested. "Don't overthink it. Jot down the first thing that comes to your mind. Make it relate to something you'd like to pass on to others."

Something I'd like to pass on to others? So many options. I settled on *hope*. I breathe it in from the One who invented the idea. I breathe it out, knowing the world desperately needs it and Jesus has hope to give in abundance (Romans 15:13).

What word would Jesus pick for Himself? *Love? Redemption? HOPE* in all caps? In John 15:9-17, Jesus said that joy defines Him and that His teaching about abiding in Him, loving one another, and responding to the Father with obedience leads to this one pinnacle—He wants to infuse us with joy. And not just any run-of-the-mill joy—*His* joy in us. In other places in Scripture, Jesus tells us that His peace isn't ordinary either (John 14:27). It's not like the faux peace the world gives. In today's passage, He lets us know that His joy is as out of this world as His peace is. My mind still wrestles with what that fully looks like. How can any of us grasp the magnitude of Jesus pouring His joy into us, so much that it's complete, full, and fills all the crevices and spaces and gaps?

I have a new answer to the assignment to describe myself in one word: *Jesus-grateful*. If it's hyphenated, it's one word, right? —CYNTHIA RUCHTI

FAITH STEP: *Write your name with a fine-tipped pen. Then with a bold marker, superimpose the word JOY over your name. Imagine His joy consuming you as you venture into the day and its challenges.*

TUESDAY, MARCH 23

Now faith is confidence in what we hope for and assurance about what we do not see. Hebrews 11:1 (NIV)

HE'S BACK! OLD PERSISTENT GRAY Cat. He turns up every morning and every evening for me to feed him. His piercing meow demands my attention, and if I don't respond immediately, he climbs up the back door. I don't know whose cat he is or if he really belongs to anyone, but he's pretty chubby for a stray. No doubt he dines at multiple homes in the neighborhood. Gray Cat exudes confidence. I peer into those green eyes of his and see his complete assurance that I will feed him. And I do!

What would it be like to have absolute assurance that I would be cared for always? As a child, I remember singing the beloved hymn by Fannie J. Crosby, "Blessed Assurance," which includes the line "Jesus is mine." I love that thought: Jesus is *mine*! I've always believed I am His, but to consider Jesus being *mine* is almost more than I can fathom. There are so many people out there who need Jesus, who yearn for His love and attention. But still, if I reach out to Him, He is mine.

Words from the third stanza speak to me: *Perfect submission, all is at rest / I in my Savior am happy and blest / Watching and waiting, looking above / Filled with His goodness, lost in His love.* I can think of no place I'd rather be than lost in His love.

How I yearn to have the assurance of that gray cat. I want to spend more time resting in Jesus and His blessed assurance.
—PAT BUTLER DYSON

FAITH STEP: *Look up the words to Fanny J. Crosby's "Blessed Assurance." Say them or sing them to yourself. Take those words to heart!*

WEDNESDAY, MARCH 24

So I will restore to you the years that the swarming locust has eaten . . .
Joel 2:25 (NKJV)

MY CHILDHOOD WAS DIFFICULT. My parents were remarkable people who struggled with substance abuse, mental illness, and their own dysfunctional histories. Our home was chaotic and emotionally unsafe. Partly because of my Italian family's expectations and partly because of my innate temperament, I assumed a caretaking role from an early age. A tiny "adult," even the way I played was seldom carefree or childlike.

Life only got more complicated as time went on. My anxious and controlling caretaking even served me for a time. I started working young, advanced through the ranks, awkwardly assumed responsibility for my mom, and sought to compensate for my childhood with achievement, relationships, and money.

It didn't work.

Thankfully, my misery led me to the ultimate satisfier of souls, Jesus. I soon got married to a kind Christian man and eventually had two boys, Pierce and Isaac—children I didn't expect to have.

Jesus is restoring my lost years (Joel 2:25) in unexpected ways, including enabling me through my own kids to have the joyous, carefree childhood I never had. Not only by observing their joy, but by enabling me to frolic right alongside them with goofy freedom. God has performed spiritual surgery on me and given me back what the "locusts" had eaten. Whether it's hide-and-seek, playing with balls or dolls, sports, make pretend, or mayhem, I can experience them all with full, unexpected delight. —ISABELLA YOSUICO

FAITH STEP: *Reflect on your losses. Ask Jesus for the ability to have faith and discern how He has or can restore them.*

THURSDAY, MARCH 25

So if the Son sets you free, you will be free indeed. John 8:36 (NIV)

WE LIVE NEXT DOOR TO the church we pastor. When our midwestern weather is either too muggy or frigid to walk outside, we exercise in the sanctuary. Three days ago, a visitor joined us.

My husband, Kevin, and I had barely started walking when we heard skittering sounds overhead. "Uh-oh, a bird is stuck between the roof and the ceiling," I said. We hauled the ancient eight-foot ladder up from the basement, and Kevin placed it under the ceiling tile where we'd heard the noises. He removed a tile, peering inside the opening. No bird.

Four times we moved that ladder—it grew heavier each time—and four times Kevin removed a new tile, trying to free the bird. I began to worry. Was it worth my husband falling and breaking his bottom, or worse, to save a silly, lost bird?

Finally the bird flew out and flapped around the sanctuary, trying to escape. I opened both front doors. But our feathered friend was so scared, it couldn't find its way to freedom. Kevin got the idea to trap the bird with the long-handled baptistery cleaning net. After I secured the bird, Kevin gently held it in his hands and released it into the bright day.

While I finished exercising I thought, *That poor helpless bird reminds me of me.* All the messes I've created. All the times I've found myself trapped in sin or silly blunders. Flapping around, scared, and looking for a way out. Forever merciful, Jesus goes to great lengths to rescue me. He never rebukes or scolds me. Instead, He gently sets me free to soar again. What love! —JEANETTE LEVELLIE

FAITH STEP: *Look up the words to the gospel song "I'm So Glad Jesus Set Me Free." Sing or say it and thank Jesus for His freeing love.*

FRIDAY, MARCH 26

How beautiful on the mountains are the feet of the messenger who brings good news, the good news of peace and salvation, the news that the God of Israel reigns! Isaiah 52:7 (NLT)

I COUNSEL OTHERS TO CARE for their feet because healthy feet are vital for a healthy lifestyle. When our feet hurt, it harms our whole body. I know because I've had four foot surgeries from neuroma, a painful pinched nerve. Most women get it from years of wearing tight, high-heeled shoes. Mine were from years of skiing moguls in hard, tight ski boots. My last surgery was the worst. The surgeon had to go through the bottom of my foot to remove the inflamed nerve.

Before my surgery I decided to get a pedicure. I vainly wanted to make my feet beautiful before the operation. When I went in for a post-surgery appointment to get the gauze and stitches removed, my foot looked horrendous. The medical tech removing the bandages remarked on my painted toes, "That's like putting lipstick on a pig."

I started to wonder if I do the same thing with my spiritual feet. The Bible mentions feet more than one hundred times, often referring to a spiritual lesson. Our spiritual feet carry us on the path of following Jesus (Psalm 119:105) and as we spread the news of the peace and salvation Jesus offers. Having beautiful spiritual feet is more than a dab of fingernail polish. Keeping beautiful spiritual feet is a long-term process of developing a secure spiritual foundation through fellowship with Jesus, prayer, and studying the Bible. Now, I remind others to take care of their physical feet but also to create beautiful spiritual feet, so our feet will carry us into old age with a vibrant, hopeful, believable message that our God reigns. —JEANNIE BLACKMER

FAITH STEP: *Pamper your feet today as a reminder to cultivate your spiritual feet every day.*

SATURDAY, MARCH 27

"But what about you?" he asked. "Who do you say I am?"
Matthew 16:15 (NIV)

I USED TO BE OBSESSED with researching online reviews before making a purchase. After a while, I found they made me a little crazy. Sometimes reviews say exactly the opposite about the same item: "This vacuum has great suction" and "This vacuum has no suction." Others are just ridiculous: "Product came today; packaging looks great." Recent articles explain how some companies pay people to write fake glowing reviews of products. Other companies pay people to write negative reviews about their competitors' products.

Consumer reviews can offer helpful insights, but I've learned they're not always a reliable foundation for purchasing decisions. The court of public opinion is also not a solid foundation for life's decisions, especially when it comes to spiritual matters. Large crowds followed Jesus in Galilee but after He tried to reveal His identity in His hometown, the people drove Him out and attempted to hurl Him off a cliff. When Jesus entered Jerusalem to celebrate Passover, crowds hailed Him. A few days later, crowds screamed for His crucifixion. During His trials, paid witnesses offered false testimony against Him.

We hear conflicting opinions about Jesus today, but in our Bibles we find reliable information about Him. Regardless of what people around us think, choosing to follow Jesus is the best decision we'll ever make. When we review who He is and what He's done for us, all the stars in the sky are not enough to rate Him as highly as He deserves. —DIANNE NEAL MATTHEWS

FAITH STEP: *Search out key Scripture passages about Jesus so you'll be prepared when you hear a false testimony about Him.*

PALM SUNDAY, MARCH 28

The crowd spread their cloaks on the road, and others cut branches from the trees and spread them on the road. . . . shouting, "Hosanna to the Son of David! . . . " Matthew 21:8–9 (ESV)

ONE EVENING ON A VACATION in Egypt, my husband and I went for a walk by the Nile River. Children played while adults relaxed under palm trees. It was a lovely, festive sight. As Stone and I made our way down steps from the road to the riverside, we caused some commotion. I still don't understand it; all I can figure is we must have looked to the locals like life-sized Ken and Barbie dolls. Men rushed over to us. They began spreading their jackets out for me to step on, which of course I refused to do. It was the sweetest—and strangest—thing anyone has ever done for me. I was embarrassed, but touched.

Two days after such royal treatment, we were scammed in Giza. Two dishonest men charged us eighty dollars apiece for a "special" tour that included a camel ride in the Sahara desert with distant views of the pyramids we were supposed to see up close. We finally got our money back, but not before haggling with the tourist police.

This kind of irony is extraordinarily mild next to what Jesus experienced during Holy Week. In the perfect illustration of humanity's fickleness, the same voices that cried "Hosanna!" would barely catch their breaths before calling out "Crucify Him!" I never see such reversals coming. What was it like for Jesus to know what would happen to Him in a week? And with that understanding, what kind of love drives someone forward to death on a cross? —GWEN FORD FAULKENBERRY

FAITH STEP: *Pray: O, Jesus, I long to be faithful, and yet I feel the tug to leave You at times—to follow the crowd, or even my own understanding. Give me the strength to love You as You deserve.*

MONDAY, MARCH 29

As he was returning to the city, he became hungry. And seeing a fig tree
by the wayside, he went to it and found nothing on it but only leaves.
And he said to it, "May no fruit ever come from you again!" And the
fig tree withered at once. Matthew 21:18–19 (ESV)

ON PALM SUNDAY, JESUS ENTERED Jerusalem with great celebration.
Oddly, to me at least, He headed straight to the temple, driving out
money changers and quoting Scripture as He capsized tables. Blind
and lame people came in next, and He healed them all while
children praised Him and the church leaders grumbled. Then He
left them, and headed to Bethany for the night.

I like to think Jesus got a good night's rest there with Mary,
Martha, and Lazarus. They were His friends—and He was comfortable there. Surely Martha cooked Him some good food. But the
next morning as He went back toward Jerusalem, He got hungry.
And when He stopped to pick figs and found only leaves, He cursed
the tree. Am I the only one who also finds this behavior odd? A clue
to what Jesus was thinking can be found later in the day, however.
As He continues teaching in parables, the religious people question
His authority again. His frustration with them—and grief, I think,
for their lost potential—is shown through the parable of the talents.
He tells them, "The kingdom of God will be taken away from you
and given to a people producing its fruits" (Matthew 21:43, ESV).
—GWEN FORD FAULKENBERRY

FAITH STEP: *Do something tangibly fruitful today. Start a Bible study, donate to*
a foodbank, volunteer to help in the nursery. Be a tender—not just a taker—of the
kingdom's garden.

TUESDAY, MARCH 30

In the hearing of all the people he said to his disciples, "Beware of the scribes, who like to walk around in long robes, and love greetings in the market-places and the best seats in the synagogues and the places of honor at feasts, who devour widows' houses and for a pretense make long prayers. They will receive the greater condemnation." Luke 20:45–47 (ESV)

SO MUCH HAS BEEN WRITTEN about Holy Week. Some of it is unusual, but a lot is beautiful. Recently, I've studied by reading, looking at calendars, and trying to piece together gospel accounts to figure out what Jesus did every day that week leading up to Easter. I discovered things I never noticed before, like Jesus spending casual time with the disciples and getting aggravated by barren fig trees, and there's also a big picture I haven't thought much about. Today's verses sum up the big picture for me: Jesus does not care for the attitudes of the Pharisees. Every time He interacts with them, their tone seems to come across as exhausting, discouraging, annoying. They exasperate Him and make Him righteously mad.

As I read about the Pharisees, I began to remember times when my own behavior reminded me of theirs. One distinct impression came over me: I don't want to have this effect on Jesus. I don't want to act like a Pharisee. —GWEN FORD FAULKENBERRY

FAITH STEP: *Read Matthew 21–27. Write down everything you notice about the Pharisees' role in the story of Holy Week. Do you ever behave in the same way?*

WEDNESDAY, MARCH 31

But Jesus . . . said to them, "Why do you trouble the woman? For she has done a beautiful thing to me." Matthew 26:10 (ESV)

WEDNESDAY OF HOLY WEEK IS less detailed in the Gospels than some of the other days, but what we are privy to is a powerful scene that becomes a metaphor for what will happen on the cross—a terrible and beautiful thing. We are told that Jesus spent time at the house of Simon the leper, where a woman came up and poured a flask of expensive perfume on His feet. The disciples fussed about it, suggesting it was too expensive for such a frivolous act. They thought it should have been sold and the money used for the poor. It's funny to me that they do this, because I think it sounds spiritual. It sounds like something they thought they should say because they were experts on kingdom economy. But Jesus wasn't impressed. Instead, He was blessed by the woman. He told the disciples not to trouble her—she had done a beautiful thing.

I can't pretend to understand all the implications of this—why this time Jesus wasn't concerned about the poor as the disciples expected Him to be. What I like about it, though, is that Jesus appreciated the woman's gift. He called it a beautiful thing. He seemed to be saying there's a time for extravagant gestures, and if there ever was one, this was it. She was preparing Him for burial. She understood sacrifice—and the beauty of extravagant love.
—GWEN FORD FAULKENBERRY

FAITH STEP: *What's the most extravagant thing you've ever done for Jesus? Was it a generous gift you gave someone, in His love? Or your time, your uninhibited worship, your surrender to His will? What beautiful thing could you offer Him today?*

MAUNDY THURSDAY, APRIL 1

Jesus took bread, and when he had given thanks, he broke it and gave it to his disciples, saying, "Take and eat; this is my body." Then he took a cup, and when he had given thanks, he gave it to them, saying, "Drink from it, all of you. This is my blood of the covenant, which is poured out for many." Matthew 26:26–28 (NIV)

WHEN MY DAUGHTER STELLA WAS a little girl, she finally cleared up something about communion that I never quite understood. Communion had always seemed so formal, even impersonal. It was a ritual I respected greatly but didn't quite understand.

We were nearly late for Maundy Thursday service. The kids hadn't eaten supper, so they were famished by the time the communion was served. We were seated on the front row of church and my daughter Stella was sitting tight beside me. I took a cracker from the plate. To my horror, Stella grabbed a handful and before I could stop her, stuffed them into her mouth, crunching loudly.

"I'm hungry," she whispered, spewing crumbs into my lap. I looked around, embarrassed, and wondered, *How many people saw what Stella just did?*

But out of the mouth of my babe, God revealed what I'd been missing. The table is not for anyone special. It's for the hungry. There's enough of Jesus to go around. And it's the one most keenly aware of her need who will have all of Him and be filled.
—GWEN FORD FAULKENBERRY

FAITH STEP: *As you take communion this week, drink deeply of His grace. Taste and see that the Lord—Jesus—is good.*

GOOD FRIDAY, APRIL 2

Joseph took the body, wrapped it in a clean linen cloth, and placed it in his own new tomb. . . . He rolled a big stone in front of the entrance to the tomb and went away. Mary Magdalene and the other Mary were sitting there opposite the tomb. Matthew 27:59–61 (NIV)

AS I CONTEMPLATED HOLY WEEK, I forced myself to walk slowly through Good Friday and think about it's meaning. The first time it's called good—or "guode" in old English—is in a text from the 1200s. The Baltimore Catechism from 1885 says it's because Jesus "showed his great love for man." The Germans, however, called it Karfreitag, or "sorrowful Friday." This seems more appropriate to me.

Easter is a good day—filled with hope, happy kids, chocolate, and ham for Sunday dinner at my mom's. I tend to not want to think about Good Friday.

This year, the verses above spoke something new to me about Good Friday. These are the moments of desolation when Jesus is gone. Really gone. It's how we feel when the funeral is over, and everyone has hugged and said goodbye. The body is in the ground. Gravesite attendants have packed up and left, and it's just us who remain. Wordless, hollowed-out, staring at the fresh dirt and flowers, or in the case of Mary and Mary Magdalene in the aftermath of the crucifixion, weeping in front of the giant rock that stood between them and the life they knew, the one they loved.

It's cliché to say we can't have dawn without the dark. The annoying thing about clichés is that they're often true. And in the case of Easter, I'm realizing it's kind of preemptory to jump to the joy before first sitting with and contemplating the loss of Good Friday.
—GWEN FORD FAULKENBERRY

FAITH STEP: *Sit with the sorrow today as Mary and Mary Magdalene did.*

SATURDAY, APRIL 3

The next day ... the chief priests and the Pharisees went to Pilate. "Sir," they said, "we remember that while he was still alive that deceiver said, 'After three days I will rise again.' So give the order for the tomb to be made secure until the third day ... " Matthew 27:62–64 (NIV)

THIS VERSE FROM MATTHEW TELLS us all we know about Holy Saturday. Pilate posted a guard at the tomb at the request of the Pharisees. The Bible doesn't tell us anything else.

As a writer, Saturday is like a great pause for me. It's a line break on a page, a double paragraph space, at least, and maybe a chapter's end. In a story that has been surging forward, building momentum and suspense, Saturday is when the writer slams on the brakes. He stops you here for emphasis. Makes you pause. So you can gather your thoughts, process what has happened, and get ready for what's next.

I imagine it was something else to Mary, Mary Magdalene, and Jesus's other loved ones. For them it must have been like the day after a funeral, when you go back to your house and face the empty chair, the closet full of abandoned clothes, the deafening quiet. We have the advantage of knowing what comes next, having heard the story a thousand times. But they didn't. All they had was what they could see and a vague notion of what Jesus promised. They must have felt numb.

It's useful, I think, to try to put ourselves in their shoes on this day. To imagine what it might have been like not to truly believe that resurrection was coming—to be unsure it was *really* an option for Jesus and, therefore, for us. —GWEN FORD FAULKENBERRY

FAITH STEP: *What difference would it make for you today if Jesus had not risen again? Write a thank-you note to Him, expressing what His resurrection means.*

EASTER SUNDAY, APRIL 4

The women hurried away from the tomb, afraid yet filled with joy. . . .
Suddenly Jesus met them. "Greetings," he said. They came to him,
clasped his feet and worshiped him. Then Jesus said to them,
"Do not be afraid . . . " Matthew 28:8–10 (NIV)

MATTHEW TELLS US THAT JESUS's first words after rising from the dead were, "Hello. Do not be afraid." That seems significant to me as a person who tends toward fear. I'm only brave if courage means you do stuff even if you're scared. I do almost everything scared.

I'm not ashamed of being afraid. I think Jesus gives us permission for that in the garden of Gethsemane, when He's hesitant to go to the cross. He did it anyway because He knew it was right; it was His purpose, and He was born for it. And He relied on God to give Him strength.

Still, I think we see a different perspective when He has risen from the dead. The women are afraid *yet filled with joy*. It's as if Jesus wants to give them fullness of joy—to take away their fear so that all that is left is joy. *Greetings. Do not be afraid.*

What must they have felt when they saw Him and heard these words? There must have been tremendous relief when they realized all He said did come true. They watched Him die. They were there as Joseph laid His body to rest. They remembered sitting outside of the tomb and staring at the stone. They hardly dared to hope, but hope they did, and now Jesus stood before them.

First John 4:18 says, "Perfect love drives out fear" (NIV). Because of Jesus, we ultimately have nothing to fear. Death is swallowed up in joy. This is the meaning of Resurrection Day, of Easter—love wins, and joy abounds. —GWEN FORD FAULKENBERRY

FAITH STEP: *Plant some seeds in the ground today and wait for them to sprout. Let all of spring remind you that love wins.*

EASTER MONDAY, APRIL 5

So even to old age and gray hairs, O God, do not forsake me, until I proclaim your might to another generation, your power to all those to come. Psalm 71:18 (ESV)

EVERY EASTER AT THE END of the church service, our congregation joins in singing Handel's "Hallelujah Chorus." I love the power of all our voices raised in full-throated praise. However, it's not easy music. I've always been a soprano, but each year it is harder to reach the high notes. This year after church, I told my husband, "I guess I better learn the alto part. I can't hit those notes anymore."

Age can steal a lot from us. Our bodies change. Activities we once loved may become too difficult. More and more of our friends go on to heaven, and we miss them. Our memory can become shaky. As technology keeps changing, and the pace of the young seems faster than ever, we can feel left behind. Yet that doesn't mean we're done living for Christ. To join in singing "Hallelujah Chorus," I had to adapt, but I didn't have to quit.

Our culture may see me as less valuable as I head into later decades of life, but Jesus doesn't. He can help me find ways to live for Him in spite of new challenges. In fact, He challenges me in Scripture to proclaim Him to the next generation. I can finish strong. I can leave a legacy for "all those to come," as the psalmist says.

Whatever our age, let's keep singing praise to Jesus. Our pitch may be lower. Our volume may be softer. Our throat may rasp. But our hearts can still lift with love for Jesus—love that has been shaped and deepened by life experience. —SHARON HINCK

FAITH STEP: *Whatever your age, think of one way you can proclaim Jesus to the next generation and do that today.*

TUESDAY, APRIL 6

So in everything, do to others what you would have them do to you, for this sums up the Law and the Prophets. Matthew 7:12 (NIV)

EARLY THIS MORNING I OPENED my Bible and continued my reading in Matthew 7. I zipped by verse 12 since it's so familiar. Like many people, the Golden Rule was one of the first verses and biblical principles I had learned as a child. Besides, I assumed I was doing well in this area. I do my best to treat everyone as I would want them to treat me. *Don't I?* But two words kept drawing my eyes and mind back to that verse: "in everything."

It's easy to look at the overall tenor of our lives and relationships and pat ourselves on the back. But Jesus didn't call us to follow the Golden Rule with only family, friends, and coworkers. He added two words to let us know He meant every brief encounter, every commonplace conversation, and every interaction in our day. That includes the driver who cuts us off, the restaurant server who messes up our order, and the faceless person on the other end of the business phone call.

The principle doesn't mean treating the other person how they deserve to be treated or how we feel like speaking or behaving toward them in that sudden flash of irritation or anger. It means extending grace, forgiving, and giving someone the benefit of doubt when they've made a mistake, sometimes speaking the truth in love with gentleness, humility, and respect. In other words, imitating the example Jesus modeled. If I let the Golden Rule guide my conduct moment by moment, maybe someone will come to know the One who treats us all far better than we deserve. —DIANNE NEAL MATTHEWS

FAITH STEP: *Think of all the people you've encountered over the past few days. Has Jesus's Golden Rule always guided your speech and behavior?*

WEDNESDAY, APRIL 7

But seek first his kingdom and his righteousness, and all these things will be given to you as well. Matthew 6:33 (NIV)

YESTERDAY, MY FRIEND MARIE FRANCE and I were driving in the car together. We have been friends since college. We are a lot alike. We love Jesus. We love to laugh and have fun. We are also perfectionists. Perfectionism is not the best commonality. Marie France asked, "Why do you think that we think being perfect is a possibility?" *Delusions of grandeur, maybe?* I told her, "I have no idea. We are setting ourselves up for a life of disappointment." Perfectionism keeps us striving for the impossible. We couldn't really laugh about that.

Achieving a perfect life…with a perfect job…a perfect house… or a perfect relationship isn't possible. We live in a world that is fractured by sin. Our own hearts and desires often work against us. Perfectionism is a way that we try to deal with our sin and inadequacies. We tell ourselves that if we only try hard enough, master our issues, and grow enough, then we can give ourselves the life we long for. We want to achieve wholeness—on our own terms. Not only do we want to be perfect, but we also hold others to our same impossible standards.

Perfectionism is a joy killer. There is no room for Jesus, the perfect One, in a perfectionist's life. But we need Him most of all. When we let go of our pride, we recognize that we desperately need Jesus, the joy bringer, and His righteousness. When we invite Him in to the broken places of our lives, He makes us whole. He heals our hearts and minds, restoring us to relationship with the One who loves us the most. —SUSANNA FOTH AUGHTMON

FAITH STEP: *Is there an area of your life where you are striving for perfection? Ask Jesus to forgive you and thank Him for His righteousness that covers all your sins and inadequacies.*

THURSDAY, APRIL 8

---

*Peace I leave with you; my peace I give you. I do not give to you
as the world gives. Do not let your hearts be troubled and do
not be afraid. John 14:27 (NIV)*

MY CAT IVY IS TERRIFIED of our new rescue kitty, Julie. Though Julie
is geriatric and small, the younger one can't bear her. Ivy's afraid to
share me with this sweet old girl, as if she thinks I can't love them
both. Now Ivy won't come into the house, leaving me to wonder if
this four-legged war will ever end. It's downright catty!

There have been times when I've walked in Ivy's padded feet,
frightened of something beyond my control. I couldn't bear to
admit it's *all* out of my control. Jesus was, is, and will be the One
in charge. He protects me from trouble, even when it's of my own
making—especially of my own making.

Like Ivy worrying that we'll stop caring about her and favor Julie,
I've forgotten Christ has love enough for me and everyone else in
the world. It's limitless. Why have I allowed myself to be threatened
by His tenderness toward others?

My husband and I are keeping a close eye on these pets, maneu-
vering them toward some sort of truce. This morning Ivy came up
from the basement for a few minutes, so we could brush her and
fuss over her. It's a start. When she's ready, we'll be able to restore
peace in our home.

Like my husband and I waiting for our scaredy-cat to trust us,
Jesus is patient. Whenever I'm ready to surrender to His wisdom,
He stills my fears and guides me back to His peace. He always has
and always will. —HEIDI GAUL

FAITH STEP: *Make a list of your fears and name them, one by one, to Jesus.
He'll grant you peace.*

FRIDAY, APRIL 9

The LORD has done great things for us, and we are filled with joy.
Psalm 126:3 (NIV)

ONLINE, I FOUND A PHOTO of a sign that read: "Welcome to Joyville." Imagine a vacation in Joyville, Maine. Ideal, right? A destination that has the Atlantic Ocean, lighthouses, and lobster. Did I mention lobster?

What must it be like to be a permanent resident of Joyville? Shopping at the Joyville grocery store. Reading books from the Joyville library. Eating at the Joyville café. I wonder what the high school fight song is, perhaps "We've got joy, joy, joy, joy down in our hearts."

Naming a town Joyville does not a joyful people make. Listing joy as one of the fruits of the Spirit, one of the evidences of the presence of Christ within, doesn't guarantee a joyful attitude. Even while writing this devotion about joy, a life event happened that made me think, *This is not what I expected "Joyville" to be like.* And I'm a local! Jesus lives in me year-round!

The Bible mentions joy an estimated 150 times. Scholars disagree on the exact number because there are eight different Greek words to describe joy and fifteen different Hebrew words for it. Isn't it encouraging that joy shows up that many times in God's Word?

What happens when we love Jesus but life feels anything but Joyville? We don't assume one horrible, awful, terrible, no good day will define every moment between now and eternity. But we may need the reminder that, because of the home—the citizenship— Jesus offers us, we don't live in Despair City. —CYNTHIA RUCHTI

FAITH STEP: *How many miles is it between you and your heart's Joyville? How will you shorten that distance today?*

SATURDAY, APRIL 10

Everyone who hears these words of mine and puts them into practice is like a wise man who built his house on the rock. The rain came down, the streams rose, and the winds blew and beat against that house; yet it did not fall, because it had its foundation on the rock. Matthew 7:24–25 (NIV)

HIKING THROUGH A GROVE OF "old-growth" trees, the forest loomed, a cool haven. I heard the brook before I saw it, the soft murmur drawing me closer as it cascaded downhill. The water's course must have shifted during the previous winter's storms, for in the middle of the stream stood two tall trees. The constant flow had eroded away the sand and pebbles, leaving the roots exposed, like giant hands digging into the ground. I glanced to the treetops and back to their base, curious who would win in this war of trees versus water, but then I noticed massive rocks weighting the trees' roots to the mountain. Those evergreens would be fine.

This season has been difficult for me. I've struggled with the loss of loved ones and battled health issues. It's as if I'm being flooded with troubles. But like those trees, I plan to keep hanging on. I'm digging deep into my faith and holding tight to Jesus, my Rock. "Truly he is my rock and my salvation; he is my fortress, I will never be shaken." (Psalm 62:2, NIV).

I know I won't fall and I won't fail. Like the trees flourishing midstream in the forest, this deluge of challenges won't shake me. Because the whole time I'm clinging to the Rock, and He's holding me even more tightly. And He'll never let go. —HEIDI GAUL

FAITH STEP: *Make a list of the problems flooding your thoughts. Give them to Jesus, our Rock, trusting Him to hold you tight.*

SUNDAY, APRIL 11

Truly my soul finds rest in God; my salvation comes from him.
Psalm 62:1 (NIV)

"WORD OF THE YEAR" IS a popular practice these days. With God's help, you choose a word for the upcoming year, and then focus on living that word for the next twelve months. This year I chose the word "rest." But a few months into the year I started to think I missed God's voice. I've done everything but rest.

I was offered several new ministry opportunities, ones I'd prayed for. *I'm so thankful for these open doors, Lord. But how can I rest when my schedule is this packed?* Jesus used a comment from my friend Beth to change my perspective. She said, "Maybe the Lord wants to teach you how to rest in Him, regardless of how full your schedule is." Of course, that was how Jesus functioned.

As I pondered His life, I realized Jesus did all God called Him to do but never became stressed. I can't imagine Jesus clapping His hands in impatience and shouting at His disciples, "Come on, you guys—row this boat faster! We have to get across the Sea of Galilee before noon. We have sixty-five healings to perform and a crowd to feed before the sun goes down." His sense of joyous peace came from within—the deep places in His heart where He often fellowshipped with God in prayer.

I rarely have the luxury of sitting in an empty room and meditating or taking a leisurely walk in the woods. But I can always—as I teach a child to pray, exercise, visit the sick, or do housework—connect with the Lord. His presence is where I find the sweetest rest. —JEANETTE LEVELLIE

FAITH STEP: *Today, instead of listening to the radio as you drive somewhere, listen to Jesus. Sing Him a song of praise and then hear His loving response in your heart.*

MONDAY, APRIL 12

So the people of Israel ate manna for forty years until they arrived at the land where they would settle. They ate manna until they came to the border of the land of Canaan. Exodus 16:35 (NLT)

SINCE I'VE CUT DOWN ON carbs, I don't need to buy bread as often as I used to. This is a good thing—most of the time. Yesterday, I decided to have a sandwich for lunch. Thankfully, I found two slices left in the bread box. Unfortunately, both had greenish spots of mold beginning to form. It looked gross, but not as gross as what the Israelites found when they tried to hoard manna.

God had rained down manna from heaven each morning and instructed the people to gather just enough for that day. Only on the sixth day, the people could gather twice as much to include their needs for the Sabbath since He didn't send the manna on their day of rest. Some Israelites disobeyed and gathered extra manna. By the next morning, it was full of maggots and smelled awful.

Both then and now, God wants His people to trust Him on a day-by-day basis to provide for their needs. Jesus's model prayer includes "Give us each day our daily bread" (Luke 11:3, NIV). He promises to provide exactly what we need and when we need it, as long as we walk humbly and obediently with Him.

Manna was a temporary fix for the Israelites; later, Jesus identified Himself as the true Bread of heaven in John 6. He added that if He is our source of nourishment, we will never go hungry. And we will live forever. Even if we're on a carb-free diet, we can never get too much of the Bread of Life. —DIANNE NEAL MATTHEWS

FAITH STEP: *Whenever you eat a meal or a snack today, thank Jesus for providing both physical and spiritual nourishment on a daily basis.*

TUESDAY, APRIL 13

Wait on the Lord; be of good courage, and He shall strengthen your heart; Wait, I say, on the LORD! Psalm 27:14 (NKJV)

WE THOUGHT IT WOULD BE a simple project. Famous last words, as they say. Convert the front porch into a four-season room. How hard could that be? We wanted to create a reading room, a comfortable place to reclaim quiet and another hangout location when kids and grandchildren visit.

What we've dubbed the *sunroom* is flooded with light. I notice the dramatic difference daily. The sunroom is visible through the window at my elbow when I sit in my dark interior office. Every day, I notice. A promised quiet, light-filled room. Still under construction more than six months after the first blow of demolition's hammer.

Last weekend, I slid the saws, ladder, hand tools, and scraps of wood out of the way so I could move a chair and small table out there and pretend the room was already finished. Ignoring the exposed insulation that will one day be covered, the subfloor that will one day be a real floor, and dangling wires that will one day be a ceiling fan, I enjoyed the promise of what's to come.

In the Bible, we're encouraged to wait with joy. Sometimes it takes courage to maintain Jesus's joy during a long wait. *Good* courage, the Bible tells us. Assuming there's no such thing as *bad* courage, we expect the idea is a good amount of courage—supersized.

Joy, amid the sawdust of an incomplete project. When we're still living in the construction zone of a promise—for a wayward child, an unanswered prayer, or a relationship's repair—it is the Promise Giver who also gives courage to strengthen our hearts to wait with joy. —CYNTHIA RUCHTI

FAITH STEP: *Find a way today to sit for a while in the construction zone of what you're waiting for. Imagine the project finished. Take joy.*

WEDNESDAY, APRIL 14

Because so many people were coming and going that they did not even have a chance to eat, he said to them, "Come with me by yourselves to a quiet place and get some rest." Mark 6:31 (NIV)

LIVING ON A SAILBOAT ALLOWS me to escape busy schedules and noise a couple of times each year. One of my favorite destinations is Wallace Island. It's a provincial park with a protected cove for safe anchorage. It also hosts hiking paths so we can explore forests and beaches.

Each morning dawns with quiet. No cars, no sirens, no airplanes flying overhead. We sit in the cockpit and read our Bibles with no distractions. Each day ends with a panoramic sunset reflected on the water. Again, we sit in the cockpit and watch God paint a masterpiece on His canvas.

Escaping now and again to a quiet place is good for both body and soul. Even Jesus recognized this to be true. He created us from dust, and He knows our human limitations. We can work and serve and rush to and fro only so long before our bodies say, "Enough."

The rest to which Jesus refers is more than a good night's sleep. It's pulling back from responsibilities, doing something different from the norm, and being refreshed from the inside out. It's escaping to a place where we can be still and think with a clear mind and regain perspective. It's providing a space where He can speak to us without competing with electronic gadgets.

I used to think resting in this way was a luxury I couldn't afford. Now I consider it as my yes to His invitation to "come with Me...and get some rest." My quiet place is a secluded cove. What's yours? —GRACE FOX

FAITH STEP: *Put your feet up and close your eyes for five minutes. Enjoy resting in God's presence.*

THURSDAY, APRIL 15

Now to him who is able to do immeasurably more than all we ask or imagine, according to his power that is at work within us. Ephesians 3:20 (NIV)

MY HUSBAND AND I ENJOY biking, and we regularly bike up a quiet road winding through a canyon near our home. One day we found a rock outcropping with a litter of baby foxes romping around. We biked down. I grabbed my camera and rode up to the spot. I took some photos and, just for fun, put one of my photos on a website that offers free high-resolution photos for anyone's use for blogs, brochures, screen savers, etc.

The following year I kept getting emails from this website, and I promptly deleted them, assuming it was spam. Finally, I decided to open one of the emails and found it was information about how many views and downloads this photo had received—more than 3 million! I was shocked; I never imagined that could happen.

This fox photo—gaining views and downloads without me doing anything—reminded me of Jesus's ability to do so much more than we ask or imagine. It's my tendency to fret over details such as where we'll live, what's my next project, and who (or *if*) my children will marry. But Jesus encourages us not to worry and just trust Him.

I still have my fox photo on the website and framed on my desk, because it reminds me God is at work in ways I don't see or imagine. This inspires me to stop fretting, trust Him, and watch for Him to do the immeasurable. When I do this, I find I'm continually and delightfully surprised. —JEANNIE BLACKMER

FAITH STEP: *Do you have faith to believe that God can do the impossible? If not, why? Journal your response and then talk to Jesus about this.*

FRIDAY, APRIL 16

Jesus wept. Then the Jews said, "See how he loved him!" John 11:35–36 (NIV)

"I FEEL LIKE CRYING, BUT I rarely let myself," I told my friends Dee and Beth as we chatted over sandwiches. The pressures of managing a ministry, caring for Mom, and helping our daughter raise three teens overwhelmed me. Ever since I'd heard a sermon warning against self-pity, I'd equated weeping with selfishness. Now, whenever I felt the need to weep, I squashed it.

Dee defended crying, saying that it releases pent-up tension and helps us relax. "I cry once a week. Afterward, I can face life." When I argued that I couldn't force tears to flow, she and Beth put their sandwiches down, joined hands, and asked God to help me weep.

That afternoon I stole away to my bedroom, where I experience my best talks with Jesus. As I poured out my heart regarding Mom's health to Him, I sensed that familiar prickle of tears sting my eyes. This time, I let them flow. Anguish over all life's challenges washed over me in waves. As I allowed myself the freedom to sob, I told the Lord I couldn't manage my messy life. He reminded me then of a story from John's gospel: Jesus on the way to Lazarus' tomb.

Although Jesus knew He was going to resurrect Lazarus in a few minutes, He lifted his voice and wept along with Martha and Mary. He entered into their sorrow as an understanding, empathetic friend. If Jesus cried along with these women, He also wept with me in the midst of my pain. He knew exactly how I felt. Better yet, He knew how to resurrect my messes.

I texted Beth and Dee. "Thanks for praying. It worked! Jesus is teaching me that it's okay to cry." —JEANETTE LEVELLIE

FAITH STEP: *Next time you feel like crying, allow the tears to flow. Then let Jesus comfort you as only He can.*

SATURDAY, APRIL 17

I lift up my eyes to the mountains—where does my help come from?
My help comes from the LORD, the Maker of heaven and earth.
—Psalm 121:1–2 (NIV)

WHEN I RECEIVED SOME UNWELCOME news, I knew life would go on, but it would be harder. My heart ached.

That weekend, my husband drove me to the mountains so I could find peace. We hiked through an old forest, rich with the scent of cedar. Birds chattered from treetops, and wildflowers bloomed. I repeated a silent prayer, each word stamped into eternity by a footfall: *Help me see You and hear You, Jesus. I feel so alone.*

No answer came. Feeling empty, I walked on.

We passed a small waterfall and sat beside a still deep pool, its water clear as glass. I leaned over the surface and spied my reflection.

I'd spent hours begging Jesus to comfort me. All the while, He'd called to me in the melody of birdsong and the sweet music of a rushing brook. I'd felt His hug as sunlight warmed my back. He'd written a love song across the sky, as sunrays shone through the puffy clouds. A wave of peace washed over me.

Jesus doesn't always speak in a way that's easy to understand. He doesn't plaster His love on billboards or purchase airtime on radio stations. Instead, He calms us with His creation, releases us from worry, freeing us to experience the sublime joy of His presence.
—HEIDI GAUL

FAITH STEP: *Step outside. Do you hear birds, see a rainbow, smell roses, or feel the sun on your skin? Notice the ways that Jesus shares His joy with you.*

SUNDAY, APRIL 18

We love because he first loved us. 1 John 4:19 (NIV)

FRIENDS, MAY I CONFESS TO you that I used to hate baseball and groaned when my oldest son decided to play? Never into sports myself, I reluctantly embraced my son's natural athleticism, but baseball made me want to nap on the bleachers. Games seemed to go on forever. There was a lot of standing around forever between actions. The rules and lingo baffled me. All-beef hot dogs were only a small comfort.

Yet, for my love for my son, I'd make myself show up and sit. At first, I admit I spent a lot of time on my phone…until my son asked me a few times if I'd seen his amazing hit or his awesome play from first base. I wanted to be there for him and forced myself to pay more attention, even when I really wanted to read a book. Again, for my love for my son.

My choosing to act out of love has blessed my son and blessed me. I've grown to love baseball—the beautiful Florida evenings, the requisite life-slowed-down leisure, the Americana, the hard work and discipline, the friendships forged with parents and kids, the life lessons gleaned.

In my flesh, I didn't want to sit at a baseball game for three hours, twice a week, plus practices. I believe it's Jesus's love in me and through me that enables me to love sacrificially. And it's Jesus's love for me that not only saved me on the cross but truly enables me to love—then rewards me with more love than my heart can hold.
—ISABELLA YOSUICO

FAITH STEP: *What large or little love sacrifice are you hesitating to make that Jesus is prompting? Can you step out in faith and trust He'll bless your response?*

MONDAY, APRIL 19

I am coming to you now, but I say these things while I am still in the world, so that they may have the full measure of my joy within them. John 17:13 (NIV)

THE IDEA DIDN'T ORIGINATE WITH him, but actor Matthew McConaughey's perspective on joy was refreshing to discover on a YouTube video. He nailed it when he said that happiness is a response to what's happening to and around us, but joy comes from within.

I found it especially refreshing because the perspective came from a person who lives and works in a cultural atmosphere that seems to consider happiness the goal of work, relationships, food, home, marriage and divorce. If happiness is absent, joy doesn't stand a chance in that environment. Or so it is assumed.

But true joy is the "full measure" of the joy of Jesus within us. Jesus established a different standard for joy. He knew few human comforts, frequently not even having a place to rest his head. His ministry necessitated He walk many miles to get to those who needed Him. He was misunderstood by more people than those who understood Him. Many mocked Him. Few thanked Him adequately when He went out of His way to help or rescue them. And we haven't even tapped into the abuse, the betrayals, the torture, the beatings, His crucifixion.

He's the One who proposed I could know inexpressible joy, *His* joy. And that stirs a passion in me to dig deeper into Scripture to discover how the life-altering concept of joy weaves its way through the most important teachings in the most important Book.
—CYNTHIA RUCHTI

FAITH STEP: *Write the word joy upside down in your nondominant hand. Hard, but possible. Jesus taught that even when life is upside down, joy is recognizable.*

TUESDAY, APRIL 20

Understand this, my dear brothers and sisters: You must all be quick to listen, slow to speak, and slow to get angry. James 1:19 (NLT)

WE ALL WANT TO BE heard. Talk shows on every channel every single day affirm that voicing our opinions is a legitimate pastime. The problem with all that talking is that we aren't usually listening. On these same talk shows, the cohosts routinely interrupt each other (though they have the benefit of the producer talking into their earbuds, telling them when to talk, when to wait, and when to change the subject—I would really like to have that—wouldn't you?). Even when we act like we are listening, most of us are thinking about what we will say next. Listening is an art and must be intentional. The passage above tells us to be quick about it too, implying that listening should be what we aim for first in any conversation.

I have spent effort trying to stop cutting people off when I'm in a conversation. I feel so sure that I know where they're going with the thought or the story that I give myself permission to preempt them. I tell myself I'm just moving things along and making the chat more enjoyable. But no matter the good-sounding excuse, I realize this is exalting myself above them, saying that my response is more important than theirs. Jesus honored people He ministered to by taking the time to listen to them. And Philippians 2:3 reminds us to think of others as greater than ourselves. So I'm training myself to keep my mouth shut and ears open. This way I allow people to share their hearts and feel heard—the way Jesus makes me feel when I talk with Him. —PAMELA TOUSSAINT HOWARD

FAITH STEP: *In your conversations today, let the Holy Spirit be like the talk-show producer talking in your ear, reminding you to listen first.*

WEDNESDAY, APRIL 21

Remember the wonders he has done, his miracles, and the judgments he pronounced. 1 Chronicles 16:12 (NIV)

As a new beekeeper, I am often awestruck because the bee-colony ecosystem is amazing! For example, one of my hives recently, unexplainably, lost its queen. Without a queen, the colony would die. Knowing this, the bees created queen cells, fed the larvae extra royal jelly and produced a new queen. Watching this phenomenal process ignited a dormant sense of wonder in me. It reminded me of the sense of wonder I had when I was a child.

Sadly, as we grow older, those moments of wonder become rare. Life can steal the awe away as we face the day-to-day grind. We put our heads down, perform our daily routines, interact with familiar people, and experience little excitement or joy. We stop being curious. We stop trying new things. Our senses become dull. Even our faith can feel dull.

Jesus encourages us to live with childlike faith. He said to His disciples, "Truly, I say to you, whoever does not receive the kingdom of God like a child shall not enter it" (Mark 10:15, ESV). I need a reminder to live life and experience my faith like a child. Beekeeping reminds me of that need.

With my renewed childlike wonder, I have begun to pay more attention to the marvels around me. I am more curious about people I thought I knew well. Most importantly, my faith has been refreshed, and I look for moments of wonder in my everyday life and intentionally give thanks for the big and small miracles surrounding me. I frequently walk out to my beehives and just watch them because they remind me that life is full of wonder. —JEANNIE BLACKMER

FAITH STEP: *Take a walk around your neighborhood today and notice the miracles around you, big or small, and thank Jesus for what you see.*

THURSDAY, APRIL 22

Are not two sparrows sold for a penny? Yet not one of them will fall to the ground outside your Father's care. Matthew 10:29 (NIV)

MY GRANDSON WINSTON CAME RUNNING through the back door with distressing news: "Honey (my grandma name), Mama, come quick! A baby bird fell out of its nest, and it's on the ground!" My daughter Melissa and I followed Winston into the backyard. Sure enough, a wobbly baby bird stood in the grass under our oak tree, moving its little head from side to side. We looked up into the tree and saw the nest but no mother bird.

We all panicked! We had to do something—but what? I thought of the verse in Matthew that says no sparrow falls to the ground without the Father noticing, and I silently asked Jesus what we should do to help this poor creature. Meanwhile, Melissa found a box and an old towel in the garage and said she'd take the bird home with her. Winston started digging for worms in the flower bed. Just then, I felt Jesus whisper in my ear, *Wait.* I repeated His message to Melissa and Winston, who looked at me doubtfully.

They ceased their frantic activity, and we all stood quietly, gazing at the tiny thing. As we watched, the bird started hopping across the yard to the nearby golf course. Suddenly it took a giant hop, flapped its wings, and flew into a nearby tree. We cheered! The bird would be fine. It was under the tender care of Jesus. And so are we.
—PAT BUTLER DYSON

FAITH STEP: *If you're having trouble trusting Jesus, read Matthew 10:29. Of how much more importance are you to Jesus than the lowly sparrow?*

FRIDAY, APRIL 23

But grow in the grace and knowledge of our Lord and Savior Jesus Christ.
To him be glory both now and forever! Amen. 2 Peter 3:18 *(NIV)*

I HAVE THREE GIANT MAN-SIZED children living at my house right now. Jack is eighteen. Will is sixteen. Addison is thirteen. Addie's shoe size matches his age. These boys are taller than my husband, Scott, and me. Scott blames me for their growth because I feed them vegetables. He said, "If it were up to me, I would feed them junk food and stunt their growth." At this stage in their lives, the amount of food they are putting away is astounding. A new box of nectarines bought in the morning won't make it past dinnertime. They need fuel in this season of growth. Their genes are at work. They are destined for tallness. If I am honest, I love that they are growing. It means that I am doing what I am supposed to do as a mom. My goal is for them to grow to their full potential.

In the same way that my boys are constantly growing, Jesus wants us to keep growing constantly. Our spiritual genes are at work. He knows who we are destined to become. Jesus designed us to grow in our knowledge of Him, trusting our lives to His care. He is enlarging our hearts with compassion and our ability to love those around us. He is cultivating our minds to think how He thinks, reframing our thoughts with grace and purpose. As we transform into the people He created us to be, it brings Him a great deal of joy. He is doing a glorious work in our lives by growing us to our full potential. —SUSANNA FOTH AUGHTMON

FAITH STEP: *Dive into His Word today and ask Jesus to continue His work in you as you grow in your knowledge of Him.*

SATURDAY, APRIL 24

Take my yoke upon you and learn from me, for I am gentle and humble in heart, and you will find rest for your souls. For my yoke is easy and my burden is light." Matthew 11:29–30 (NIV)

THIS PAST YEAR, MY PRAYER life has taken a remarkable turn with profound impact on my life. I hope it shows in these pages.

I've always prayed. Well, before I knew Jesus, I prayed with fervent expectation that God heard me, even after my prayers weren't answered the way I wanted. Yet, deep in my seeking heart, I sometimes glimpsed an answer that was deeper than I could fully grasp. That's still true.

Since then, I've prayed with good outcomes in mind—I thought. I've kept lists in journals, using prayer acronyms like ACTS and PRAY. I've punctuated prayers with "God willing," more or less sincerely.

Then, honestly, I'd muster all the self-will I could to see my prayer answered the way I wanted. Convinced my prayer was good, I fought hard to see or act against what was actually unfolding.

It's only recently that I've seen how this anxious and misguided method was painful and took me out of God's will. Not outright sin, just someplace less than the best. Moreover, it was a hard way, always fighting against the flow.

I wish I knew then what I know now. When I truly let go, life is so much better! He can truly accomplish things I can't begin to imagine, and He does it in remarkable ways that aren't as exhausting as my way.

Today, praying expectantly is more like quiet, submissive curiosity—I no longer force or finagle. Faith is really life without scheming. Jesus's leading is humble, gentle, and restful. —ISABELLA YOSUICO

FAITH STEP: *Pick one persistent prayer, and entrust it to Jesus, letting it go entirely.*

SUNDAY, APRIL 25

And he said, "The kingdom of God is as if a man should scatter seed on the ground. He sleeps and rises night and day, and the seed sprouts and grows; he knows not how." Mark 4:26–27 (ESV)

JESUS TEACHES THAT YOU AND I are like farmers. One of our roles is to sow seeds. Most often we do it without even realizing it. For instance, a mother sows seeds by caring for her home and for little people as she goes about her normal routines. Those seeds take root and sprout and grow in the lives of her kids. I see evidence of this in my granddaughters' lives when they cradle and dress their dolls in the same manner that their mother cares for their younger siblings.

A pastor or parent sows seeds of love for God's Word. My mother sowed these into my life when she sat at the kitchen table and prepared her lessons for the women's Bible study she attended.

Folks who clean up after the church potluck sow seeds of servanthood. Those who give thanks even when it's hard sow seeds of gratitude. Those who sit at the bedside of a dying loved one sow seeds of compassion.

We don't consciously think about our actions as sowing seeds, but Jesus says that's what they are. He says those seeds take root in other people's lives. They sprout, they grow, and eventually they produce a harvest (Mark 4:29). We really have no idea when or how this all takes place. It just does. It's a spiritual mystery in which our actions and attitudes play a part in other people's lives, so let's sow seeds that result in a harvest of righteousness. —GRACE FOX

FAITH STEP: *Take one intentional action to sow seeds of joy in someone's life today.*

MONDAY, APRIL 26

Jesus was led by the Spirit into the wilderness to be tempted by the devil. After fasting forty days and forty nights, he was hungry. Matthew 4:1–2 (NIV)

THE LORD SENT ELIJAH TO safety in an isolated area (1 Kings 17:2–6). David, a man after God's own heart, spent years in solo worship as he tended sheep. Jesus also sought solitude with the Father as He fasted and prayed in the wilderness. Each one of them found shelter in desolation and gained strength in communion with God.

I, too, need alone time with Jesus—the more the better. My soul craves it. When I go without, my mood shifts. My effectiveness as a Christian and a friend suffers. I'd love to go someplace quiet, away from the world's bustle, as Elijah, David, and Jesus did—but I can't. I don't have forty days to offer the Lord. I have closer to forty minutes.

Today, I set aside half an hour while my husband worked. I sat on my porch rocker and watched neighbors walking their dogs pass by. Birds gathered straw for the front yard birdhouse as my cat dozed in the warmth of the sun. I read the Bible, prayed, and waited. Tomorrow, I'll get up early to watch the sunrise with Him.

These aren't the extended periods I'd prefer, yet they're all I—and many of us—can carve out. Whatever time I offer to Jesus, He rewards generously. In the intimacy of silence, I feel His love, His presence. It's during those precious moments of stillness that He touches me most deeply. They aren't many. But they are His. And they are full. —HEIDI GAUL

FAITH STEP: *Set aside a block of time every day this week for Jesus. After you've prayed and listened, bask in the intimacy of simply being with Him.*

TUESDAY, APRIL 27

He did only a few great miracles there, because of their unbelief.
Matthew 13:58 (TLB)

THERE IS SO MUCH MORE Jesus wants to do in the earth through us, but as a body we struggle with unbelief. In the context of today's Scripture verse, Jesus was trying to preach and heal people in His hometown of Nazareth, but they wouldn't receive Him. He was too familiar to be so anointed. If you've ever tried to minister to your family or close friends, you understand! They know you too well sometimes to listen to the wisdom you've gained, and they won't believe you. The shoe can also be on the other foot. We can be the ones whom God sent, but like Moses, Sarah, Gideon, and many others, we have a hard time believing we are chosen.

When I was in my third year of Bible College, a visiting professor's wife known for her prophetic gifts prayed over me. She said, "You have been a student a long time. It's time to be a teacher." Wow. I realized I had enough faith to sit under great teachers each day, but not enough faith to step out and share the wealth. (I recall hiding in a bathroom one day when I was scheduled to teach on an overseas missions trip). Thankfully, I took that word in and my confidence grew. Just like Jesus in Nazareth, I stepped forward to minister to people, but found that many weren't ready to receive. Some I prayed with had long-standing illnesses and they just couldn't see themselves well. Others heard the Word and shouted "Amen" but remained unchanged years later. The hidden beauty in this is that Jesus is still able to do "a few great miracles," despite our unbelief.
—PAMELA TOUSSAINT HOWARD

FAITH STEP: *Ask the Lord to reveal areas of unbelief. Rely on His faith to get you over the hump.*

WEDNESDAY, APRIL 28

So that Christ may dwell in your hearts through faith—that you,
being rooted and grounded in love . . . Ephesians 3:17 (ESV)

AS MY HUSBAND AND I were home shopping, we found some land with a spectacular view of the mountains that can be subdivided into two building lots. It's too much for us to do alone, so we've been talking with a couple who have had a longtime dream of building a retreat center and providing soul care for leaders in ministry. We've been prayerfully asking Jesus to show us if this is a place He wants us to pursue. I've been waffling because the portion of the land we would buy has a house on it that needs work.

While praying with my close group of girlfriends about this, one friend led us in a Lectio Divina exercise, which is a prayerful reading of the Bible. She had a compilation of verses she read three times, inviting us to listen to what Jesus was saying to us through those particular Scriptures. When she read the words "that you, being rooted and grounded in love," I sensed Jesus had a message for me.

I've been focused on planting myself in a physical place. This Scripture verse reminded me to plant myself in knowing Jesus and His love, rather than a temporary home. Our physical homes often change. We can be uprooted for all sorts of reasons, and if our roots are planted deep in an earthly place, it will be painful when they are uprooted. But by being planted in His love and developing deep roots in faith in Him, we will find joy and fulfillment wherever our homes are.

Whether this plot of land is our next home or not—as I plant myself in His love—I believe I'll feel at home wherever I land.
—JEANNIE BLACKMER

FAITH STEP: *Prayerfully read Ephesians 3:16–19. What is Jesus saying to you today?*

THURSDAY, APRIL 29

The winds blew and beat on that house; and it did not fall, for it was founded on the rock. Matthew 7:25 (NKJV)

A RECENT PROJECT AT OUR house has tested our mettle as a couple, as I've heard is true for most remodeling projects. I now straighten crooked pictures in the dentist's waiting room and notice if a floor is an inch lower on one side of the room than the other. Turning a circa 1913 farmhouse porch into a four-season room has proven the veracity of the nursery rhyme "There was a crooked man in a crooked little house." (Except for the crooked man. It's just the house that's askew.)

So installing straight, factory-squared windows into an opening that is anything but perfectly square has been cause for... discussion.

I point out, calmly, that it's crooked. He points out, calmly, that the house is crooked, not the window. I mention, gently, that we can't go according to the house, since it's "off," and if we measure using the house's quirks, the windows won't open. He mentions, gently, that the house is immovable, so the windows have to follow that line.

What a telling picture of the reasons Jesus was so adamant that the foundation needs the most attention. The foundational layer of our souls has to be built plumb and true, more meticulously than anything that will come after.

Jesus said that joy is foundational to our lives as Christ followers. If joy is solid, anchored well, and secure because of our trust in His promises, anything else we build on top of that will have much greater chance of aligning with His purposes for us. We won't be "half a bubble off" if His joy bubbles inside us. —CYNTHIA RUCHTI

FAITH STEP: *Is anything in your house noticeably crooked? When you pass that spot, use it as a reminder of the importance of building your life of faith on Jesus, who is plumb and true.*

FRIDAY, APRIL 30

---

*All those the Father gives me will come to me, and whoever comes to me
I will never drive away. John 6:37 (NIV)*

THE HAND-LETTERED SIGN SAID: "12-YEAR old female cat, declawed,
free to a good home." Hmmm. Why would someone who'd had a
cat for twelve years want to give her up? Had the cat grown mean?
Was the owner ill and no longer able to care for her? It was all very
puzzling. This cat was middle-aged, trending toward old. Being
declawed, she would need to be an inside cat, which necessitated a litter box. Nothing about this cat sounded very appealing. Who would
want this cat?

Jesus would! Jesus included people that everyone else left out:
thieves, outcasts, lepers, the unclean, the poor. Not only did He
include them, He embraced them. It feels great to be included, to
be part of the in-group. There've been times in my life when I've
felt like an outsider—not an outcast exactly, just insignificant. It's
not a good feeling. It's hurtful. Romans 15:7 urges, "Accept one
another, then, just as Christ accepted you, in order to bring praise
to God" (NIV).

Jesus Himself understood what it was like to be shunned. Even
in His hometown of Nazareth, people scorned Him and drove
Him out of town. Maybe Jesus had even more compassion for the
unwanted because He knew how it felt to be rejected.

I need to remember that seeking approval from others and trying
to be part of the in-group can become tiresome and meaningless.
Acceptance from Jesus is really all I need.

And maybe I'll inquire about that free cat. —PAT BUTLER DYSON

FAITH STEP: *Meditate on today's verse and embrace the fact that Jesus will
never drive you away.*

SATURDAY, MAY 1

Because of the LORD'S great love we are not consumed, for his compassions never fail. They are new every morning; great is your faithfulness. Lamentations 3:22–23 (NIV)

MY DRIVE INTO WORK TAKES me down the California coastline. The view is spectacular. The cliffs to my right disappear into the crashing waves below. As I drop into the small coastal valley, the beach curves past the mountain range that frames the seaside town Pacifica. The expanse of blue-green ocean sits beneath a brilliant blue sky. Some mornings the endless stretch of surf is hemmed in by rolling fog. The ocean stretches far beyond where my eyes can see. I can't comprehend its greatness.

The same is true of Jesus's love for me. I catch glimpses of His great love for me, but I can't comprehend it. Some moments I feel engulfed by His compassion, but when I truly think about it—it is beyond me. The apostle Paul wrote, "I pray that you, being rooted and established in love, may have power, together with all the Lord's holy people, to grasp how wide and long and high and deep is the love of Christ, and to know this love that surpasses knowledge..." (Ephesians 3:17–19, NIV) Jesus' love for us is so great that we can't truly know its depths or heights. His mercies renew daily. His faithfulness is unending. We can't begin to understand how much Jesus loves us, but we can revel in it. Wherever you are right now, whatever you have or haven't done, rest in the knowledge that you are deeply and truly loved by the One who created you—more than you could ever begin to imagine. —SUSANNA FOTH AUGHTMON

FAITH STEP: *If you have never been to the ocean before, scroll through some pictures online. Try and comprehend the vastness of it and know that Jesus loves you even more.*

SUNDAY, MAY 2

After this, Jesus traveled about from one town and village to another, proclaiming the good news of the kingdom of God. The Twelve were with him. Luke 8:1 (NIV)

I LOVE VISITING NEW PLACES and seeing new things. When I observe different cultures than mine, it widens my perspective. I become more open to contrasting views and choices, and as a result, I learn acceptance. And I delight in trusting Jesus to guide me as I navigate faraway shores.

Right now, I'm planning a trip abroad. We'll visit Germany, my mother's homeland, and Czechia, the country where my husband's grandparents were born. I can't wait to walk those ancient streets.

So many Bible characters traveled: Abram, Moses, and Joseph in the Old Testament, and in the New Testament, the Samaritan, the disciples, Paul... and Jesus. Every time our Lord visited another town, He furthered His calling.

My reasons for travel aren't quite as noble. I go to free my mind of the endless intricacies of life, to find freedom away from home. Replacing the mundane and ordinary with unfamiliar sights, sounds, and tastes restores my soul. But in a way, I'm seeking after Jesus just as the crowds did (Matthew 4:25, 8:1, 14:13). Traveling, I catch glimpses of Him in the shy smile of a child hiding behind her mother's dress. I hear Him in the happy chatter of an open-air market. I sense dogged devotion in the construction of ancient cathedrals. I see the diverse beauty of His creation in foreign faces. In turn, I pray these people I meet—whose language I can't speak—will see His joy in my eyes and His love in my acts, that they'll know Him a little better because of me. —HEIDI GAUL

FAITH STEP: *Travel somewhere unfamiliar, even if it's a neighboring county. See how Jesus opens your mind and your heart.*

MONDAY, MAY 3

Come, see a man who told me everything I ever did.
Could this be the Messiah? John 4:29 (NIV)

AS OUR BUS NEARED THE entrance of the orphanage in Uganda, we heard cheering. We rounded the corner to see hundreds of kids shouting and waving at us. They chased our bus yelling, "Muzungu, hi!" (*Muzungu* means "traveler" in Swahili). The joy of these children overwhelmed me. After nearly forty-eight hours of travel, this was my first moment experiencing the organization our church has supported for ten years. Tears filled my eyes. When we got off the bus, the children hugged us, then grabbed our hands and proudly showed us their bunkrooms and classrooms. It was one of the most precious moments of my life.

I'd been invited to visit with our church's Come and See team. We were sent to simply *see*, not to *do*. After being there, meeting the people and seeing transformed lives, I wanted others to come and see too. A year later, I led the team.

This reminded me of the woman at the well, whom Jesus amazed by what He knew about her. After time with Jesus, she went back to her village and told others to come and see Him. She introduced Jesus to her community.

When we're excited about something, it's easy to invite others into it, so why is it so scary to invite others to come and see Jesus? Like the woman at the well, He's transformed my life. I only need to joyfully share with others my experience with Jesus and invite them to come and see Him themselves. —JEANNIE BLACKMER

FAITH STEP: *Take a bold step and invite someone to see Jesus through you.*

TUESDAY, MAY 4

The second is this: "Love your neighbor as yourself." There is no commandment greater than these. Mark 12:31 (NIV)

AUTHORS, LIKE PREACHERS, OFTEN SHARE the truths they need to practice in their own lives. I discovered this fact when I wrote *Hello, Beautiful! Finally Love Yourself Just As You Are*. Over the course of a year, my coauthor, Beth Gormong, and I wrote stories about how God sees us through His eyes of unconditional love. During that time, Beth and I repeatedly felt challenged to believe the words we had written. When we made disparaging remarks about ourselves, I laughingly reminded us to read our own book. We didn't want to be hypocrites!

Instead of simply writing about loving ourselves, Beth and I started practicing what we'd learned from Jesus's example of grace. Gradually, sometimes painfully, we grew in our ability to love ourselves. Now we can even look in the mirror and say, "Hello, Beautiful!" and mean it. I believe that makes Jesus smile.

As women, we excel at helping others. We nurture, cheerlead, and patch everything from broken kites to broken dreams. But when it comes to loving ourselves, we often run the other way. We've been taught that putting the needs of others first and our needs last leads to joy.

Yet, Jesus taught us to love others as we love ourselves. We can't fully love those around us if our own self-esteem is in the gutter. When we embrace Jesus's high opinion of us, we will find the joy we crave. —JEANETTE LEVELLIE

FAITH STEP: *Find a Scripture that speaks of Jesus's unconditional love for you. Write it on a sticky note and put it on your mirror. Read it aloud until it's embedded in your heart.*

WEDNESDAY, MAY 5

I consider that our present sufferings are not worth comparing with the glory that will be revealed in us. Romans 8:18 *(NIV)*

I LIVE IN A PARADISE for beach lovers. Our family's regular beach is Honeymoon Island, which has topped several "Best Beach" lists over the years and is a mere fifteen-minute drive from our house. But it's a deceptively rough-looking route to get there. This is an apt and amazing metaphor for my walk with Jesus, who Himself endured an awful road to Calvary on His way to glory.

Getting to Honeymoon means taking one of several major arteries west. These big boulevards are full of commercial buildings unburdened by zoning laws or good taste. On the way to the beach, one could almost get dejected by some of the sights, when suddenly, another vista appears. Future glory indeed!

The approach to Honeymoon Island is breathtaking, as are so many along the Florida Suncoast. Crossing the causeway to the island still fills me with wonder every time. Palm trees slung with colorful hammocks line the road where sand meets shimmering sea. Gulf-side tailgaters unload kayaks, paddle boards, and jets skis and set up colorful canopies for the day. Dozens of people are fishing. Families are frolicking in the clear shallow water that stretches far and is interrupted only by tiny islets lush with life. All beneath a beautiful sky bathed in sunshine. Spectacular!

Life can be a lot like that. We have to navigate uneventful routines or downright ugly spots, sometimes punctuated by unspeakably beautiful moments. Hard or happy though this earthly plane may be, Jesus, the Way, leads to the glory of heaven. —ISABELLA YOSUICO

FAITH STEP: *Recall a situation that turned out better than you imagined while you were experiencing it. Thank Jesus.*

THURSDAY, MAY 6

Now may the God of hope fill you with all joy . . . Romans 15:13 (NKJV)

IS HOPE EVER A BAD shopping decision? At a bookstore hours from home, I noticed the word *hope* in a beautiful script font on the wall, high above the shelves of books and racks of cards and gift items. It was an exact duplicate of a sign I have, but this one was in white, which would contrast more strikingly the chocolate walls of my dining room than the black version I already own.

I asked the salesperson to get it down for me. Did I really need another hope sign in my house? The other day, my college-student grandchild told a visiting friend, "This is one of Grammie's quirks. As you can see, she collects hope." The white hope sign, which had a reasonable price tag, would raise my collection to forty-eight, if I'm counting correctly. The black version could move to the front porch and the white version could take its place—light against the dark wall.

Moments later, the salesperson approached me apologetically. "I'm so sorry, but . . ." As she was boxing up the sign, it broke. Hope broke. I wonder how many people feel that way. They have hope, but it's busted. They still know what it is, but they can't display it in that condition.

The incident reminded me that real hope—the kind rooted in Christ—is invisible but strong. It's unbreakable. It fiercely protects the breakthroughs we long for. It holds brokenness to keep it from flying apart. It anchors the strongest and most fragile vessels through the fiercest storms.

Symbolically, I love being surrounded by the word *hope*. Far more important is being held by Jesus, hope personified. —CYNTHIA RUCHTI

FAITH STEP: *Fill in this blank and repeat it often throughout the day to feed your hope: "The hope Jesus gives is _____."*

FRIDAY, MAY 7

Love the Lord your God with all your heart and with all your soul and with all your strength. Deuteronomy 6:5 (NIV)

YEARS AGO, I GAVE MY mom a journal called "Reflections from a Mother's Heart: Your Life Story in Your Own Words," which had pages that asked specific questions. On a recent visit, she returned the book filled out. Although I already knew much of the information, I enjoyed gaining new insights into her memories. Mom's answers painted a typical picture of a poor farm family in the 1930s and 40s. She had worked in the fields and garden, milked the cows, and as the oldest of seven children, helped care for her younger siblings. She did homework by the light of the fireplace. She walked across pastures to catch the bus and in high school rode three different buses to school.

Pages about vacations, traveling, and music lessons were blank. The wedding/honeymoon page told of exchanging vows before a justice of the peace, returning to her in-laws' house, and going to work in their cotton fields. Yet, when asked to choose one word to best describe her life, she wrote, "Wonderful—I haven't been perfect and have had some bad times, but I think I've had a wonderful life." Despite poverty, hardships, disappointments, and the grief of losing siblings and her husband of sixty-nine years, my mom can look back and say that. How?

The answer is on the page in the book that asks for life advice to share. She wrote, "Love the Lord with all your heart, soul, mind, and strength and your neighbor as yourself." The theme of this memory book? The surest way to have a wonderful life is to have a love of Jesus scattered across all the pages of our days and chapters of our lives. —DIANNE NEAL MATTHEWS

FAITH STEP: *Thank Jesus for your good memories and ask Him to heal any hurtful, negative memories with His love and grace.*

SATURDAY, MAY 8

To every thing there is a season, and a time to every purpose under the heaven: a time to be born, and a time to die; . . . a time to weep, and a time to laugh; a time to mourn, and a time to dance. Ecclesiastes 3:1–2, 4 (KJV)

TODAY ON MOTHER'S BIRTHDAY, I thank Jesus for the legacy she left with her journals—thirty years' worth. For months, I couldn't look at them. Then one day I opened one of them from 1990. Mother and Daddy had both endured cancer, and the entries I read spoke of the painful side effects of chemotherapy. I turned another page and read about how devastated Mother was about the loss of her beloved cat. That did it! I couldn't bear to relive the sadness. I closed the journal and put it away with all the others, in Daddy's old sea chest.

Months later, while searching for a photo in the chest, I came across the journals. A nudge from Jesus made me open a journal from 1993. "I made a hole-in-one on number 9 today! Bill was with me! This is my second and he only has one!" The glee my mother felt at besting Daddy at golf flew off the page and made me smile. As I looked further, I read entries about my parents enjoying a sunset on the dock at their lake home, about the fish Dad had caught, about a delightful visit from friends they hadn't seen in ages.

Paging through another journal, I read about Mother's time in her prayer closet. I hadn't known she had a prayer closet! She wrote of praying for family and friends and how close to Jesus she felt.

I realized Mother's journals revealed a balance between the joy and sadness each of us encounters in life. Through it all, Jesus is with us. —PAT BUTLER DYSON

FAITH STEP: *Keep a journal or a prayer journal. Leave a legacy.*

MOTHER'S DAY, SUNDAY, MAY 9

When Jesus therefore saw His mother, and the disciple whom He loved standing by, He said to His mother, "Woman, behold your son!" Then He said to the disciple, "Behold your mother!" And from that hour that disciple took her to his own home. John 19:26–27 (NKJV)

IF YOU ARE A MOTHER or mother figure to someone today, know that your heavenly Father sees you, loves you, and greatly honors you! My husband and I do not have biological children together yet, but when I received my first-ever Mother's Day card from my stepchildren, it was a wonderful new feeling of being appreciated as a mom. Jesus was dying on the cross, but the sight of His mother Mary crying moved Him. He chose His disciple John to take her in and care for her. He made sure Mary would be loved and protected as she aged.

Sometimes we don't do a great job showing our moms or mother figures in our lives our appreciation. As a child, I recall the panic I felt one year when I realized I'd let my mom's birthday go by without remembering. I rummaged through her jewelry box, wrapped up a pair of her own fancy earrings, and presented them to her sheepishly. She smiled and said, "Thanks for the thought." Yikes. Don't let that happen to you!

Years later, I had the privilege of throwing my mom a huge surprise birthday party, complete with old friends and relatives who had flown in for the occasion. Seeing the delight on her face was priceless. I am humbled and grateful that afterward she said to me, "This was the best day of my life!" Love big on your mother today as Jesus would. —PAMELA TOUSSAINT HOWARD

FAITH STEP: *If your mother is still alive, think past a Hallmark card or a gift. What can you do to spread joy into her life and share the love of Jesus?*

MONDAY, MAY 10

God can testify how I long for all of you with the affection of Christ Jesus.
Philippians 1:8 (NIV)

IT WAS A TYPICAL MOTHER'S Day for me. As usual, I didn't get to
be around anyone who shares my DNA. The best parts of the day
were the phone calls to four different cities that allowed me to talk
with my three children and my own mom. I couldn't help thinking
about all the holidays and special events I've missed over the years.
Later in May, I would miss my oldest granddaughter's drama club
awards banquet (where she won top honors), my middle granddaughter's first dance recital, and my grandson's birthday celebration (of which I've only made two out of nine).

I've done a lot of heartfelt longing since my husband's job change
moved us away from our families in 1982. More relocations and
my children scattering have only worsened the situation. But the
apostle Paul has given me new insights about missing my loved
ones. He told his spiritual "children" at Philippi that he longed for
them with the affection of Christ Jesus. I liked the sound of that,
but I wondered how to put it into practice.

The affection of Christ goes beyond earthly affections. I think it's
more than simply wanting to spend time with someone; it's a desire
to see them find God's best and follow Christ as closely as possible,
regardless of where that might take them. It also means thanking
God for our loved ones, praying for them with joy, and trusting God
to complete His good work in them (Philippians 1:3–6). So even
when I can't hold my grandchildren in my arms, now I understand
better how to hold them in my heart. —DIANNE NEAL MATTHEWS

FAITH STEP: *The next time you're missing loved ones far away, ask Jesus to help*
you love them with His affection. Then pray Philippians 1:9–11 over their lives.

TUESDAY, MAY 11

His mother used to make for him a little robe and take it to him each year when she went up with her husband to offer the yearly sacrifice.
1 Samuel 2:19 (ESV)

LIKE MANY WOMEN, HANNAH AGONIZED in prayer for a child. When little Samuel was born, she responded in remarkable ways. She rejoiced, and her beautiful song of praise is recorded in Scripture. She also gave her precious son to God's service. And she continued to care for Samuel by bringing him a new robe each year. I can only imagine the tender care that went into weaving fabric and sewing tiny stitches as she prepared for her visit with him.

All of us who are parents have felt the painful moments when we have to release our children. Perhaps it is when they ride the school bus for the first time or when they go on a class trip or when they leave for college. Perhaps it's at their wedding or when they take a job across the country. Parenting is often about letting go while our hearts are still full of love and longing.

Jesus has given us a wonderful way to continue to pour love into our children—or other loved ones—even as they grow up and move away. He assures us that we can ask our Father anything. We can pray in Jesus's name over our children—no matter their age. Even from a distance, we can support them, encourage them, and ask for blessings in their lives.

Our prayers for our children are like Hannah's coats delivered to little Samuel. They cover and protect our loved ones, even from afar. What a joy to have prayer as an avenue to continue to bless our loved ones! —SHARON HINCK

FAITH STEP: *Pray for a loved one today, imagining a beautiful, soft, warm coat that will surround him or her with love.*

WEDNESDAY, MAY 12

*Because Your lovingkindness is better than life, my lips
shall praise You. Psalm 63:3 (NKJV)*

MY CROSSWORD PUZZLE CLUE *WAS* "a four-letter word for foul
mood." Ha, that was easy: *snit*! The perfect word to describe my
mood yesterday. You've heard the old saying, "A face only a mother
could love?" Yesterday I was a person only Jesus could love.

The burned toast started it, along with the boiled egg that wouldn't
peel right. I read a devotion, wrote in my prayer journal, then hopped
on my bike to exercise. It was too windy to sustain a good speed and
that frustrated me. Back home, I grew crabbier as I wasted forty-five
minutes on the phone with our cell-phone provider.

Settling in front of my computer screen, I prayed for inspiration for
an article whose deadline loomed. My mind had never felt emptier.
Then I got a call from someone on my worship committee, telling
me she couldn't be there on Sunday, so I had to find a sub. Brilliance
continued to elude me with my article, so I gave up and ran to the
cleaners to pick up some shirts my husband, Jeff, needed for a trip.
When I got home, I discovered the cleaners hadn't sent his favorite
shirt. Dinner was baked chicken, undercooked, and brown rice, dry.
When Jeff suggested we take the grandkids to a see a movie, I wailed,
"I don't deserve to have fun! I haven't gotten a thing right all day!"

I skulked to the bedroom, sat on the bed, and picked up my
prayer journal. "Thank you, Jesus, for always loving me," I'd written, only that morning. My life might be unpredictable, unproduc-
tive, and frustrating, but the one thing I could count on was Jesus's
love for me. —PAT BUTLER DYSON

FAITH STEP: *Thank Jesus for His steadfast love, through sunshine and snit.*

THURSDAY, MAY 13

Keep your conscience clear. Then if people speak against you, they will be ashamed when they see what a good life you live because you belong to Christ. 1 Peter 3:16 (NLT)

ONE MORNING MY DAUGHTER, HOLLY, helped my eight-year-old grandson straighten up his room. Later that day, she glanced in Roman's room and found it a wreck. Several books had been pulled off the shelf; some were turned upside down to mark the spot where he'd been reading. Toys, papers, and clothes were scattered over the floor, as well as petals of a fabric lei Roman had taken apart. And Nerf bullets—Nerf bullets were everywhere! Holly asked Roman what had happened to his room. His solemn response: "Mom, didn't you hear about the tornado that passed through?"

Our natural instinct to blame others (or the weather) instead of taking responsibility for our actions goes all the way back to the Garden of Eden: "It was the woman You gave me who gave the fruit to me." "It was the serpent who deceived me." Sometimes people give downright outlandish excuses for their behavior. We can also maintain a false impression of innocence simply by manipulating words or presenting a slightly twisted version of the facts.

The Bible urges us to confess when we've done something wrong instead of excusing our actions, or our failure to act. We can't fool Jesus no matter how good our alibi because He sees into our hearts. He invites us to come to Him and lay down our burden of guilt. Thankfully He promises to forgive and cleanse us. Then we can know the joy and freedom of going through life with a clear conscience. —DIANNE NEAL MATTHEWS

FAITH STEP: *Have you avoided taking responsibility for your own unwise actions? Confess that to Jesus and accept His forgiveness and grace.*

FRIDAY, MAY 14

Cast all your anxiety on him because he cares for you. 1 Peter 5:7 (NIV)

MY OLDEST GRANDSON, WESLEY, WAS turning sixteen and our large, rambunctious clan had gathered to celebrate him. Wes ran track, had good grades, played guitar, and was about to get his driver's license. That last part worried me. Teen drivers often drive too fast, and even if they know better, they sometimes text or talk on the phone. Wesley's parents had bought him a safe car to drive. He'd taken drivers' education and demonstrated good driving skills. Still, I worried. Every day I asked Jesus to protect Wes.

Awaking with a start on Saturday night, I looked at the clock—11:15 p.m. Wes had a curfew of 11:00 p.m. Was he at home? Was he safe? Fear overtook me as I thought of all the scary things that could happen to a new driver. Weekend nights were especially dangerous with more impaired drivers on the road. I got up and started to pace the floor. How many nights had I done this when my own kids were teenagers? I thought about calling him, but that would have been over the top. I thought being a grandparent was supposed to be easier than being a parent!

There was only one thing for me to do. I crept back into the bedroom, grabbed my Bible from the bedside table, went into the living room, and turned to Psalm 91, a Scripture passage of protection. Reading Psalm 91 never failed to calm me when I was most worried. I loved the image of being covered with heavenly feathers and finding refuge under those wings. I read this, my favorite Psalm, three times. Finally, my anxiety soothed, I was ready to go back to bed and sleep, secure in my Lord's promise of protection for Wesley. —PAT BUTLER DYSON

FAITH STEP: *Read Psalm 91 aloud when you are feeling anxious.*

SATURDAY, MAY 15

But those who wait on the Lord Shall renew their strength . . .
Isaiah 40:31 (NKJV)

I'M WAITING FOR THE ELECTRICITY to kick on. Like many others in our neighborhood who survived a massive storm, my husband and I are living a back-to-basics life. Temporarily disconnected from traditional sources of communication, work, leisure, and entertainment, we're reading more. We're eating simpler meals. (Who knew you can boil beans fresh from the garden in an aluminum foil "bowl" on the barbecue grill?) We're finding enjoyment in talking about the books each other has read.

For the first day or two, we were a little lost. Nothing in the house works without electricity—not the water pump, water heater, lights, stove, microwave (gasp!), or our landline phones. Not even the footrest on my husband's recliner. It's stuck in the raised position until the power comes back on. Now, that's a first-world problem!

The electricity outage may last a few more days, we're told. So we've settled into calm and quiet routines. Yes, the laundry is piling up. Yes, we miss being able to regulate the temperature in the house. But we're making do while we wait for the electricity to kick on.

And while I miss many creature comforts, I've discovered a deeper joy in Jesus as I wait. Time is passing in a marvelous way as I linger with Him; abiding in His presence, and resting and nesting in Him in a way that's not possible with technology always at hand. Waiting with Jesus brings peace, joy and renewed strength. It turns out that waiting for the electricity to be restored isn't so bad after all. —CYNTHIA RUCHTI

FAITH STEP: *Trust Jesus to strengthen you while you wait—and find joy.*

SUNDAY, MAY 16

For just as each of us has one body with many members, and these members do not all have the same function, so in Christ we, though many, form one body, and each member belongs to all the others. Romans 12:4–5 (NIV)

THIS SPRING, MY SIXTH-GRADE BIBLE class put on a play about the prophet Jonah for our middle school. My friend Alexis was the director. A theater arts major in college, she brought all her gifts to the table: creativity, humor, drama, and fantastic set design. Every student was assigned a part; there were acting roles as well as props, sound, and lighting responsibilities. Weekly rehearsals began with an acting exercise. Even the tech crew and props team had to participate. Alexis created a sense of purpose and connectedness with the whole class. She said, "You have to be all-in. Unless you all give one hundred percent, this play will not work." She was right. If someone missed a cue or forgot his lines, it held everyone else up. Working together, the kids told a funny, poignant, and beautiful story of mercy and forgiveness.

Jesus invites us to tell the same merciful story with our lives. We need to know our part and work together. When we go "off script," embracing our own selfish desires, it affects the whole body of Christ. When we are all in, we forgive those around us. We radiate peace. We lift one another up in moments of joy and share one another's burdens. We are a collective force of love that tells the story of Jesus's grace toward humanity. And that is beautiful.
—SUSANNA FOTH AUGHTMON

FAITH STEP: *What is your part in telling Jesus' mercy story? Journal your thoughts about what He is asking you to do right now. Thank Him for including you in His great work of love.*

MONDAY, MAY 17

Let us therefore come boldly to the throne of grace, that we may obtain mercy and find grace to help in time of need. Hebrews 4:16 (NKJV)

HAVE YOU EVER FELT TONGUE-TIED? Perhaps you approached your employer to ask for a raise. You longed for someone to stand beside you and make your case because all the words you planned had slipped from your mind. Or perhaps you faced a difficult conversation with aging parents who needed more care than they were willing to accept. You wanted another relative to sit with you and offer support. Or maybe you were in the midst of a health crisis and hoped for someone to tell your friends that you needed help, so you wouldn't have to do the asking.

Making a request can feel risky or difficult, even when approaching the King of kings. Do you ever find it difficult to ask for His help? Do you stumble over your words like a clumsy peasant in a glorious court?

There are times when I'm awkward drawing near to God. I believe He is a loving Father, yet I still feel daunted. At those times, I remember that I'm not approaching the throne alone. The Prince of heaven takes my arm and leads me forward. He speaks on my behalf. What a relief to know that Jesus intercedes and claims me as His own!

When our voices crack and we stumble over words, Jesus speaks with authority and conviction. When we pour out our failings, Jesus announces our forgiveness. When we timidly offer our petition, He boldly asks the Father for more than we can ask or imagine. There is no better advocate, and none more willing to fight for us than Jesus. —SHARON HINCK

FAITH STEP: *Write down some of the deepest longings of your heart. Thank Jesus for interceding on your behalf and watch for answers to unfold in the coming days.*

TUESDAY, MAY 18

Those who sow with tears will reap with songs of joy. Psalm 126:5 (NIV)

WHEN HEALTH ISSUES FORCED ME to give up gardening in my beloved vegetable garden, I mourned. I loved pulling funny-shaped carrots from the soil, loved the smell of tomato plants on my hands, and loved kneeling in the warm earth as I weeded, butterflies dancing around my face.

But when back pain and the cost of chiropractor visits increased, I knew it was time. This summer, I traded my vegetable seed packets for potted flowers and tomato vines. I was excited to watch the plants as they grew. But I still missed my veggie plot.

Then I remembered the weekly farmers' market on our town square. Family farms and individuals sell their produce and crafts from card tables and the beds of pickup trucks. Not only do we get fresh veggies and fruit every Saturday but we also make new friends and chat with people we have known for years. Plus, we're helping our neighbors make a little money.

I no longer grow the veggies I use in my salads and stews. That is a joy I must savor in my memory and hope for in heaven. Still, Jesus compensated for my loss by giving me a new form of joy, fellowshipping in the town square.

When we experience loss, we may be tempted to think we'll never find another person, hobby, church, or job to take the former one's place. It's true, we won't. But if we open our hearts to Jesus's new beginnings, He will enrich us with experiences that delight and surprise us. He's the Master Gardener, willing to share His bounty with all. —JEANETTE LEVELLIE

FAITH STEP: *Think of a friend who's experienced a recent loss. Give them a gift of fresh produce or flowers, and then sit and talk with them for a while.*

WEDNESDAY, MAY 19

All Your works shall praise You, O LORD, and Your saints shall bless You. They shall speak of the glory of Your kingdom, and talk of Your power. Psalm 145:10–11 (NKJV)

EVERY SPRING OUR MISSIONS STAFF gathers for a conference somewhere in Eastern Europe to provide encouragement through networking, participating in corporate worship and Bible teaching, and hearing stories about what God is doing through one another's ministries. The latter is a personal highlight.

Thanks to technology, staff unable to attend can Skype for a few minutes at the start of each main session. Their faces are cast onto a large screen, and then one of our leaders interviews them so we can get acquainted with them and their work.

Every story declares Jesus's power to heal and transform broken lives. Jesus is opening doors to talk about Him in places where sharing the Good News is forbidden, and people are coming to faith despite their government's attempt to stifle them.

Between sessions, our staff visit in small groups. Some have undergone cancer treatment, lost a spouse, or sent kids off to college. Most have dealt with financial issues and the challenges of living on faith donations. Difficulties have deepened their intimacy with Jesus, and their testimonies encourage.

Our annual conferences are an opportunity to celebrate Jesus's presence, power, and provision. Praising Him together encourages everyone. —GRACE FOX

FAITH STEP: *Gather friends and celebrate your love for Jesus and His faithfulness. Thank Him!*

THURSDAY, MAY 20

When anxiety was great within me, your consolation brought me joy.
Psalm 94:19 *(NIV)*

MOVING IS NEVER EASY, AND moving to Florida two years ago was extra hard. Apart from the usual stress, it all happened so quickly, leaving little time to process, pack, and plan. I found and made an offer on a house over a weekend, uncertain I was making the best choice. My carefully researched school selection for the two boys fell apart. By the time I got in the car to drive south, my hopeful anticipation had morphed into weary worry. My husband stayed behind to work.

Adding exhaustion to anxiety when we arrived, I discovered the long-term hotel room I'd reserved was gross, so I scrambled to find a rental. Thankfully, I did, but we had to wait to check in. I took my boys and Bichon rescue Katie to a dog beach, fighting the flood of tears and angst I feared would level me. I walked along the beach while Katie and boys played in the shallow water. I started to question God. *Why did we face all these challenges? Was it an omen? Had we made a terrible mistake?* Please, *comfort me, Lord.*

My painful pondering was interrupted by my son Pierce, "Mommy, Mommy, look what I found!" In his hand was a very beautiful, perfectly formed, large whelk seashell, something you'd buy in a store. I love seashells and felt a sudden sense of joyous relief and deep peace that God was answering my heart's prayer with this beautiful shell.

The Airbnb was charming, cheap, and convenient. The house we bought turned out to be perfect. The boys' new schools were great. Moving to Florida has proven to be one of the best decisions ever. The whelk sits on my dresser, a reminder that God can be trusted. —ISABELLA YOSUICO

FAITH STEP: *If you're in the midst of an overwhelming challenge? Look expectantly for creative answers from Jesus.*

FRIDAY, MAY 21

Do not neglect to show hospitality to strangers, for thereby some have entertained angels unawares. Hebrews 13:2 (ESV)

How could I have run out of vanilla? I realized it right in the middle of mixing the dough for my sugar cookies. In baking, you can substitute some ingredients but not vanilla. I dashed to the car and headed for the grocery store. Just one item. This shouldn't take long. *Jesus,* I prayed, *please don't let me run into anyone I know or encounter anything that will slow me down.*

As I snatched the vanilla off the shelf, I noticed a young woman browsing in the baking aisle. In fact, the way her shopping cart was positioned, I couldn't get past her. I was in the process of squeezing around her when she touched my arm. "Excuse me," she said in halting English. "Can you help me?"

Just my luck. "Sure," I said, not very cordially. "What do you need?" She held up a package of flaked coconut. "What is *desiccated*?" she asked. "It sounds bad!" I smiled and replied, "No, it's not bad. It just means dried. When you use the coconut in a recipe, it will fluff up."

"Oh, thank you," she said. "I'm just learning English and I don't know all the words." I laughed and said, "Me either, and I've been here all my life!"

I grinned at the little boy in her cart. "He's a cutie," I said. She thanked me, and I made my way to the checkout. Somehow it didn't seem so important to hurry home anymore. My cookies could wait, but a fellow traveler had needed assistance, and Jesus put me there to help her. —Pat Butler Dyson

Faith Step: *Ask Jesus to place people in your path to whom you can offer kindness or assistance. And slow down! You might just meet an angel.*

SATURDAY, MAY 22

In My Father's house are many mansions; if it were not so, I would have told you. I go to prepare a place for you. John 14:2 (NKJV)

IN MAY 1983, MY HUSBAND, young sons, and I set out for our first visit with our families since moving to the Midwest six months earlier. Unfortunately, our air conditioning stopped working two hours into the trip. I was hot, miserable, and grumpy until we crossed into Tennessee. Then a familiar scent filled the car, and my eyes filled with tears. For miles the smell of wild honeysuckle vines growing along the interstate drifted into our open windows. I knew I was getting close to home. Today the fragrance of honeysuckle still affects me the same way.

Whether we're returning to the place where we grew up or coming back to our house after a trip, we find comfort in the familiar sights, sounds, and scents of home. Even if we had a wonderful time, we're ready to sleep in our own bed and sit in our favorite recliner, surrounded by the things we know. Yet no matter how comfortable we are, we are not really home—not yet.

If we are a Christ follower, our true home is with Him. He's preparing a home that will be perfect in every way. In heaven we'll be free from pain, fatigue, worry, fear, death, and sin. Most importantly, we will no longer be separated from the One who loved us enough to die in our place. Although we have never seen heaven, when we get there it will be more familiar than any place on earth ever felt. And then we will find out what it means to really come home. —DIANNE NEAL MATTHEWS

FAITH STEP: *Take a few minutes to think about the perfect home Jesus is preparing for you. Thank Him for loving you so much that He desires to be with you for eternity.*

SUNDAY, MAY 23

For in this hope we were saved. Now hope that is seen is not hope. For who hopes for what he sees? But if we hope for what we do not see, we wait for it with patience. Romans 8:24–25 (ESV)

ON A LOVELY SPRING DAY, my hubby and I stopped at a local park. Volunteer gardeners who maintain the park were hosting a plant sale. Unlike at a garden center, most of the green seedlings didn't have photos of what they would grow into. Most had only a Popsicle stick saying "blue" or "lavender" or "yellow." I love blue irises, so we searched for those. We purchased them without seeing proof of what they would look like in bloom. When we got home, we planted the rhizomes in our garden, and I trust that next year beautiful iris blossoms will bring me joy.

Jesus has promised us many things. He promises He is with us to the ends of earth. But we can't see His presence. He promises us a home in heaven, but we have no realtor listing with a photo of what that will look like. He promises our sins are forgiven, yet we continue to be harassed by our sinful nature. Like a young plant, we are not yet fully all we're intended to be. This time between—the time between when we hear promises and when we will see them—gives us a wonderful opportunity to grow in faith.

We plant bulbs and rhizomes that look nothing like the blooms for which we long. Yet we trust that in time the promised beauty will appear. If we can have faith that a gnarled root will produce flowers in the spring, we can also hope in the true and trusted promises of Jesus. —SHARON HINCK

FAITH STEP: *Plant something today and thank Jesus for all the promises He has planted in our lives.*

MONDAY, MAY 24

For we are God's handiwork, created in Christ Jesus to do good works, which God prepared in advance for us to do. Ephesians 2:10 (NIV)

IT SEEMS LIKE EVERYONE EITHER is a life coach or has a life coach. If I had more time and money, I'd love to have some savvy visionary inspiring me, coaxing me to create and stick with a plan, and cheering me on. One can find a coach for just about anything, and coaching courses and certifications abound.

My husband, Ray, an addictions counselor, is a Florida-certified recovery coach. He's explained to me that one of the principles of coaching is to support clients in their own approaches. In fact, even life coaches often just support you in your pursuit of your goals. I have a coach at my new teaching job, and while she does share some helpful tips and tools, she mostly just supports me as I find my way. Herein lies a potential downside of coaching. Looking back on my life, I see that at least some of my goals have been self-serving or otherwise misguided.

But wait just a minute—in today's verse Paul assures me that I have the ultimate Life Coach! One who not only knows me intimately but actually created me (Psalm 139:13) with a perfect and specific plan in mind (Jeremiah 29:11).

In fact, God can and does give us aspirations and desires according to His purpose for our lives. We can discern them through our close relationship with Him, cultivated through Bible study, fellowship with Him, healthy friendships and—especially for me personally—time spent earnestly seeking Him. This is no complimentary one-hour consultation; this is an intimate, ongoing, and sometimes messy personal relationship with Jesus, the perfect Life Coach. —ISABELLA YOSUICO

FAITH STEP: *Do you have a dream or goal you're longing to achieve? How can you let Jesus coach you into realizing it?*

TUESDAY, MAY 25

May the God of hope fill you with all joy and peace as you trust in him,
so that you may overflow with hope by the power of the Holy Spirit.
Romans 15:13 (NIV)

BECAUSE OF MY MOTHER'S HISTORY, I get an annual mammogram at MD Anderson Cancer Prevention Center. Some years back, a doctor asked if I'd participate in a study for women at low-risk for ovarian cancer. It would require blood to be drawn once a year at the time of my mammogram. I readily agreed.

As I walked into the lab waiting room for my blood test, I asked Jesus to be with me. It wasn't the needle I dreaded; it was the heartache that would be in that room. Cancer patients filled every chair, awaiting various lab tests. As a participant in a study, I was there to help, but I felt guilty for being healthy. I'd brought a crossword puzzle so I could look down until the nurse called my name.

The woman next to me, wearing a bright scarf wrapped around her head, wanted to visit. She was ecstatic because she'd had her last chemo treatment and was looking forward to a cruise. When her name was called and she got up, I stole a glance around the crowded room. To my surprise, people were smiling, even laughing, and no one seemed to be despondent. Patients chatted cheerfully with one another and the staff. Without a doubt, I was the gloomiest person in the room.

The longer I observed the patients around me, the more optimistic I felt. There was something in that room I hadn't noticed before. Hope! I thanked Jesus for making me look up to see the joy and hope around me. —PAT BUTLER DYSON

FAITH STEP: *When things look bleak, trust Jesus to restore your hope and joy.*

WEDNESDAY, MAY 26

Now to him who is able to do immeasurably more than all we ask or imagine, according to his power that is at work within us, to him be glory in the church and in Christ Jesus throughout all generations, for ever and ever! Amen. Ephesians 3:20–21 (NIV)

AS A HIGH SCHOOL FRESHMAN, my oldest granddaughter, Lacey, signed up for theater class and joined the drama club. In the fall, the class began preparing a short play for the regional competition. Lacey decided to try out just to gain auditioning experience. She ended up with a major role, and the judges awarded her an Outstanding Performance medal. For the spring musical, Lacey auditioned for a supporting role; she was shocked when the teachers cast her as one of the two female leads (a first for a freshman). Lacey was even more surprised at the end-of-the-year banquet when she received the Best Voice and Best Overall Actress awards.

Those of us related to Lacey were not surprised that she did well; we expected that. But we were amazed at how comfortable she seemed on stage, and how flawlessly she performed while recovering from bronchitis. We enjoyed seeing her self-confidence and the sheer joy she feels when performing. I asked her, "Who would have thought your first year in drama would have encompassed so much?"

It's wonderful when things turn out even better than we'd imagined. But that's the hope we should have every day. Jesus did warn that we will have trouble in this world, but He also said He has overcome the world. Nothing is too much to hope for when His power is at work within us. And we shouldn't be surprised that Jesus has greater plans for us than we do for ourselves. —DIANNE NEAL MATTHEWS

FAITH STEP: *Think of a difficult decision or problem you're struggling with now. Imagine the best outcome possible. Now ask Jesus to do even more than that.*

THURSDAY, MAY 27

For here we have no lasting city, but we seek the city that is to come.
Hebrews 13:14 (ESV)

I RECENTLY SAW A DECORATIVE sign with the familiar message "Home Sweet Home." I smiled. That message carries a whole new meaning since my life became so transient. In the last year, I've averaged about only half of each month at home due to ministry travels and time spent with family.

Nowadays, home is where I touch base between trips, where I pack and unpack my suitcases, and where I catch up on emails before heading out again. Don't get me wrong, please. I love the life Jesus has entrusted to me. It gives me many opportunities to see where He's working around the world. I consider that a privilege. However—a little piece of my heart yearns for the day I'll put my suitcases away.

No longer will I need packing lists lest I forget something important. No longer will I wait in airport security lines or fear losing my passport. No longer will I need to get up early, head to the gym, and hoist weights so I can stay strong enough to lift those fifty-pound suitcases!

Someday my transient lifestyle will end. I'll move to my permanent home in heaven and stay put for a long, long time. The yearning in my heart to settle down will be satisfied once for all.

That sounds enticing, but meeting Jesus face to face will best it. He's ready and waiting to welcome me with the words "Home sweet home!"

Is heaven your real home too? If not, it can be. Acknowledge that you're a sinner, ask Jesus to be your Savior, and give Him control over your life. Imagine the joy of hearing Jesus say, "Welcome home, My child." —GRACE FOX

FAITH STEP: *Ask Jesus to give you a hunger for heaven even while enjoying life on earth.*

FRIDAY, MAY 28

"Do not grieve, for the joy of the LORD is your strength." Nehemiah 8:10 (NIV)

A FRIEND FROM HIGH SCHOOL sent an unexpected email. My delight quickly turned to sadness. Her daughter, not yet forty, was battling an aggressive breast cancer and faced another critical round of treatments. My friend was asking for prayer, hoping to widen the circle of the many who were already praying.

What could have been the saddest email in my inbox that day turned a corner when I checked out my friend's daughter's blog. The young woman had been keeping a public gratitude journal during her journey. The posts were cleverly written, even on the worst of days. They celebrated life in all of its messiness and pain, all its hidden joys and unexpected humor. She'd invited each of her siblings and her parents to guest post to commemorate her final chemo treatment before surgery. And she wouldn't take "No," "I can't," or "That's too hard" for an answer. She knew "too hard" well. And writing a blog post wasn't it.

But the assignment would have challenged any of us. She asked her family members to write a blog post titled "What's So Good about Cancer?" They each discovered something profound they could say. I read the series of posts as if unearthing treasures of love and respect these family members shared and their resilience in the face of a formidable enemy. Overarching all was joy irrespective of the young woman's circumstance. It was the kind of joy only Jesus can give.

That's one of the marvels of following Him. The joy He provides isn't a reflection of circumstances. Many times, it is completely, utterly contrary to our circumstances. A joy people notice. I did.
—CYNTHIA RUCHTI

FAITH STEP: *Consider the most trying difficulty you're facing right now. Dare to ask, "What's so good about it?" Find a buried nugget of gratitude.*

SATURDAY, MAY 29

Jesus Christ is the same yesterday, today, and forever. Hebrews 13:8 (HCSB)

IT'S A TIME OF TRANSITION for our family. My oldest daughter, Grace, just graduated from high school. This whole year has been a series of last times, juxtaposed with all of the possibilities open to her for the future. I've been a bit of a train wreck. Don't get me wrong. I'm excited for Grace and extremely proud of her. She was valedictorian of her class, and scored so highly on national tests that she could go anywhere in the country she chooses to go to school. As she's answered invitations from Ivy League schools, I've held my breath. I never want to discourage my children from dreaming or reaching their potential. But if I could keep them under my wings—or at least close by—while they pursue those things; well, that's what I'd call the best of both worlds. Thank God she decided to go to the University of Arkansas, about an hour away. While thankful, my husband, Stone, and I still dread her empty bedroom, her empty seat at the table, and all of the days empty of her hugs. We're living proof you can be excited and thankful even as your heart is breaking.

My deepest comfort is the faith that just as Jesus was with me as she came into my life and He has been with me every day of her life at home, He will also be there when she goes off to college—here with me and there with her. He'll be loving, protecting, leading, listening—working all things together for good. Everything changes, but Jesus stays the same through every season.
—GWEN FORD FAULKENBERRY

FAITH STEP: *As you look forward to the next season of your life, make a list of the changes you anticipate, whether new joys or new challenges. Next to each one, write "Same Jesus." Tuck the list into your Bible in Hebrews 13.*

SUNDAY, MAY 30

"Again I tell you, it is easier for a camel to go through the eye of a needle than for someone who is rich to enter the kingdom of God." When the disciples heard this, they were greatly astonished and asked, "Who then can be saved?" Jesus looked at them and said, "With man this is impossible, but with God all things are possible." Matthew 19:24–26 (NIV)

I LOVE THIS PASSAGE BECAUSE it offers me hope for a wealthy unsaved friend. My husband used to do her yardwork. Two years ago, disappointed by the poor condition of her massive iris garden, she requested David remove it. I had to agree with her. The area was sloppy and never bloomed. But my spouse asked her to give the flowers one last chance. He dug them up, split and trimmed every rhizome, then replanted them.

Soon after, he accepted a different job and quit gardening. We stayed in touch with our friend, but life kept us too busy for visits.

Last week, she called, her voice tinged with excitement. There was something she wanted us to see. We hurried over, wondering what was going on. Upon rounding her corner, we couldn't believe the scene before us. At least a hundred irises blossomed in colors so vibrant they almost hurt our eyes. The flowers I'd given up on were now a delicate sea of purples, yellows, whites, and burgundies.

If I'd had my way, they'd have been thrown away. But my husband saw the possibilities and saved them.

Like those irises, sin once kept me from blooming. But Jesus saw my potential and instead of discarding me, He redeemed me. Salvation is possible for everyone, including my well-to-do, unbelieving friend. God's needle, threaded by Jesus, is big enough for anyone to pass through. —HEIDI GAUL

FAITH STEP: *Seek opportunities to help thread God's needle this week. Don't regard anyone's salvation as impossible—God doesn't.*

MEMORIAL DAY, MONDAY, MAY 31

Since we are surrounded by such a great cloud of witnesses, let us throw off everything that hinders and the sin that so easily entangles. And let us run with perseverance the race marked out for us. Hebrews 12:1 (NIV)

TODAY I SENT A BIRTHDAY card to a man I don't know. I saw on the Aggie Network that Colonel Tom "Ike" Morris was celebrating his 109th birthday, making him the oldest living Aggie. (An Aggie is a graduate of Texas A&M University.) Aggies, current and past, share an intimate bond. A&M's school colors are maroon and white, and it's said that Aggies bleed maroon. For generations, everyone in my family, including me, has gone to A&M. On Ike's birthday card, I mentioned my dad, Bill Butler, and my uncle, O. D. Butler, both from the class of 1939 and like Ike, World War II veterans. I'm fiercely proud of those men and how bravely they served.

I've always cherished the reference to the "great cloud of witnesses" in Hebrews. During trying times, I'm comforted by thinking of all who have gone before me, lining the streets of heaven and cheering me on as I strive to finish the race of life. Along the route, I imagine not only Abraham, Isaac, and Jacob but also my parents and grandparents, Amelia Earhart, Jimmy Stewart, President Kennedy—and, of course, Jesus, the most encouraging one of them all.

Myriads of people today are fascinated by tracing their roots, finding out who their relatives are, and what countries they came from. It might be exciting to find out you were kin to someone famous, but I really don't have a desire to trace my roots. Just knowing I come from Jesus is good enough for me. —PAT BUTLER DYSON

FAITH STEP: *Make a list of the people who comprise your great cloud of witnesses. Thank Jesus for them.*

TUESDAY, JUNE 1

You make known to me the path of life; in your presence there is fullness of joy; at your right hand are pleasures forevermore. Psalm 16:11 (ESV)

I CAN STILL FEEL THE warmth of that freshly baked cookie in my hands. It was the perfect accompaniment to my second cup of coffee that morning as I prepared to facilitate a brainstorming workshop a few weeks ago. Days earlier, the retreat team had included a single individually wrapped gourmet cookie in our registration packets. With an allergy that prevents me from most treats, I was delighted to find gluten-free options of the gourmet offerings. I passed up the chocolate chip and picked the gluten-free toffee cookie I savored to the last crumb.

Fast-forward to the day of the brainstorming workshop. The husband of a woman already seated at the round table of attendees was late. His wife explained that they'd noticed how much I enjoyed that single toffee cookie. He'd walked to the bakery early that morning to get me a repeat of that delight. "He just texted," she said. "He had to wait for the cookies to come out of the oven."

He walked. He waited. He purchased. He walked back… simply so he and his wife could bless me. That overt thoughtfulness meant far more than the warm toffee goodness in the bakery bag when he finally arrived, breathless but smiling.

That couple modeled the way Jesus delights in blessing His people. He's not stingy, and He sets a high standard for generosity. He too walked (this earth), waited (for His Father's timing for His ministry), purchased (us for His own), and will one day "walk back" with unimaginable joys in hand. His reward? The joy on our faces.
—CYNTHIA RUCHTI

FAITH STEP: *Fullness of joy comes in His presence. What seemingly small delights can you notice and thank Jesus for today?*

WEDNESDAY, JUNE 2

Therefore, there is now no condemnation for those who are in Christ Jesus, because through Christ Jesus the law of the Spirit who gives life has set you free from the law of sin and death. Romans 8:1–2 (NIV)

MY JOB AS A MIDDLE school teacher this year was both exciting and challenging. Its challenges took a toll on my family life. I was exhausted by the time I got home. Stress affected my relationship with Scott and the boys. My inability to cope left me feeling like a failure as a wife and mom. Even though I repeatedly apologized to my family for my exhaustion and short temper, I finished the year feeling raw with guilt and shame. I shared this with my friend Marie France, who is a master teacher. She knows the struggle of balancing work and home life. I said, "I know I have messed up. I have a whole lot of repairing to do." Marie France thought for a moment and then said, "Sue, I don't think it is up to you to repair this season. I think you need Jesus to redeem it."

Those words brought tears to my eyes. When we fall short and repent, Jesus steps in and says, "I'll take over from here." He shoulders the weight of our wrongdoing and somehow and someway redeems it. He didn't come to set us free so that we would still carry the burden of sin with us. He doesn't condemn us. He saves us. Condemnation is the work of the enemy, stifling the joy of Jesus's salvation. Jesus forgives us, setting us on a new path of freedom, redeeming our past and enabling us to become the new creation He created us to be. —SUSANNA FOTH AUGHTMON

FAITH STEP: *Jesus doesn't condemn you. He wants to set you free. Take a freedom walk outside, knowing that who the Son sets free is free indeed.*

THURSDAY, JUNE 3

---

*Even to your old age and gray hairs, I am he, I am he who will
sustain you. I have made you and I will carry you; I will sustain you
and I will rescue you. Isaiah 46:4 (NIV)*

WHEN MY CHILDREN WERE IN college and weary of school, I'd remind them to "finish strong." The temptation to coast arose in the final semester. I understood their struggle, because years ago I went through the same impulse. I didn't think I could face one more class, one more test, or one more paper. But it was well worth the final push.

Today a friend and I were commiserating about aging. Not about the things you might expect like wrinkles or forgetfulness or health issues. We were disheartened by how chronological maturity hadn't automatically produced spiritual maturity. We had hoped that by this stage of life we would have become more like Jesus, learned from our life experiences, and mastered more Christlike qualities. Instead we continue to struggle. We still forget to trust Him. We continue to fight battles with envy. We give in to selfishness far too often.

The longer I live, the more aware I am of the ways I fall short. What a blessing that I'm not alone in my efforts to grow! Jesus knows that no matter how long we've followed Him, our old nature continues to give us trouble while we're on this earth. We need His Word for daily reminders about how to follow Him. We need worship to direct our attention away from ourselves. We need fellowship to give accountability and encouragement. We never stop learning, practicing, and growing.

Whatever our age, Jesus gives each day meaning and purpose. He promises to help us finish strong. —SHARON HINCK

FAITH STEP: *Draw a picture of your life's finish line, with Jesus welcoming you home. Ask Him to help you finish strong.*

Friday, June 4

"For I know the plans I have for you," declares the LORD, "plans to prosper you and not to harm you, plans to give you hope and a future."
Jeremiah 29:11 (NIV)

A FEW MONTHS AGO, I took my daughter and two granddaughters to a paint-your-own-pottery studio. Recently, at a different studio, I had painted a napkin holder, and now I wanted matching salt and pepper shakers.

The method I'd used on the napkin holder was unique: I dipped a long brush in various glazes and slung it onto the pottery, creating a kaleidoscope of colorful splotches—glorious!

When Tammie, the studio assistant, showed us to our tiny table, I inwardly groaned. I politely asked her for a larger table so I could use the same glaze-slinging method.

Instead, she positioned three clipboards on their sides in a U-shape to give me my own space. But the only brushes she had were too large for the slinging method. I splattered glaze on my clothes, my oldest granddaughter, and even the pottery on the shelf behind me. I was angry at Tammie for not accommodating me, and I grumbled as I worked.

After the pottery was fired in the kiln, my daughter brought me the shakers. They'd turned out lovelier than I could have imagined, and matched the napkin holder perfectly. I repented of my terrible attitude toward Tammie, who was only doing her job, then thanked Jesus for reminding me that no matter how my plans get upset He always has a solution. —JEANETTE LEVELLIE

FAITH STEP: *Think of a time when your plans were changed and Jesus replaced your disappointment with delight. Thank Him for His creative problem solving.*

SATURDAY, JUNE 5

*In My Father's house are many mansions; if it were not so, I would
have told you. I go to prepare a place for you. John 14:2 (NKJV)*

A COUPLE OF OUR MINISTRY coworkers visited us for five days.
During that time, Gene and I took them sailing among the islands
dotting British Columbia's coastline.

Houses of all shapes and sizes sit along the shore. Some are multi-
million-dollar mansions. Others are tiny abandoned cabins inhabited only by mice and spiders.

One huge house was nestled on a landscape filled with flower-
ing plants. The lawn sloped gently toward a beach where a covered
pagoda beckoned guests to its shade. "Oh, so beautiful," I gushed.

My coworker smiled and said, "That's nothing compared to what
our heavenly mansions will look like."

Human architects design houses that leave us in awe, but their
most magnificent creations cannot compare with the home Jesus is
preparing just for us. As long as we're alive, we'll never comprehend
the scope and beauty of our heavenly residence.

When Jesus welcomes us into heaven and ushers us to our new
home, its beauty will leave us breathless. Perhaps its design will be
perfectly suited to our personality and uniqueness. Maybe its walls
and floors will be embedded with pearls and precious stones. Who
really knows? The fact is, it will far exceed our expectations.

We'll experience joy indescribable when Jesus opens our mansion's
door and says, "Enter." But the joy we'll experience when we finally
meet Him face to face will be far greater. —GRACE FOX

FAITH STEP: *Jot down a description of your ideal home. Thank Jesus for
preparing one that supersedes that design.*

SUNDAY, JUNE 6

He made known his ways to Moses, his deeds to the people of Israel.
The LORD is compassionate and gracious, slow to anger, abounding in love.
Psalm 103:7–8 (NIV)

OUR FAMILY IS EMBARKING ON a new adventure. After fourteen years of living in California, we are moving to the foothills of Boise, Idaho. This past week, my husband, Scott, a full-time pastor and part-time marketer, accepted a job at a tech company, shifting his ministry to the marketplace. I will move from being a middle school teacher to a freelance writer and editor. Our younger sons Will and Addison will attend a new school. Our eldest son, Jack, is staying behind in California to launch his college career. Our dog and cat? Hopefully, they will survive the upending. We have discovered this past year that Jesus was at work, pulling our hearts in a new direction. *But how could it all come to pass? How could we transition our family cross-country? How could we move forward without work, a house, or a plan?*

So much of this process has been mysterious. I have frequently asked God, *What in the world is going on?* But Jesus is not weary of my questions. Instead, He is moving on our behalf. He knows that the most complex thought processes of my brain cannot encompass the greatness of His ways. He is flinging open doors and creating opportunities and crushing doubts and fears. In the boundlessness of His love, He is telling a new story with our lives. In the vastness of His grace, His mind-blowing works are being revealed. In the midst of uncertainty and change, Jesus remains the same, making His ways and deeds known to those whom He loves. —SUSANNA FOTH AUGHTMON

FAITH STEP: *What out-of-reach plans are you pondering in your heart right now? Offer both your dreams and doubts to Him today. Believe that in the mystery of your life, Jesus will make His ways and deeds known to you.*

MONDAY, JUNE 7

Carry each other's burdens, and in this way you will fulfill the law of Christ.
Galatians 6:2 (NIV)

RECENTLY, A FRIEND OF MINE experienced an unexpected, life-changing setback. In an instant, her world was flipped upside-down. As she struggled with loss, her family and I helped in small ways, such as walking the dog, visiting her, or simply sitting with her in silence. Jesus worked inside her and mended her heart, just as promised in Psalm 147:3.

Soon, she and I ran some errands together. Last week, we sat together on my porch rocking chairs chatting while the world passed by. Birds chirped as my cats watched through slitted eyes, too lazy to leave their patches of sunlight. Yesterday we shopped for silly things—bed pillows, the perfect pretzel—and stopped for coffee at what's become our favorite place for heart-to-heart talks. When I reflect on the path she and I have walked these past few months, I'm grateful and a bit surprised. In the past, though friendly, we rarely spent time together. Now, our friendship has gained value, deepening into a relationship of mutual trust and support. Her tears appear less often and have been replaced by smiles, proof of slow but steady healing. I'm blessed to share in a measure of hope as I witness the return of her strong spirit.

Jesus has softened her pain and muted her anguish. Family and friends keep her moving forward, one step at a time. On days when the road ahead looks too hard for her to walk alone, we come alongside and hold her up, following where He leads. We are His, and it's our honor and privilege to share the weight of her burden, to live out His perfect law in love. —HEIDI GAUL

FAITH STEP: *Consider friends whose burden you can help carry. Can you run an errand, or spend time together in quiet conversation? Pray for—and with—them.*

TUESDAY, JUNE 8

For no matter how many promises God has made, they are "Yes" in Christ... 2 Corinthians 1:20 (NIV)

JUST SAY *"NO."* I REMEMBER this phrase plastered as a slogan on posters around my high school. Saying "no" was believed by authority figures to be a talisman that would ward off all manner of teenage vices. Later I built on the power of "no" as I increased my efforts to not be a people pleaser, to draw boundaries, and keep from overloading myself with more commitments than I could handle. "No" definitely has its perks.

But because I am a parent, I've lately been pondering the power of "yes." Although it's hard to say "no" to vices and pleasing people, sometimes I get into a rut with my kids where "no" just feels like the easiest answer. "No, you can't go" keeps me from having to worry about my child's safety away from me. "No, you can't make slime" can keep a mess out of my house. "No, we can't afford that." "No, it's not good for you." "No, not today; I have to work." I caught myself recently saying "no" as my default—my first and quickest answer. My kids were unhappy and I felt like a pretty crummy mom.

I think we often imagine God like a grumpy parent whose default position is "no." Or maybe we assume what we want is inherently wrong so we expect Him to say "no" to the desires of our hearts. But Jesus is the resounding "Yes!" God speaks over us. Everything He's promised is fulfilled in Jesus, and that's a lot. —GWEN FORD FAULKENBERRY

FAITH STEP: *Google "God's promises" and read up on all of the things that are yours for the asking in Jesus. Need more grace, more wisdom, more joy, more courage? Then ask! And hear Him answer with a resounding "Yes!"*

WEDNESDAY, JUNE 9

After the earthquake came a fire, but the LORD was not in the fire.
And after the fire came a gentle whisper. 1 Kings 19:12 (NIV)

OUR FRIENDS HAD JUST GOTTEN a new fishing boat and invited us on an outing. The forecast was sketchy: storms would be skirting our fishing grounds throughout the day. We delayed our departure, hoping it would clear but ended up heading out in the overcast weather. Our native Floridian hosts weren't concerned, even as we passed boats heading into shore. Florida's weather is notoriously erratic, but life goes on.

I'm not a nervous Nellie, but I prayed before we left and kept a close eye on the storm radar app, a common practice down here. We soon dropped anchor, and the guys cast their lines while we ladies chatted. Not getting any bites, we paused for lunch, then moved farther out to a nearby islet where another boat bobbed in the mildly choppy waves.

My phone's weather alert pinged overly cautious warnings that I mentally ran by Jesus. But the sky didn't change, so we stayed put, relaxed. This went on for a while. Then I sensed a little quickening. Nothing had changed, but I just knew it was time to go. I told the captain and indulging me, he promptly made for port.

Just as we set foot on land, there was a crash of thunder. We scurried to the marina hut and crossed the threshold just as the skies opened. I never once felt afraid. I thanked Jesus for keeping us safe.

I'm learning to discern and obey these subtle prompts that have awesome results. —ISABELLA YOSUICO

FAITH STEP: *Next time you feel a little nudge from the Holy Spirit, act on it and note the results.*

THURSDAY, JUNE 10

Therefore, since we are surrounded by such a great cloud of witnesses, let us throw off everything that hinders and the sin that so easily entangles...
Hebrews 12:1 (NIV)

MY CREDIT CARD BILL THIS month was three times larger than usual. When I lamented to my husband, he tried to reassure me. "You had several large ministry expenses, Jeanette." But I knew better.

For me, overspending is what the writer of Hebrews calls a "sin that so easily entangles." If I'm not vigilant, I spend money like some people use drugs. To make even a small purchase—a few packs of gum, a three-dollar blouse at a thrift store, a used book—lightens my heart and gives me a sense of importance. If I let myself career out of control, the guilt that accompanies my self-indulgence fills me with shame.

The only cure is to confess to Jesus that I did it again, ask His forgiveness and cleansing, and commit to live within my means. Sometimes it helps to look in the mirror and say, "I forgive you, Jeanette."

If I was addicted to alcohol or nicotine, I think quitting would be easier—I could go cold turkey. But I need to spend money for groceries, clothes, and hair color (that *is* a necessity).

Only Jesus can fill the holes in my heart I try to fill with my inadequate methods. Saying no to impulse buying and saving up for large purchases forces me to rely on His power. When I can walk away from a clearance rack of clothes or a 75-percent-off display of jewelry, I'm overjoyed. When I let Him love and help me, I feel His pleasure too. —JEANETTE LEVELLIE

FAITH STEP: *If you have one sin you constantly wrestle with, ask Jesus to show you someone to call when you're tempted, someone to hold you accountable. Pray for His power to live big in you.*

FRIDAY, JUNE 11

Pride goes before destruction, and a haughty spirit before a fall.
Proverbs 16:18 (NKJV)

I SCURRIED DOWN THE POLISHED mahogany staircase, with my daughter Melissa's bridal gown draped over one arm and her veil over the other. The next thing I knew, I lay sprawled in a crumpled heap at the bottom of the stairs. I couldn't move my arm, and my head throbbed. *Why me, Jesus? Why now?*

My daughter Melissa, her fiancé, Daniel, my husband, Jeff, and I had gone to the wedding venue that morning to decorate tables for the reception. Hours later, I sat slumped in a chair in the Emergency Room, waiting for test results.

"You were lucky," the doctor said, as he fitted a sling over my shoulder. "No broken bones and no concussion." I didn't feel lucky. I felt mortified and sick inside.

As I iced my shoulder back at home, I told Jeff and my younger daughter, Brooke, I wouldn't attend the wedding in a sling.

"I can help you dress and do your hair and makeup, Mom," Brooke offered. Brooke is twenty-five, with long, straight hair. Full makeup for her is lip gloss and a touch of mascara. Could Brooke squeeze me into my Spanx? No way. Just then, I felt Jesus speak to me: *Pat, are you really going to miss the biggest event in your daughter's life because of pride?*

"You're on!" I said to Brooke. An hour later, I was at the wedding in my sparkly outfit, coifed and made up, toasting the happy couple, greeting guests, and thanking Jesus and Brooke for getting me where I needed to be. —PAT BUTLER DYSON

FAITH STEP: *Are you letting pride prevent you from doing something you should do? Ask Jesus to help you rise above it.*

SATURDAY, JUNE 12

"Truly I tell you," he said, "this poor widow has put in more than all the others. All these people gave their gifts out of their wealth; but she out of her poverty put in all she had to live on." Luke 21:3–4 (NIV)

I RETURNED FROM SPEAKING AT a women's retreat, filled to overflowing. We were strangers at the start of the retreat, but fast friends at the end. We were from different denominations but shared the most important common ground—our love for Jesus.

In the final program, the coordinator asked the women to share ideas they'd used to live generously and reach out to others, as He did.

One group started an aquaponics mini-farm to raise fresh fish, lettuce, herbs, and tomatoes to give to families in need. Another group takes on a new community mission every month, and last month the focus was "lightbulbs." They volunteered to change burned out interior and exterior lightbulbs for the elderly and infirm in their community. The ideas flowed as the women helped each other brainstorm, with no ulterior motive—except to bless people in Jesus's name.

When Jesus experienced disappointment in His ministry, it was over people who focused on themselves rather than on pouring themselves out, people who hoarded their possessions and their time rather than demonstrating the love that could change lives.

What made Jesus beam with joy? Expressions of faith (Matthew 8:10), when we care for the needs of others (James 1:27; Matthew 25:40), obedience to His teaching (1 John 5:3), and, like the widow in Luke 21, irrepressible generosity to His cause. Lord, keep me faithful to the things that bring You joy. —CYNTHIA RUCHTI

FAITH STEP: *Perform an act of kindness or generosity. Repeat daily.*

SUNDAY, JUNE 13

About midnight Paul and Silas were praying and singing hymns to God, and the prisoners were listening to them. Acts 16:25 (ESV)

RAIN BLURRED THE WINDSHIELD AS we drove home. The road was slick; highway traffic, cautious. Suddenly a car zoomed past us and the two trucks ahead. It swerved into our lane and cut off the first truck. Both vehicles stopped abruptly to avoid a collision. My husband, Gene, tried to do the same, but our tires slid. *Crash!*

Our car was totaled, but we expressed thanks when we prayed later that night. We thanked Jesus for protecting everyone involved, for sending first responders, for quickly sending a tow truck, and for stopping the rainstorm as we waited roadside for a taxi.

It's easy to give thanks and praise when the story ends well—but not so much when bad stuff happens. Paul and Silas experienced terrible circumstances. Stripped and beaten with rods and then locked in stocks in the worst cell, they had reason to complain. Instead, they sang hymns and prayed.

Luke 6:45 says, "Out of the abundance of the heart his mouth speaks" (ESV). Clearly Paul and Silas's hearts were filled with hope and joy. The only explanation for their ability to respond as they did was their faith in the risen Christ (Acts 16:31). They'd encountered Him and understood the power of His resurrection (Philippians 3:10–11). His Holy Spirit lived in them, and the hope and joy He produced spilled over under pressure.

Apart from Jesus, few can respond like Silas and Paul. When love for Jesus fills our hearts, we, too, will praise Him under pressure.
—GRACE FOX

FAITH STEP: *Identify one pressure facing you today. List as many things as possible that you can be thankful for in the midst of it.*

MONDAY, JUNE 14

Set your minds on things that are above, not on things that are on earth.
For you have died, and your life is hidden with Christ in God. When
Christ who is your life appears, then you also will appear with him in glory.
Colossians 3:2–4 (ESV)

"THIS HOUSE IS IN YOUR price range, and it's been on the market for a while." The realtor ushered us into a dark kitchen. Battered avocado-colored appliances were wedged against a grimy brick wall. A strange plastic sliding barrier outlined a tiny eating area.

The bathroom had an ugly green sink and tub. The whole house looked dingy and forsaken. But when we stepped into the living room on the back of the house, we stopped short.

Beyond the ample backyard, the water of a public pond rippled in the breeze. Ducks swam, willow branches bobbed, and beyond the pond a protected wetland held native grasses, reeds, and endless trees. My husband and I looked at each other and knew this was our new home.

We spent years remodeling, first the main floor and then the basement. When the work was frustrating, we'd stop and look out the window. The beauty energized us to keep going.

Sometimes the view is everything. Life can be dingy, cramped, and ugly more times than we'd like to admit. The work of our hands is often repetitive and seems unrewarding. Relationships can wound us like rusty nails. Loss and grief can darken our vision like a blown fuse. But when we set our gaze beyond, the glimpse of Jesus's glory carries us through. No matter how ugly our present circumstances, we can focus on where He is guiding us—to beauty beyond imagination.
—SHARON HINCK

FAITH STEP: *Shift your gaze today. Find a beautiful view and thank Jesus for that reminder of the glory ahead when He returns.*

TUESDAY, JUNE 15

But ask the animals, and they will teach you, or the birds in the sky, and they will tell you; or speak to the earth, and it will teach you, or let the fish in the sea inform you. Which of all these does not know that the hand of the LORD has done this? Job 12:7–9 (NIV)

HOW HAD THE DAY GOTTEN away from me? It was almost dusk, and I hadn't exercised. With darkness encroaching, it was too risky to ride my bicycle, so I'd walk. I grabbed my headphones and set out, anxious to catch up on the news of the day as I exercised. About the time I reached the end of the block, my phone died. How would I occupy my mind? The silence was deafening.

I hustled along the empty street, preoccupied with worries. My route took me to a wooded area of the subdivision that hadn't been developed. As I rounded the bend, a slight movement caught my eye, and I stopped. A doe and two fawn grazed in the clearing not twenty yards away. The sight took my breath away. I stood watching for several minutes before the deer bounded away. *Jesus, was that You? How I needed You to tell me to slow down, to appreciate the beauty around me!*

I remembered a sonnet by nineteenth-century poet William Wordsworth, "The World Is Too Much with Us." Guilty as charged. How long had it been since I'd looked at the clouds, sniffed a flower, or paused to listen to a bird's song? On my way home, I slowed to a stroll and talked to Jesus. As always, He showed me the way. —PAT BUTLER DYSON

FAITH STEP: *Go for a nature walk. Take a bag with you to collect leaves, feathers, and rocks. When you get home, look at all the items and thank Jesus for nature's bounty.*

WEDNESDAY, JUNE 16

Every good and perfect gift is from above, coming down from the Father of the heavenly lights, who does not change like shifting shadows. James 1:17 (NIV)

"IF HE WERE MY DOG, I wouldn't want him to suffer anymore," our vet advised tenderly. It was time to say goodbye to our thirteen-year-old Labrador. I'd been holding back tears, but when the vet spoke those words, I felt them slip down my cheeks.

I looked at Mogul, who was named after the bumps on a ski mountain because our family loves to ski. *How had he gone so quickly from being the chubby puppy we'd brought home to the handsome yellow lab that hiked miles with me—to now?* He had lost fifteen pounds in the last eight weeks and his face and sides showed signs of muscular deterioration.

My throat hurt. I couldn't speak. I just nodded and dabbed at my eyes with a tissue.

I decided the next day to give Mogul the best day ever. We went on a hike overlooking the city, and when it was time to head down, Mogul was sniffing something underneath a rock. I saw he'd found a plastic bag. I picked it up, assuming it was trash, but instead I found a gift card for new hiking boots. A shoe company was hosting a scavenger hunt, and Mogul had found the treasure! He had given me a gift to remind me of him. More than that, I knew Jesus was giving me the perfect gift to comfort me as I was having to say goodbye to a beloved family pet.

Whenever I wear the hiking shoes, I think fondly of Mogul and of Jesus, who knows me so intimately and faithfully that He gives me meaningful and perfect gifts. —JEANNIE BLACKMER

FAITH STEP: *What is a gift you've received that can be from only Jesus? Write about it in your journal.*

THURSDAY, JUNE 17

Be kind to one another, tenderhearted, forgiving one another,
even as God in Christ forgave you. Ephesians 4:32 (NKJV)

MY DAD WAS A TORMENTED writer, an alcoholic who shunned religion until his deathbed. His antique desk, intricately carved and inlaid with mother-of-pearl now stands in my living room, a veritable monument to the art of writing. A tarnished old key grants entry to several drawers.

For years, I couldn't bring myself to open them. Every time I'd peek inside those private spaces, scarred-over hurts engulfed me like a tsunami. I'd start, but minutes later I'd need to walk away, undone by grief.

Last week I determined to open the drawers and empty them. I first found a photo of my late mother's face. I paused to pray and then dug deeper to find more pictures, receipts, and greeting cards. Somewhere in that pile of stuff, I rediscovered my dad's core goodness. It was evident in the one place where, as a writer, he felt safe. At last I could view his turbulent life journey through his perspective.

Daddy had done his best. He'd loved us in his imperfect way, just as I'd loved him. And that was enough. I sighed—the ancient scars inside me were healed at last.

What transpired inside me as I cleaned the desk that day was a gift from Jesus. He's not afraid of or disgusted by what He'll find when He looks deep inside us. He frees us from past hurts and generously forgives us forever. I owe my father that same grace—complete and permanent, with no strings attached.

Because once I pulled the pain out of the drawer, all that was left was joy. Pure, precious joy. What more could I ask for? —HEIDI GAUL

FAITH STEP: *Ask Jesus to heal your internal scars. Forgive just as our Lord would (Matthew 6:12) and as He has forgiven you (Ephesians 4:32).*

FRIDAY, JUNE 18

Instead, they need to hope in God, who richly provides everything for our enjoyment. 1 Timothy 6:17 (CEB)

CONFESSION TIME: I JUST NOW used a rubber spatula to scrape ice cream off the sides of its paper carton and eat it. Even though it's late afternoon. Even though I had a bowl of the black walnut ice cream this morning.

I can explain.

My freezer drawer is overcrowded right now; this morning the upper drawer fell off the roller track when I pulled it out. This afternoon I saw that the ice-cream carton was in the way. So I scooped out the ice cream into a small glass container. When I saw how much was stuck on the sides, I did the logical thing. I ate it!

Instead of feeling guilty, I have a smile on my face. My earliest memory is of me sitting on my knees on a kitchen chair in front of an ice-cream carton that someone had flattened out. I'm scraping the sides with a spoon while my dad, an ice-cream lover himself, watched and laughed. I still remember how his eyes twinkled as he said, "You like that stuff, don't you?" Like many fathers, my dad didn't talk much about feelings. That's why sixty-five years later, I treasure that image of him smiling as he watched me eat ice cream out of the carton.

Sometimes it's easy to get fixated on the aspects of following Jesus that have to do with taking up our cross and dying to self. We may forget that the Christian life also means embracing the blessings He's given us. If we could see how much pleasure He receives from watching us enjoy the gifts He sends our way, we would gain a clearer image of how much He loves us. —DIANNE NEAL MATTHEWS

FAITH STEP: *As you go through your day, thank Jesus each time you find yourself enjoying something He created or has sent into your life.*

SATURDAY, JUNE 19

But seek first his kingdom and his righteousness, and all these things will be given to you as well. Matthew 6:33 (NIV)

TUCKED INTO THE MIRROR FRAME in my bedroom is the only note I ever received from my dad, who is now with Jesus. Dad was not a writer. Nor did he express himself fluently in other ways. But I cherish the words he wrote in his elementary-style script. "Thanks for the 5 Bibles for my birthday. Love, Dad."

The whole family knew that for every birthday, Christmas, and Father's Day, Dad asked for the same gift: Bibles. He was a Gideon— part of a worldwide group of businessmen who place Bibles in hotel rooms, doctor's offices, and prisons. The Gideons have a program where you can donate Bibles to be given away in honor of someone. You then send a card to the person you want to honor, telling them how many Bibles you bought in their name.

Dad didn't care about anything on this earth as much as seeing people receive the Word of God. He passed up scores of opportunities to get all manner of gifts. But ties, candy, movies, and other presents weren't important to him. His heart was in heaven long before he walked on its gold streets.

I admire Dad's attitude of laying up treasures in heaven (Matthew 6:20). I know it gives Jesus immense joy when someone makes sharing His Word a priority. Although I will ask for dark chocolate and funny romance DVDs for my birthday this year, I often purchase Bibles in honor of others. As long as I'm here, Dad's legacy will continue. The light of God's Word will cover the earth, one Bible at a time. —JEANETTE LEVELLIE

FAITH STEP: *Find a Bible you aren't using or buy one. Give it to someone who needs to hear the Good News of Jesus's love for them.*

FATHER'S DAY, SUNDAY, JUNE 20

A father to the fatherless, a defender of widows, is God in His holy dwelling. Psalm 68:5 (NIV)

FATHER'S DAY CAN BE BITTERSWEET for me. I joyfully celebrate my husband's loving fatherhood, but I sometimes grieve for my own father and the father I didn't have.

My dad was a remarkable man: charming, funny, brilliant, and full of life but also a deeply troubled alcoholic who was often angry, unpredictable, and absent for much of my childhood. He died nearly twenty years ago—about the time I met Jesus and was reconciled to my heavenly Father—no coincidence, for sure. I also had a surrogate dad who was rather similar to my own dad, and although well-meaning, he also left a bruise. He died three years ago. Honestly, I've always felt fatherless.

I've lived with the consequences of hanging my hopes on these very human paternal figures. The void led me to seek to know my perfect heavenly Father all the more. The Scripture confirms that the perfect father is unconditionally loving, supportive, wise, generous, merciful, concerned with our well-being, always available... the list goes on.

Through Jesus, we are forever reconciled to our perfect Father. Whether we had a great earthly dad or not, we can rejoice in our standing as truly adopted sons and daughters of our perfect heavenly Father, who satisfies our deepest need as no human can. Truly internalizing this truth is transforming my life emboldening me to lean into Jesus and trust Him more and more. —ISABELLA YOSUICO

FAITH STEP: *Today, invoke your privilege as a child of God, mindfully reframing your prayers as though speaking to your very real and perfect heavenly Dad.*

MONDAY, JUNE 21

Jesus called the children to him and said, "Let the little children come to me, and do not hinder them, for the kingdom of God belongs to such as these." Luke 18:16 (NIV)

THE CHURCH WHERE I WORK is famous for its floor-to-ceiling stained glass windows. My favorite one depicts Jesus as He blessed the children. They range in age from an infant on His lap to an older child sitting in the grass at His feet. One small girl stands beside Him, waving for His attention.

Sometimes as I pass that window, colored light streaming down upon me, I imagine myself in the scene. Last week I identified with the older child, secure enough to sit and watch Jesus bless the others. Today I feel like the baby, needing all the assurance Jesus can offer. Next week I may relate to the girl who waves to Him, saying, "Look at me. Notice me. Please, tell me I'm significant."

I wonder if we all have a child inside, full of changing needs and levels of security. We would like to feel grown up all the time—never envious, never anxious. But life happens. We find ourselves acting out of childish attitudes we thought we had overcome (I do, anyway). Jesus never shakes His head in disappointment or harshly scolds us to "grow up." His love is custom-made to bless our little hearts at each level of maturity we go through—even if we seesaw between them.

When Jesus returns to take us home with Him, we'll leave our childish ways behind. Thank God! But until that day, we can trust Him to understand. And to be there for us, blessing every one of us. —JEANETTE LEVELLIE

FAITH STEP: *Find a painting of Jesus blessing the children. Pick which child you identify with in this moment of your life. Now, thank Jesus for accepting you just as you are.*

TUESDAY, JUNE 22

When the cares of my heart are many, your consolations cheer my soul.
Psalm 94:19 *(ESV)*

MY HUSBAND, GENE, AND I had just returned from Slovakia where we'd helped host an English-learning evangelistic family camp. We'd come home tired, and jetlag added to our fatigue. So did thinking about our upcoming schedule. It included hosting evening informational meetings for our ministry, traveling to Bible colleges to engage with students seeking mission opportunities, and speaking at retreats and conferences. I also anticipated helping my mom for a week.

Taking a break before hitting that schedule seemed necessary, so we prepared our boat and launched out. Several days of sunshine and soft breezes seemed the perfect antidote for our weary bodies and souls.

One morning Gene put up the sails and set the steering to autopilot. I poured two cups of hot chocolate. We sipped our drinks and marveled at the beauty of water and mountains. Suddenly a fin surfaced about 100 feet away. An orca whale!

The creature swam straight toward us. A second fin appeared. And a third. Within seconds, a pod of perhaps thirty orcas surrounded us. They swam in front of the boat, under it, and then one leaped out of the water behind us and landed with a giant splash.

The chances of encountering an orca pod in that vast expanse of water were slim. Could it be that Jesus whispered to the whales and sent them to swim across our path?

Jesus knows when we need encouragement, and He's masterful at sending it our way. His consolations always come through His Word. But sometimes they come as an unexpected phone call or email, a favorite song, or a hug. They come in the form of a baby's giggle, a bird's trill, and a rose's scent. Sometimes they even show up as a pod of orca whales. —GRACE FOX

FAITH STEP: *Identify one consolation by which Jesus has cheered your soul recently.*

WEDNESDAY, JUNE 23

"All the earth worships you and sings praises to you; they sing praises to your name." Selah. Psalm 66:4 (ESV)

I'VE BEEN TRAINING OUR NEW puppy, Ody. He's a chocolate lab with beautiful hazel-green eyes. He's our third Labrador. We trained the other two while raising three rowdy boys. Suffice it to say, our dogs didn't get much training. They were loved, but they were rowdy too. They pulled when we walked, and they ran away, ate trash, and especially went nuts for squirrels.

With our sons out of the house, I decided to hire a dog trainer to help me. I wanted to avoid those same bad habits. One of the strategies the trainer has taught me is to have Ody sit and look at me and then praise him before releasing him.

I've been practicing this rhythm with him. Pause, focus, praise.

Then, the other morning I was reading Psalm 66. As I read, I noticed the word *Selah* at the end of verses about singing praises to God. *What does "Selah" mean?* I wondered. I searched on Google and found it appears seventy-one times in the Psalms, and some Bible scholars believe it means "pause and praise."

Hmmm. Reading that made me realize that I needed training too. I began to take moments in my day to pause and stop whatever I was doing, especially in chaotic moments when I feel the pull of life. Focus my thoughts on Jesus. And praise God for a specific blessing in that moment. Practicing this has helped me find peace, clarity, and direction. Just as Ody is growing up as a calm puppy who consistently looks to me for direction, I'm continually looking to Jesus throughout my day and giving Him praise. —JEANNIE BLACKMER

FAITH STEP: *Set your alarm for three times today. Stop whatever you're doing to pause, focus on Jesus, and praise Him for something specific.*

THURSDAY, JUNE 24

And his name will be the hope of all the world. Matthew 12:21 (NLT)

SINCE MOVING INTO THE MARINA, we've intentionally built relationships by being hospitable and helping with fix-it jobs on our neighbors' boats. We've made lots of friends, but we've yet to find another believer.

Our neighbors' lives are difficult and varied. Some are unemployed, and others work full-time. Some are here because they can't afford rent anywhere else, and others live here because they love boats. Many are estranged from family. Alcohol and marijuana are common coping mechanisms.

Our conversations are deepening. We listen to their stories, look for cue words that indicate Jesus is creating a spiritual thirst in them, and respond as the Holy Spirit leads.

One fellow asked how long we'd been married. I said, "Thirty-seven years." His face registered shock. He said that he'd been married twice but couldn't get past fifteen years. "What's your secret?" he asked. His question provided an ideal opportunity to point him toward Jesus as our only hope to stay well-married.

Jesus truly is our only hope—and not just for a successful marriage. We all need Him to give wisdom for decisions, patience and forgiveness for relationships, and strength to resist temptation. We need Him to free us from the bondage of trying to earn God's favor through good works. We need Him to give us our next breath.

Jesus is the hope of the world. Sadly, most of the world doesn't know it. As we live among unreached people in the marina, we pray for more opportunities to share Jesus so our neighbors, whom we've grown to love, will find the hope their souls crave. —GRACE FOX

FAITH STEP: *Ask Jesus for a divine appointment with someone who needs hope. Listen for cue words as he or she speaks, and respond as the Holy Spirit leads.*

FRIDAY, JUNE 25

*Whoever listens to me will live in safety and be at ease,
without fear of harm. Proverbs 1:33 (NIV)*

WHEN TRAVELING THE BACKROADS OF North Carolina with a friend, we stopped at historical markers, adding time and enjoyment to the trip. Nearing our destination, we drove past a marker that read, "Pon Pon Chapel of Ease." We looked at each other. My friend turned around at the next wide spot in the road to investigate the curious sign.

We discovered a small brick chapel in the backwoods built to serve as temporary worship facilities after a fire destroyed the parent church. In the 1700s, John Wesley was among the noted itinerant preachers who had spoken in the Pon Pon Chapel of Ease.

We took pictures as late sunlight bored through holes in the once-solid brick facade that stood as a reminder of sermons preached, souls saved, and weddings and funerals and revivals conducted in that hallowed spot.

Despite internet searches, we never did discover *why* it had that curious name. Jesus didn't portend His house would be a place of ease but of prayer. Was it a place of comfort, solace for the parishioners who'd lost their original church building? Was "Chapel of Ease" a reference to a southern version of Psalm 23—"He maketh me to lie down" under the live oaks and "restoreth my soul" (vv. 2–3, KJV)? We may never know. But we'll never stop honoring those who have loved and served Jesus before us, leaving a legacy we aspire to follow.
—CYNTHIA RUCHTI

FAITH STEP: *Can you trace a spiritual legacy in your family? Share the story, thanking the Lord for allowing you to be part of that thread.*

SATURDAY, JUNE 26

I can do all this through him who gives me strength. Philippians 4:13 (NIV)

THIS WEEKEND, I VISITED A new friend at her beachfront home. The tide in the harbor appeared nonexistent, almost as smooth as glass. I relished sitting in her Adirondack chair, peace skimming over me as gently as the water lapping at the seawall.

The next moment, she mentioned how much fun I'd have kayaking.

My stomach flipped, and I tried to explain the idea was out of the question. I'm clumsy, and a terrible swimmer. My arms are strictly ornamental.

Every argument I offered was met with a firm but logical response.

The safety vest fit well. As I plopped into the tandem kayak, I offered silent thanks for the years I'd been granted. Then we were off.

While she steered, I helped paddle, and before long we'd skirted the bay and entered an estuary via a slow, deep stream. She pointed out kingfishers perched on low-lying branches, and we searched the murky banks for an otter's den. Listening to my friend, I forgot to be afraid.

Too soon, the time came for us to paddle home. By now, I'd become used to the quiet, the rhythmic dipping of the oars, and the seals bobbing in the surf. I returned to shore a braver, stronger person.

It wasn't until today that I realized I'd faced a mighty fear and conquered it—and was eager to face another.

Just as my friend did, Jesus stretches me beyond my comfort zone in my everyday life and my faith walk. He nudges me to come closer to the way He sees me: a complete, powerful woman. —HEIDI GAUL

FAITH STEP: *Is Jesus asking you to face a fear? Think of ways you can pick up your oar and start paddling. You'll be surprised at the wonderful places He'll lead you.*

SUNDAY, JUNE 27

---

*Whatever happens, my dear brothers and sisters, rejoice in the Lord.
I never get tired of telling you these things, and I do it to safeguard
your faith. Philippians 3:1 (NLT)*

I WILL NEVER FORGET THE video a church member shared one Sunday after returning from a missions trip to Africa. First, he described the harsh conditions these believers faced: extreme poverty, persecution for their beliefs, and threats of violence. Then he showed footage of a typical Sunday morning service. These Christians did not have a church building; they gathered under a tree and sat on the dusty ground or stood. Yet they sang, clapped, and shouted praises to God as though they didn't have a care in the world. The faces of each man, woman, and child radiated one thing: pure, unadulterated joy.

We often rely on material possessions or favorable circumstances to bring us joy. But these African believers had none of these things. Neither did Paul, who wrote his letter to the Philippians while imprisoned in Rome. He had learned the secret of true contentment and lasting joy: choosing to focus on our relationship with Jesus, not on what we lack or what is happening around us. Ironically, our material possessions and busy lives often steal our joy.

There are many things we can rejoice in—some good and noble, some trivial. But the greatest reason we have to rejoice is that we know Jesus and He knows us. What could be a better way to start our day than by concentrating on what He means to us? This will set the tone for a day well-lived and filled with joy.
—DIANNE NEAL MATTHEWS

FAITH STEP: *Jot down all the reasons you find joy in Jesus. Each morning for the next week, choose one item from the list to pray about and meditate on throughout the day.*

MONDAY, JUNE 28

I urge, then, first of all, that petitions, prayers, intercession and thanksgiving be made for all people. 1 Timothy 2:1 (NIV)

WHEN MY HUSBAND JEFF AND I saw the SOLD sign on the house across the street, we cheered! We'd missed the large, lively family who'd moved away, and we were anxious to meet our new neighbors. When newlyweds Tim and Virginia, along with their big friendly dog, moved in, we couldn't wait to get to know them. I took them a tin of my chocolate chip cookies to welcome them to the neighborhood.

Several months later, a friend told me Tim was very ill and that his prognosis was poor. We wanted to reach out to our neighbors, but as relative strangers, we didn't want to intrude. I asked Jesus to show me what I could do for Tim and Virginia. Several times I slipped over and left a tin of cookies at their back door. We saw Tim in a wheelchair one day, and he looked very frail. We felt helpless and heartsick. I continued to wait for Jesus's guidance for what to do.

In the meantime, every morning when I rode my bike past our neighbors' house, I prayed for healing for Tim. Every evening when I walked past their house, I asked Jesus to be with them. Every time I drove past their house, coming or going, I prayed for comfort for Tim and Virginia. Jeff and I prayed for strength and courage for them each morning during our devotional time. *Still* there was no direction from Jesus. Finally, it dawned on me that maybe my lack of an answer from Jesus *was* an answer. Maybe praying for Tim and Virginia was the best thing I could do. —PAT BUTLER DYSON

FAITH STEP: *Pray for a stranger—the clerk at the grocery store, the delivery man, the homeless woman. We all need prayer.*

TUESDAY, JUNE 29

Give thanks to the God of heaven. His love endures forever.
Psalm 136:26 (NIV)

I GRABBED MY COMPUTER BAG and dashed out the door. I had a two-hour work window because my son Jake offered to watch our new pup, Ody. I had already played with him, fed him, and walked him a few times.

I didn't have the chance to shower, but I had dressed semiprofessionally for my meeting at a coffee shop. As I walked in to order my coffee, I realized I had been in such a hurry, I forgot to change my shoes. I was still wearing my rubber, neon colored, mud covered gardening shoes I wore to tromp around the yard in the dewy morning grass as I coaxed the pup to do his business.

Trying to act calm and collected, I stood at the counter and ordered my cappuccino. Embarrassed by my bright shoes, I wondered what the woman I was meeting would think of my shoe choice. I could easily explain it, but why did I care so much? Then, I had a brave thought. *What if I don't say anything?* Recently, I had been learning I put too much value on what others think about me. I know Jesus doesn't care about what we wear, where we live, or what degrees we hold. He simply loves us. Here was a chance to practice accepting His love and letting go of what someone else might think. So, I didn't say a word. After she left, I glanced at my muddy shoes and thought, *Uh-oh, that might not be mud.* I smiled and thanked Jesus for loving me no matter what. —JEANNIE BLACKMER

FAITH STEP: *Today, if you're tempted to say something to impress someone else, practice not saying it and remind yourself of God's enduring love.*

WEDNESDAY, JUNE 30

My Father's house has many rooms; if that were not so, would I have told you that I am going there to prepare a place for you? And if I go and prepare a place for you, I will come back and take you to be with me that you also may be where I am. John 14:2–3 (NIV)

FOR THE FIRST TIME IN twenty-two years of marriage, my husband, Scott, and I are buying a house. We are moving 637 miles northeast of the California coast to Idaho. It is brand new house that is twice the size of the midcentury rental we live in. It smells of new paint and joy. Our forever home.

Scott and I are completely overwhelmed. We keep asking each other, "Can you believe it?" Each of our boys will have his own room. There is a great sense of anticipation to get there and begin living in our own home. But the truth is, this will not be our *last* new home. We are still traveling toward that destination. Before Jesus left His disciples, He made them a promise. He was going to prepare a place for them in His Father's house, and then He was coming back for them. The place He was fixing up for them was a kind of space they had never seen before. Built with love and forgiveness and crafted in perfect peace and joy, it has rooms filled with grace and jubilation. This is the same house that Jesus invites us to live in. *Can you believe it?* This forever home will be a place where we will be wholly loved, free of pain, and fully in the presence of Jesus. —SUSANNA FOTH AUGHTMON

FAITH STEP: *Meditate on this love-filled Scripture. Whatever your address is here on earth, know that you are journeying to a place of peace and hope that Jesus is designing specifically for you.*

THURSDAY, JULY 1

Through him all things were made; without him nothing was made that has been made. John 1:3 (NIV)

AT OUR LAST PRAYER MEETING, two friends and I decided we needed to step out of our familiar ways and take more risks. "Let's do something brave this month, then report to each other next month," I suggested.

So this afternoon—robust with sunshine and birdsong—I ate my lunch in the park. I took only my food. No book. No mp3 player. Not even my phone—a very brave thing for me.

I sat on an ancient stone bench, grape vines dripping from the arbor above. A breeze tickled my face. I thought, *I wonder what that bush with the tiny red flowers is called…I think that's a red-winged blackbird up on the telephone wire…I wish I had the energy of the squirrel skittering up that fat tree—I believe it's an elm.*

Wonder surrounded me as I ate, and crispy greens, a tender avocado, and crunchy almonds delighted my tongue. *Is this the best salad ever? Or have I always focused on everything but my food?*

Something happened as I sat alone. My thoughts filled with Jesus: *Thank You for fashioning all this beauty, Lord. Your endless creativity amazes me. And to think You made it for Your children's enjoyment—I will never get over how good You are.*

I'm not sure what my friends will report about the brave thing they did this month. It might prove more spectacular than my unplugged lunch in the park. But focusing on Jesus's love through His creation wasn't as brave as I'd imagined. Instead of stepping out of my comfort zone, I stepped into the presence of greatness—Jesus Himself. The most comfortable place to be. —JEANETTE LEVELLIE

FAITH STEP: *Next time you leave the house, leave your phone behind. Or go an entire day without using social media. Ask Jesus to fill the empty places.*

FRIDAY, JULY 2

I can do all this through him who gives me strength. Philippians 4:13 (NIV)

BIBLE MEMORIZATION WAS A BIG part of my sixth-grade Bible class curriculum this year. My students started out the year memorizing a single verse each week. On Friday, they would recite the week's verse. As the year progressed, the verses got longer and more complex. A communal groan went up in the class when I told them we would be memorizing Psalm 103:1–12 during the last six weeks of school. There were outbursts of "We can't do it!" and "Mrs. Aughtmon, you are trying to kill us!" I assured them, "I am not trying to kill you. You can do this!" I knew they were capable of that, and more. Each week, I would cheer them on, encouraging and reminding them that I knew they could do it. In the face of a daunting task, they persevered. Pushing through their fear and doubt in themselves, they did more than they ever thought they could. The look of accomplishment on their faces when they recited all twelve verses was fantastic.

This world can be overwhelming. We shoulder pressures at home and at work. We struggle with relationships and finances. We battle temptation and sin. At times, it feels as if life is trying to kill us. *How can we make it? How can we accomplish all that we need to?* We persevere to accomplish everything that Jesus assigns us, and everything that He's created us for. Yet, we have to remember that we are not alone in our struggles. Jesus is with us. His Spirit is ever-present, strengthening us, encouraging our hearts, reminding us that with Him and in Him, we can do all things.
—SUSANNA FOTH AUGHTMON

FAITH STEP: *What daunting task are you facing right now? Memorize Philippians 4:13. Say it throughout the day, anytime you feel overwhelmed.*

SATURDAY, JULY 3

Jesus said to them, "Come and have breakfast." Now none of the disciples dared ask him, "Who are you?" They knew it was the Lord. John 21:12 (ESV)

THREE THINGS I LOVE. BEACHES, breakfast, and Jesus. Maybe that's why this story of Jesus preparing breakfast for the disciples on the beach resonates so deeply with my soul. Imagine how discouraged and depressed the disciples were after the death of Jesus. Even though He had appeared to them after His resurrection, He had come and gone. So, a group of them were together on the shore of the Sea of Tiberias: Peter, Thomas, Nathanael, James, John, and two others. Peter announced he was going to go fishing, and all the others went with him. They fished all night and caught nothing—adding salt to their already hurting souls.

Then Jesus showed up, but the motley crew didn't know it was Him—yet. He called out to them and asked if they'd caught any fish. "None," they replied. Jesus suggested they throw the net on the right side of the boat. They did, and the net became so full of fish they couldn't haul it in. Then their eyes were opened, and they saw Jesus. Peter, of course, jumped in the water and swam to Him. The rest dragged the boat and the net to the shore. When they arrived, Jesus had bread and was tending a charcoal fire, cooking fish. Jesus had fixed them breakfast.

He provided nourishment for their bodies and refreshment for their souls. When I feel downcast due to circumstances, such as a wayward child, death of a loved one, or an ailing elderly parent, I spend time in the Word, feasting on His bread, and Jesus nourishes and restores my soul. —JEANNIE BLACKMER

FAITH STEP: *Make a plan to have breakfast with Jesus this week. Pack food and go to a favorite spot, or stay in your cozy kitchen and commune with Him.*

SUNDAY, JULY 4

[Jesus,] who purchased our freedom and forgave our sins. Colossians 1:14 (NLT)

THE ANNUAL FIREWORKS DISPLAY WAS rained out. So much for Independence Day. All that money the Firefighters Auxiliary paid for the planned fireworks—wasted. Now, there was nothing to see but storm clouds, and sheets of rain.

Families packed up picnic baskets and lawn chairs and high-tailed it for their vehicles, scanning weather channels to see if the storm and winds would pass so they could resume celebrating America's freedom.

Is it possible that the thunder and lightning, the rain and misery, the spoiled plans and disappointments were a more fitting tribute? Our country's independence came at a high price. Lives were upended. Courage was tested. Battles were won and lost. We've made Independence Day a celebration of excess with lavish displays in the sky and fun. It's so easy to forget the price paid when a party is on our minds.

What about our soul's freedom? We say we're conscious of the price Jesus paid to set us free. But do we celebrate only with flashy experiences and fun stories about how Jesus freed a parking space for us just when we needed it? Or do we give the honor and reverence He deserves for what it cost Jesus emotionally, physically, and spiritually to win our freedom? Do we pause to imagine the moment when midday turned to the blackest night, when the air chilled as if all warmth had been sucked from earth's atmosphere, when tremors unlike any a human has known coursed through Christ's dying form? Do we ponder the torment of both body and soul that the King of glory endured so we could live free?

Fireworks? Or sober silence? Jesus, our hearts explode with gratitude.
—CYNTHIA RUCHTI

FAITH STEP: *Sit in silence today and consider the high price tag of your freedom.*

MONDAY, JULY 5

Praise the LORD, my soul, and forget not all his benefits— who forgives all your sins and heals all your diseases, who redeems your life from the pit and crowns you with love and compassion, who satisfies your desires with good things so that your youth is renewed like the eagle's. Psalm 103:2–5 (NIV)

MY HUSBAND, SCOTT, STARTS HIS new job at a tech company in a month. The company has a wellness program as part of the benefits package. They want their employees physically, mentally, and emotionally whole. Scott read the varied list of things that the wellness program allocation can be used for, such as a gym membership, life-coaching sessions, and even house-cleaning services. I immediately put in my vote for the house-cleaning services. I lobbied for the fact that clean toilets and sparkling fixtures would help my well-being immensely, which would ultimately help our marriage…because of my wellness. Scott rolled his eyes at me and said, "Stop trying to steal my benefits." That was hurtful but true. The wellness program is for employees only.

Fortunately, the benefits of following Jesus apply to all of us. The benefits of loving Jesus are life-altering. He forgives every sin that we have ever committed, giving us open access to our heavenly Father. He heals our hearts and our minds, filling us with goodness and peace. He takes our brokenness and frailty, restoring us to wholeness. He fills us with overflowing compassion. He surrounds us with His immense love. He fills the deep well of need within us, satisfying our desires with good things and renewing our strength. True wellness begins the moment we invite Jesus into every nook and cranny of our lives. —SUSANNA FOTH AUGHTMON

FAITH STEP: *Remember all the benefits you have received in your own life since you began following Jesus. Praise Him for all that He has done.*

TUESDAY, JULY 6

According to his great mercy, he has caused us to be born again to a living hope through the resurrection of Jesus Christ from the dead, to an inheritance that is imperishable, undefiled, and unfading, kept in heaven for you. 1 Peter 1:3–4 (ESV)

WITH OUR FOUR-SEASON SUNROOM NEARING completion, I'm contemplating the interior design—chair and pillow fabrics, loveseat upholstery, window treatments for the six large windows.

My dilemma is that what I most want—light—can be a problem for many fabrics that are prone to fade in UVA and UVB exposure. Those deep-red throw pillows will be a mottled pink if left exposed to sunlight day after day. You'd think bright white would be the answer. But white can turn yellow if overexposed to sunlight.

The stronger the color, the more prone it is to fading, even in the washing machine. "Cold water only; hang out of direct sunlight to dry; store in light-blocking container." That's not an actual fabric care label. But it's a fact that fabric fades.

House paint fades over time. Even asphalt parking lots fade.

But Jesus provides for us an inheritance—hope, joy, peace—that is unfading. It comes pretreated with fade-resistance. It's protected from decay, defilement, and the natural consequences of life exposure.

The next time I need to lay a chenille throw over the window-shaped faded spot on the quilt in the spare room, I'm going to stop and thank Jesus for providing the unfadable. —CYNTHIA RUCHTI

FAITH STEP: *The hope Jesus provides cannot fade—have you thanked Him?*

WEDNESDAY, JULY 7

The precepts of the LORD are right, giving joy to the heart. The commands of the LORD are radiant, giving light to the eyes. Psalm 19:8 (NIV)

SEVERAL INTERSECTIONS WITH TRAFFIC LIGHTS interrupt a section of the freeway along my husband's commute. Cars travel at sixty miles per hour on that freeway, so authorities have placed speed reduction signs along the road prior to the first intersection. Drivers obey the "slow down" message because they understand the potential for accidents. They know the traffic laws are meant to protect, not impede, their journey.

Just as authorities have established traffic rules to protect us, so Jesus gave rules designed to guard our well-being. For instance, His command to forgive our offenders protects us from bitterness and ensures God's forgiveness toward us (Luke 6:37). His command to love others as He loves us prevents us from becoming self-centered creatures (John 15:12–13). His command to remain connected to Him as the grapevine remains connected to the branch means we'll avoid the emptiness of an unfruitful life (John 15:4–6).

Our human nature tends to chafe when we're given rules. It may tell us that commands hamper our fun and hinder our independence, but that's a lie. Jesus didn't invent rules to make us miserable— He gave them to ensure our well-being and bring us joy.

Obeying Jesus's commands helps us avoid the pitfalls of sin, and that's cause for joy in itself. We also experience joy when we reap the benefits of obedience, such as a clear conscience. But there's more. Obedience demonstrates our love for Jesus. Surrendering to His ways proves that we trust Him and naturally deepens intimacy with Him (John 15: 9–11). His rules are designed to protect us on our journey through life, and nothing produces more joy than obeying them. —GRACE FOX

FAITH STEP: *Ask Jesus to make you willing and able to obey His commands.*

THURSDAY, JULY 8

Keep your heart with all diligence, for out of it spring the issues of life.
Proverbs 4:23 (NKJV)

GOD IS SERIOUS ABOUT WHAT we allow to captivate our hearts. He wants us to give Him and His Word first place because He knows this is best for us. "Keeping" our heart involves guarding it from being consumed by even good things, such as work, hobbies, ministry, or even family. Even a godly desire can capture our hearts in an ungodly way. When every prayer and every conversation revolves around "that thing," that may be the thing we need to bring to the Lord and set down.

When Netflix became big a few years ago, a friend offered me a subscription. I was fascinated because I desired to write for television someday. So, for "research" purposes, I started watching one show after another and soon found myself binge watching into the wee hours. (The streaming services are great at "suggesting" new programs you might like even before you've finished the last one: click here for the next binge.) So for months I let crime stories, mysteries, dark political dramas, and unholy romances into my heart nightly. What started as an innocent pastime became more like a drug. I forgot about other after-work obligations in order to have my fix.

Fortunately, Jesus is the friend who sticks closer than a brother. He helped me see how these shows were slowly warping my view of real people and my attitude toward life in general. Sarcasm and negativity were creeping into my heart and coming out of my mouth. Thank God, He interrupted my binge and turned my heart back toward things that are pure, lovely, and of good report (Philippians 4:8). —PAMELA TOUSSAINT HOWARD

FAITH STEP: *What are you bingeing on? Talk to Jesus. Listen and obey.*

FRIDAY, JULY 9

Throwing off his cloak, he sprang up and came to Jesus. And Jesus said to him, "What do you want me to do for you?" And the blind man said to him, "Rabbi, let me recover my sight." And Jesus said to him, "Go your way; your faith has made you well." And immediately he recovered his sight and followed him on the way. Mark 10:50–52 (ESV)

IN RECENT MONTHS, I'VE BEEN impressed with the palliative-care team that is helping a family member. They explained their focus is on asking the patient, "What do you want?" Instead of arriving with assumptions and pushing drastic interventions on someone, they invite their client to consider what he or she truly desires. Then they develop options to provide that care.

The first time I met the team nurse and she asked that question, I heard echoes of today's Scripture passage and the blind man's encounter with Jesus. I've always been intrigued by the way Jesus asks questions. As the true God, He knows the answer. Yet, He still asks—probing people to evaluate what they truly desire. In this instance, a very eager blind man sprang up when he heard Jesus approach. He revealed the deepest desire of his heart, one that probably felt so impossible that it felt too daring to mention.

The blind man's boldness gives me the courage to respond to Jesus. There are deep needs that I'm almost afraid to speak. Things I long for, for my loved ones and myself. But as I hear Jesus gently ask, "What do you want me to do for you?," I bare my soul and tell Him, trusting in His timing and His wisdom.

If you were sitting near the dusty road and heard Jesus ask you this important question, what would you answer? —SHARON HINCK

FAITH STEP: *Respond to Jesus's question today and tell Him what you want from Him.*

SATURDAY, JULY 10

Trust in and rely confidently on the LORD with all your heart and do not rely on your own insight or understanding. Proverbs 3:5 (AMP)

I APPRECIATE ROAD CREWS WHO post bright yellow signs warning me of bumps on the highway. It helps to know what's ahead, so I can slow down and avoid a huge jolt. I sometimes wish Jesus would warn me about all the impending bumps—relationship issues, sickness, money troubles—in my future. Then I could prepare myself. How lovely life would be if no calamity ever caught me unaware.

But Jesus is too wise to grant my wish. He knows if He forewarns me about future problems, I'll do one of two things. I'll worry myself into a state of panic. Or I'll create a giant list of possible solutions. Either way, I won't be trusting Him. When I rely on my own limited understanding to repair the broken places in my life, it's as if I am telling Jesus, "Your love and power aren't enough. I need to fix this myself." Does He laugh at my childishness or shake His head in sadness that, once again, I'm settling for an inferior solution?

In over five decades of following Jesus—some days more closely than others—I've discovered how dependable He is. No matter what kind of upset I experience, He has the wisdom and strength to help me through it. Not only does He possess what I need, He willingly shares, through the power of His Holy Spirit within me, all of Himself.

I know I can trust Him and calmly rest in His love. Whatever life may bring and whatever bumps loom in my future, Jesus will always be more than enough. —JEANETTE LEVELLIE

FAITH STEP: *Look up the words to the song "I Know Who Holds Tomorrow." Either sing or say the lyrics aloud. Remind Jesus that you trust Him with all your tomorrows.*

SUNDAY, JULY 11

They shall still bear fruit in old age; they shall be fresh and flourishing.
Psalm 92:14 (NKJV)

THE OTHER DAY I DECIDED it might not be too bad that my hearing is getting less sharp—maybe I'll be less bothered by the creaking noises my bones make when I get up from the floor after cleaning. These days I seem to get more frequent reminders of my advancing age. Sometimes I mentally compose a list of things that probably will never happen at this point: places I won't travel, books I won't write, new skills I won't ever learn. Then I remember Harry Bernstein's story.

Motivated by the death of his wife after sixty-seven years of marriage, Mr. Bernstein started writing a memoir of his early life when he was ninety-three. The book was published three years later. Two more books of his were published over the next two years; a fourth one released after his death at age 101.

The Bible includes stories of people whose "golden years" brought some special ministry or reward. At age ninety, Sarah gave birth to Isaac, through whom the Jewish people came. Miriam was around ninety when she helped her younger brothers, Moses and Aaron, lead the Israelites to the Promised Land. Elizabeth was well past childbearing age when she had John the Baptist, who prepared people for Messiah's coming. Simeon and Anna, two elderly people at the temple, enjoyed the privilege of seeing and recognizing the promised Messiah when He was just over a month old.

In Isaiah 46:4, God promises to care for His people. If we walk closely with Jesus, we don't need to worry about what we've lost through aging. We can look forward to what He has in store for us.
—DIANNE NEAL MATTHEWS

FAITH STEP: *Don't long for "the good old days," instead focus on your future in Jesus.*

MONDAY, JULY 12

Let no debt remain outstanding, except the continuing debt to love one another, for whoever loves others has fulfilled the law. Romans 13:8 (NIV)

"I OWE YOU ONE," I told my friend Jim, who'd agreed to fill in for me at my church job while I was out of town. Jim probably didn't expect me to pay him back, but he'd done me a favor. If he needed someone to substitute for him, he wouldn't hesitate to ask me. And I'd be glad to return the favor. That's what friends do.

"I owe you one." How easily those words slip off the tongue. It may be convenient to forget when we owe someone, or a debt can hang over our heads like a heavy weight. How amazing it is when someone does something for us with no expectation of collecting on that debt! When Jesus gave His life for us in the ultimate sacrifice, He asked nothing of us but that we love one another.

Hmmm, Jesus. Easier said than done.

I'm learning to rely on Jesus and the power of the Holy Spirit to help me love others, such as the girl who sent out a cruel group text about my daughter, the neighbor who kicked my cat, and the teacher who embarrassed my son in front of the whole class.

Jesus didn't specify *which* others we are supposed to love. He simply asked us to love one another—such a small thing to request in return for the huge favor He did for mankind. I'm betting Jesus is especially pleased with us when we love the people who are hardest to love. But really, isn't it the least we can do? We owe Him—*big time*! —PAT BUTLER DYSON

FAITH STEP: *Show your appreciation to Jesus today by being kind to someone who isn't easy to love.*

TUESDAY, JULY 13

He cuts off every branch in me that bears no fruit, while every branch that does bear fruit he prunes so that it will be even more fruitful. John 15:2 (NIV)

WE ARE IN THE MIDST of a great crisis in our home. In other words, we are packing up to move. Everywhere I look, I find complete chaos. Dishes are stacked on the counters. Papers and detritus litter every flat surface. Clothes are flung about in complete disarray. On the phone yesterday, I told my mom, "Every room is a mess. I can't stand it!" She laughed and said, "With moving, it always gets worse before it gets better." This is so true. The sorting process is critical. Everything has to be evaluated. *Do we need it? Should we give it away? Should we trash it?* It is a huge pruning process that takes us back to the essentials. We want to take only the things we need and love to our new home. We want room to grow and thrive in this new space.

Jesus is also constantly sorting us out. He is clearing out the detritus and nonessentials that crowd our lives. He wants to trim back any area that is hedging out His love and purpose in us.

Sometimes this can be a painful process. We may need to let go of toxic relationships or old dreams or destructive habits. But He knows the shape that our lives need to take. He lovingly pares away the parts of our lives that are stunting our growth in Him. Jesus wants us to thrive in every way. —SUSANNA FOTH AUGHTMON

FAITH STEP: *Are you in a sorting season with Jesus? With a willing heart, let Him do His work. As you pray today, ask Him to take you back to the essentials, giving you room to grow and thrive.*

WEDNESDAY, JULY 14

Therefore I tell you, do not worry about your life, what you will eat or drink;
or about your body, what you will wear. Is not life more than food, and the
body more than clothes? Look at the birds of the air; they do not sow or reap
or store away in barns, and yet your heavenly Father feeds them. Are you not
much more valuable than they? Can any one of you by worrying add a single
hour to your life? Matthew 6:25–27 (NIV)

YESTERDAY I WOKE UP AT 3:30 AM. My anxious mind woke me from
a troubled sleep. My brain was racing with questions about our
upcoming move: *Will our loan go through for our house? Will our two*
younger boys be able to adjust to their new school? How will Jack do
at college when we are out of state and he can't visit on the weekends?
Will Scott like his new job? How will I find a new job? I tossed and
turned for the next several hours. I finally got out of bed exhausted.
(Anyone else awake at 3:30 AM out there?)

Worrying subtracts joy from our lives. It exhausts our minds and
spirits, leaving us depleted and anxious. But Jesus is all about addition. Adding hope. Adding peace. Adding strength. In the presence
of Jesus, there is fullness of joy...not worry. We can bury our worries in the knowledge that He always will be the ultimate problem-
solver, the absolute answer-giver, and the over-the-top provider of
all good things. When we turn our anxious thoughts into prayers,
we invite Jesus into the worrisome conversations going on in our
minds. His words of love and hope still the nervous chatter and
replace it with peace. —SUSANNA FOTH AUGHTMON

FAITH STEP: *What anxious thoughts are stealing your joy? Meditate on Jesus's*
words in Matthew 6:25–34. Let His loving truth replace your worries. Decide
to trust Jesus and live worry-free.

THURSDAY, JULY 15

If your hand causes you to stumble, cut it off. It is better for you to enter life maimed than with two hands to go into hell, where the fire never goes out. And if your foot causes you to stumble, cut it off. It is better for you to enter life crippled than to have two feet and be thrown into hell.
Mark 9:43–45 (NIV)

JOGGING IS MY PRIMARY AND beloved form of exercise, prayer meditation, and therapy. I recently had a bout of plantar fasciitis so agonizing that I could barely walk, much less run. I've had a milder version before. Among other things, I was told to stretch before running and not to wear unsupportive shoes like flats or flip-flops. Did I follow that advice? For only a short spell. Then my plantar fasciitis came back far worse than before, and I finally got rid of the flip-flops... but my cute flats?

A few years ago, I had searing shoulder pain. The physical therapist recommended wearing a light posture-friendly bag and not scrunching the phone in my shoulder. Did I follow that advice? Yes, but only until the pain went away. It happened twice again; finally so bad that I couldn't feel my fingertips because nerves were compressed. A bad thing for a writer! I finally got the message and now only wear crossbodies and fanny packs.

Sin can be like that. Like the Israelites, I can heed God for a while and then slip back into complacency, but the consequences get more and more painful until I finally comply. Even so, Jesus never stops loving me when I sin, but the consequences remain.

Shouldn't I avoid the ill effects altogether by heeding Dr. Jesus?
—ISABELLA YOSUICO

FAITH STEP: *Are you dealing with a correctable physical, emotional, or spiritual pain? Pray and follow the Great Physician's suggestion for immediate relief.*

FRIDAY, JULY 16

Because the Lord is my Shepherd, I have everything I need! Psalm 23:1 (TLB)

DID YOU KNOW THAT WHEN Jesus went to the cross and rose from the dead, He purchased everything we need—our soul's salvation *and* our passport to a fruitful life?

At the time the Bible was written, the culture was very agrarian. Many Old Testament figures, from Abraham to David, were shepherds and farmers. The shepherd anticipates all of the sheep's needs, from finding the best place to graze and drink to keeping bugs from getting caught in their fur. Sheep aren't considered very bright animals. For example, they might see a rolling river and jump in to get water, not realizing they could drown. Sheep are also known to wander off. Jesus teaches us in Matthew 18 that a good shepherd leaves the ninety-nine to search for the one who got lost. That is the heart of a shepherd—he doesn't rely on the sheep to figure things out for themselves but sees it as his responsibility to provide their daily needs and to keep them safe.

In my own life, I've found this challenging because it requires me to surrender and be dependent on Jesus to come through—without my help. But this is how the Lord desires to be with us, if we will let Him. He already knows the best place, the best mate, and the best course of action for us to take when we have a problem. If we accept this, we won't need to rush to the pastor, the prayer line, or the next Christian conference for "a touch from God." We would be calmer during the waiting period, too, knowing that our Shepherd will not let us lack. —PAMELA TOUSSAINT HOWARD

FAITH STEP: *Allow yourself to be led by your Shepherd today in something small. Then build on that reliance for the larger things that may come tomorrow.*

SATURDAY, JULY 17

Let us not become weary in doing good, for at the proper time we will reap a harvest if we do not give up. Galatians 6:9 (NIV)

I WAS READING IN MY living room when I heard some clanging in the kitchen. Everyone was home, so I didn't think much of the noise until my son Isaac called my name. I walked in to find he'd pulled a stepstool to the counter, pulled out a bowl, gotten a spoon, and taken the applesauce and cottage cheese out of the fridge. He stood smiling, wrestling with the applesauce lid and needed help. My heart swelled, my eyes got wet, and I clapped my hands, beaming, forgetting that he hadn't asked permission to snack.

"Great job, Isaac!" I said, giving him a big hug. He grinned proudly.

You see, my son Isaac has Down syndrome, and while he's ten years old, he's more like a five or six-year-old in most ways. Even so, thanks to Jesus, I prize Isaac's unique gifts and perspective. His languid learning has some unexpected perks, including the jump-for-joy delight we all feel when he attains some milestone that most kids gain effortlessly.

In the trenches of teaching Isaac, repeating lessons countless times, potty training for years, or seeing him struggle to grasp simple skills, I sometimes get discouraged. I've been afraid he would never learn a particular something, but Jesus always urges me onward. Then suddenly, Isaac gets it, and we all cheer and celebrate with true delight. There are too many examples of this to recount. While there may be things that Isaac never does, I entrust them to Jesus. Meanwhile, I'll keep on enjoying his hard-won victories. —ISABELLA YOSUICO

FAITH STEP: *Are you discouraged? Make a list of your own hard-won victories. How did you press forward? What was the reward?*

SUNDAY, JULY 18

Make every effort to live in peace with everyone and to be holy; without holiness no one will see the Lord. See to it that no one falls short of the grace of God and that no bitter root grows up to cause trouble and defile many.
Hebrews 12:14–15 (NIV)

A FEW WEEKS AGO, WE flew to Boise, Idaho, in preparation for our upcoming move. We had the joy of going to our friend's church on Sunday and hearing him speak. Mike's message was about cynicism. He said that most cynics are wounded optimists, embittered about their disappointment in life. I was convicted as I sat in my seat, hearing my own past thoughts parade before me. *Why hasn't my life turned out the way I thought it would? How can I trust Jesus when He doesn't come through for me in the way that I want Him to? Why are Christ followers the people who have hurt me the most?*

Sometimes Jesus takes us out of state to get our attention. He is not okay with my bitterness. Or yours. He wants us to stand in a place of grace, recognizing that He is enough for us, no matter what the situation. When we are cynical, it seeps into our conversations with others and affects our relationships. Words that drip with confusion, hurt, and anger cultivate a bitter root in our heart, shutting out joy. Jesus wants us on His path of grace, recognizing that He is enough even in the face of pain, suffering, and disappointment. He leads us into a place of hope, killing the root of bitterness and inviting us to flourish. —SUSANNA FOTH AUGHTMON

FAITH STEP: *Take a walk through a park. Notice any weeds that are trying to choke out the beautiful flowers and plants. Ask Jesus to yank out the root of bitterness in your heart and to surround you with His grace.*

MONDAY, JULY 19

Let your work be shown to your servants, and your glorious power to their children. Psalm 90:16 (ESV)

WHEN FACING IMPOSSIBLE SITUATIONS, I sometimes pray, *Father, accomplish Your purposes in a way that leaves onlookers dumbfounded.* My heart's desire is for the answered prayer to be so big and so unexplainable that God receives all the credit. So that people who might otherwise doubt His existence or His involvement in our lives have no choice but to admit His presence and power.

Sometimes believers need a little encouragement too, so I pray this on my kids' behalf when they're facing something major. I prayed it for Gene and myself when we needed a place to moor our sailboat. Every broker said there'd be a seven-year wait. But, God swiftly gave us the moorage we'd wanted, and everyone who hears the story is amazed whether they believe He exists or not.

The disciples saw Jesus do something that dumbfounded them. They were in a boat in a storm, and in a panic they believed they would drown. They woke the sleeping Jesus and begged Him to save them from certain death.

Matthew 8 tells us, "Then he got up and rebuked the winds and the waves, and it was completely calm. The men were amazed and asked, 'What kind of man is this? Even the winds and the waves obey him!'" (vv. 26–27, NIV).

We often dread impossible situations because we can't see our way through them. Let's change our way of thinking. Let's consider them the ideal opportunity to see God's glorious power displayed. Let's ask Him for an answer that will leave us in awe of who He is. —GRACE FOX

FAITH STEP: *Go ahead! Ask the Lord to do something that will leave you amazed.*

TUESDAY, JULY 20

My sheep hear My voice, and I know them, and they follow Me.
John 10:27 (NKJV)

I VISITED MY DAUGHTER'S FAMILY for a few weeks while they awaited the birth of their fourth child. Their three other children and I arrived at the hospital about an hour after Leona was born. I snapped photos while the family took turns holding the new baby girl, amazed at how alert and content she seemed—considering what she had just gone through. She'd left her cozy environment for an open space filled with bright lights, noises, and all sorts of strange sensations on her skin. Yet, each time Leona was passed around, she usually seemed calm, quietly moving her arms around.

Finally, my anxious arms got to hold the baby. Both then and over the next couple of days, I noticed a difference when I talked to her: She didn't recognize my voice. She didn't necessarily cry, but she didn't appear to feel as calm and settled. Although Leona couldn't focus her eyes to see faces clearly at first, she knew when a family member held her because she had been hearing their voices for months. And that familiar voice made her feel safe.

Jesus said that His followers hear and recognize His voice. Since we live in a world full of noise and distraction, it's not always easy to hear our Shepherd's voice speaking to us. If we're not thoroughly familiar with His voice, we may confuse it with others that try to lead us astray. It's crucial to stay attuned to Jesus's voice by spending time in prayer, Bible reading, and active listening for His guidance. Then, even if we can't clearly see His presence in our situation, we will remember that we are safe in His arms. —DIANNE NEAL MATTHEWS

FAITH STEP: *Take time today to listen to Jesus's voice. Thank Him for holding you in His loving arms.*

WEDNESDAY, JULY 21

Rejoice always, pray continually, give thanks in all circumstances; for this is God's will for you in Christ Jesus. 1 Thessalonians 5:16–18 (NIV)

MY FRIEND SUZIE RECENTLY HIKED with her fourteen-year-old daughter. "I was excited to hang out with her and imagined having meaningful conversations," she said. But on the hike, her daughter walked one hundred yards in front of her the entire time, and Suzie was fuming. She imagined the snarky things she would say when they got back to the car, such as, "How was *your* hike?"

Then she remembered a new practice she was trying to implement to change her mind-set from anger to thankfulness. She had been keeping a gratitude journal to refocus her emotions when she felt angry. She told me, "I decided to not let my mind dwell on how angry I was while I was hiking but to turn my thoughts to thankfulness in the present moment." Suzie took her eyes off her daughter ahead of her, and focused instead on the lush green grass in front of her. Suzie stopped and looked at the blanket of purple flowers and the magnificent mountains. She expressed gratitude for everything that brought beauty to that moment. She prayed, *Thank You, Jesus, for this flower. Thank You for the rain that's made the grass so green.* Released from anger, Suzie's heart was filled with joy.

When she returned to her car, her daughter was sitting on the hood waiting. Instead of feeling angry, Suzie had enjoyed her hike by rejoicing in the moment and giving thanks. When she saw her daughter, she sincerely asked, "How was your hike?" Keeping her mind-set on Jesus and practicing a grateful attitude helped Suzie overcome frustration and discover joy instead. —JEANNIE BLACKMER

FAITH STEP: *Are you angry? Focus on Jesus and give thanks.*

THURSDAY, JULY 22

His mother said to the servants, "Whatever He says to you, do it."
John 2:5 (NKJV)

MARY HAD A LOT OF confidence in her son Jesus. Long before this passage, that trust began when the angel Gabriel appeared to her, an unwed teenager, and said she would bear a Son, a King, the Savior of the world. In response to this amazing announcement, she had the courage to say, "Let it be to me according to your word" (Luke 1:38, NKJV). Mary is an example of someone who was totally submitted to the Lord.

In today's passage, Mary and Jesus were at a wedding, and the hosts had run out of wine. Jesus got involved and performed His first miracle there, turning water into wine. But first, He asked them to fill some empty pots with water. Mary paved the way for the miracle she knew was about to happen by tipping off the servants: no matter how odd Jesus's request might seem, it would be best that they cooperate. And they did. The master of the feast ended up with more wine than he could pour!

It's no different today. When I submit to Jesus and what He tells me to do, my life is much richer and filled with more peace, joy, and wonder than when I don't do what He says. Obeying Jesus opens the door to His miracles and majesty.

I think Jesus would have found a different place for His first miracle if the servants hadn't cooperated. It was important for them to *do* what He said in order to experience a miracle. I want to be a person Jesus can count on to do what He says when He speaks.
—PAMELA TOUSSAINT HOWARD

FAITH STEP: *Be sensitive to hear His voice. Be quick to do what you hear Him say, even if it sounds impossible! Jesus is waiting for us to obey!*

FRIDAY, JULY 23

He said to them, "Watch out! Be on your guard against all kinds of greed;
life does not consist in an abundance of possessions." Luke 12:15 (NIV)

FRIENDS INVITED US TO SPEND a weekend at their cabin. Tall trees
framed a beautiful view of the lake, and the call of loons invited us
to leave behind the worries of the city. Our friends had hung a few
hummingbird feeders from the roof of the screened porch. We sat
and relaxed, entertained by the buzzing visitors as they hovered for
a drink.

"One of them is a real bully," our friend Jon told us. Sure enough,
one plump bird dove aggressively at the others near the feeder and
chased them away. There was a generous amount of sugar water in
the feeder, and plenty of room for all the birds. Yet, the one greedy
bird insisted on harassing everyone else and prevented them from
eating. The irony was, he was so busy being sure no one else got
more than he did, that he didn't have time to eat either.

I shook my head at his antics but acknowledged that I'm not that
different. Jesus has filled my life with blessings, but sometimes I get
drawn into the greed of wanting more, sometimes in ways that keep
me from enjoying the gifts right in front of me. I may even struggle
to share with others—my time, my home, the last chocolate cookie
on the plate.

Jesus is so wise to warn us to be on guard. Greed can slip in and
become a regular thought and habit before we realize it. He calls
us to a life of much greater joy than what possessions can bring us.
—SHARON HINCK

FAITH STEP: *Walk through your home and select a few items to give to someone*
else. Include a note, telling your loved one how much you appreciate her or him.

SATURDAY, JULY 24

Lift up your eyes and look to the heavens: who created all these? He who brings out the starry host one by one and calls forth each of them by name. Because of his great power and mighty strength, not one of them is missing.
Isaiah 40:26 (NIV)

WE HAD SAILED FOR THE day with friends and then anchored for the night in a harbor off Thetis Island, British Columbia. The air was warm and our sleeping berth felt stuffy, so my husband opened the hatch above our bed to allow airflow.

Gene fell asleep immediately, but I remained wide awake for a couple of hours. My thoughts flitted from one topic to another: last night's conversation, the next day's menu, upcoming deadlines, and more.

Finally, I knelt on the bed and poked my head through the open hatch. Tiny lights twinkled against the midnight backdrop as far as my eyes could see. I admired the heavenly canopy and adored its Creator. *Jesus, You are greater than the galaxies,* I whispered. *You created and named every star and hung each one in place. My mind cannot comprehend Your strength and intelligence. Neither can it fully grasp the truth that You—almighty God—love me and care about my needs.*

The Psalmist's words came to mind: "When I consider your heavens, the work of your fingers, the moon and the stars, which you have set in place, what is mankind that you are mindful of them, human beings that you care for them?" (Psalm 8:3–4, NIV).

Wonder led to worship, and worship focused my busy thoughts on Jesus. Filled with renewed awe at His splendor and secure in His love for me, I crawled under the sheet, closed my eyes, and fell asleep. —GRACE FOX

FAITH STEP: *Stargaze tonight. Praise the One who placed them there.*

SUNDAY, JULY 25

Jesus entered the temple and drove out all who were selling and buying in the temple, and he overturned the tables of the money changers and the seats of those who sold doves. Matthew 21:12 (NRSV)

THIS SCENE OF JESUS ON a rampage in the temple holds endless fascination for me. I'm glad the story was included in the Gospels because alongside washing feet, healing the sick, and suffering on a cross, it rounds out the picture. Without examples of behavior like this, it might be tempting to paint Jesus as only meek and mild, like a lamb.

And He is the Lamb of God. I'm thankful for that too, of course. A lamb is soft, innocent, and warm. It's a nonthreatening animal you can cozy up to. But let's not forget that the Lamb of God is also the Lion of Judah. He's king—the boss and scary powerful. A lion's roar can make your blood chill in your veins. I heard the sound one time on a safari in Kenya, and I have never forgotten it. That kind of thing stays with you.

Why is this dual nature so important? It's because in Jesus we find a balance. Tough and tender, gentle yet firm, and power under control. When kindness worked, that was His way. But He knew there were times one can't "nice" His way through—especially when the problem is a whole corrupt system like the one in the temple, which had to be broken down. We are builders in His kingdom, and sometimes that means overturning the old to make way for the new. —GWEN FORD FAULKENBERRY

FAITH STEP: *Read the entire chapter of Matthew 21. Note all of the aspects of Jesus' character you see in this chapter. Consider how to implement them into your life, discerning what is called for in particular situations.*

MONDAY, JULY 26

That is why, for Christ's sake, I delight in weaknesses, in insults, in hardships, in persecutions, in difficulties. For when I am weak, then I am strong. 2 Corinthians 12:10 (NIV)

WHEN I WASHED A NEW blouse I'd only worn twice and it fell apart, so did I. In tears, I called my husband, Kevin. "We're leaving for our trip in six days, and I have forty-five things on my plate this week. I can't take time to return this," I said, wailing. True to the meaning of his name—kindness—Kev assured me that he would help get everything done. When I apologized for acting like a baby, he simply said, "It's okay."

I tried to argue with him. Shouldn't I be strong all the time, no matter what kind of pressure I'm under? Since I'm an author of devotional books, an inspirational speaker and pastor's wife, meltdowns shouldn't be part of my life—at least when it's something as insignificant as a blouse gone south. But Kevin wasn't buying my unrealistic notions of "should be." My husband realizes I am human, which means I have limits. Both he and Jesus make allowances for those days when I'm anything but strong.

Times of stress make us aware of how much we need Jesus's grace and power. We're desperate for His help, so we lean on Him more than we do on a carefree day. The truth is, we need Jesus during the seasons we feel like a warrior as much as we do when we're basket cases. When we confess our dependence on Him, He's more than willing to help.

Annie Hawks and Robert Lowry wrote a hymn in the 1800s that says, "I need Thee, O I need Thee; Every hour I need Thee." Let's change that to every *moment.* —JEANETTE LEVELLIE

FAITH STEP: *Look up the words to the hymn "I Need Thee Every Hour" and sing or say them aloud to Jesus.*

TUESDAY, JULY 27

God saw everything that he had made, and behold, it was very good...
Genesis 1:31 (ESV)

I WALKED IN THE HOUSE after being gone for a few hours and let Ody, our puppy, out of his crate. He can hardly contain himself when he sees me. He runs between my legs, rubbing against me while his tail vigorously wags. He romps around the room and picks up his toys and brings them to me. His whole being exudes joy. He clearly delights in being with me.

I read a quote recently from Jim Wilder, a neuroscientist, who said, "Joy is being with someone who delights in being with you." Ody truly exemplifies this phrase. As I reflected on this, I thought about the people in my life who most of the time delight in being with me. My husband, my boys, close friends, and others came to mind.

Then I thought, *Jesus delights in being with us so much more than any pet or person on earth.* He delights in being with us all the time, from the beginning of time. After God finished creating everything, He declared it was very good. Not just good, but *very* good. He delighted in His creation. He delights in us. He desires to be with us. Even in those times when we may feel as if no one delights in us, we can know Jesus does. When we believe this, we can live with an unwavering sense of joy.

And, because joy is contagious, let's make sure others know we delight in being with them. We may not bounce around and wag our tails, but we can make intentional efforts to let those we love know we delight in being with them. —JEANNIE BLACKMER

FAITH STEP: *Who is someone you delight being with? Write them a note today and let them know how much joy they add to your life.*

WEDNESDAY, JULY 28

Have I not commanded you? Be strong and courageous. Do not be afraid; do not be discouraged, for the Lord your God will be with you wherever you go. Joshua 1:9 (NIV)

WHAT WERE *INDETERMINATE LESIONS*? THEY'D appeared on my husband Jeff's routine MRI and now the doctor wanted a closer look at Jeff's spine. Years of sports and walking on concrete floors at the family hardware store had created disc problems. Jeff needed a CT scan.

If there's a worry gene, I'd inherited it. Both my parents were big worriers; I grew up surrounded by worry. Intellectually, I knew it was foolish to agonize about things I couldn't control. But worry had become a habit with me. After I searched *indeterminate lesions* on Google, my worry gene kicked in bigtime.

It took eight days for the insurance company to authorize the CT scan. I seesawed between panic and despair. I couldn't eat and didn't sleep. One day Jeff sat me down. "Pat, I'm in good health. If this is something serious, we'll deal with it. We live an hour from one of the best medical centers in the country. Besides, Jesus has this."

One of the daily devotions I read said, "Pray without ceasing." Every day, many times a day, I asked Jesus to spare Jeff. I discovered I didn't have to be on my knees to pray. I could be in the car, at the grocery store, or riding my bike. Every time I felt worry about to overtake me, I prayed. I was amazed that a quick prayer could restore calm before anxiety engulfed me.

Finally, the insurance company responded, and Jeff had the CT scan. One day later, thanks to a friend in the imaging department at the hospital, Jeff learned the lesions were benign. Jeff was right. Jesus had this. —PAT BUTLER DYSON

FAITH STEP: *Ask Jesus to help you replace worry with prayer.*

THURSDAY, JULY 29

On the same day Jesus went out of the house and sat by the sea.
Matthew 13:1 (NKJV)

I LOVE SUCH GLIMPSES OF Jesus. The chapter before this verse shows us that He's under tremendous stress. It feels like the kind of week I've had as I type this. When even though I know I have all of His resources, nothing seems like enough. I feel misunderstood, powerless, and overwhelmed by the problems of the world. What would Jesus do? Everywhere He turns there's a critic, a need for healing, and someone with a burden for Him to bear. But He handles it all with grace and courage, of course.

And still that chapter ends with unresolved conflict. And a new one begins and we find Jesus out by the sea. I don't know why this image is so dear, but it is. Perhaps it's His humanity it reveals. I can see Him sitting in the sand at the edge of the water. Maybe He takes off His shoes and lets the sand tickle His feet. He hugs His knees. He looks out over the vast expanse of water—the sea He created—and squints at a gull. Closing His eyes, He breathes deeply. He waits and listens to the sound of the waves as His peace returns.

Maybe it's time for me to step out of the conflict. To be still and quiet and wait for peace. In this, as much as in His patience, boldness, compassion, and honesty in the previous chapter, Jesus leaves us an example. —GWEN FORD FAULKENBERRY

FAITH STEP: *Set aside time today to be still until your peace returns.*

FRIDAY, JULY 30

As he sat on the Mount of Olives, the disciples came to him privately, saying, "Tell us, when will these things be, and what will be the sign of your coming and of the end of the age?" Matthew 24:3 (ESV)

WORKING AS A WRITER INVOLVES a lot of waiting. I submit an idea to my agent and wait to hear his thoughts. He sends a proposal to publishers, and we wait for a response. I turn in my manuscript and wait for my editor to return it with feedback. Even when my part is finished, I have to wait for the book to be published. And I'll let you in on a secret: I don't enjoy waiting.

The other day, I settled in a lawn chair, relaxing in my backyard. Time slowed. Goldfinches darted past. A chipmunk peeked from around the corner of the shed. A rabbit ventured out from the day-lily patch, rooting for clover. A quick glance out the window during the day rarely reveals so much activity. It was only when I decided to sit quietly that some of the treasures of the backyard revealed themselves. I grudgingly admitted that waiting can be valuable.

The disciples had their own issues with waiting. They asked Jesus when all His purposes would be fulfilled—even if they didn't fully understand what those were. I can relate to those disciples. I often want to say, "Get on with it, Lord!"

Yet when I sit in His presence, quietly and watchfully, I begin to see His hand in so much of life—just as I noticed new things in my sunny backyard. His timing is perfect. His purposes are loving. If waiting helps me lean into Him more, then I will learn to find joy in it. —SHARON HINCK

FAITH STEP: *Set a timer and sit quietly and watchfully. Ask Jesus to unfold new glimpses of His hand at work in your life.*

SATURDAY, JULY 31

I know what it is to be in need, and I know what it is to have plenty. I have learned the secret of being content in any and every situation, whether well fed or hungry, whether living in plenty or in want. Philippians 4:12 (NIV)

GETTING READY TO MOVE NEXT week has me rethinking my home decor. One of my passions is decorating. I could spend hours poring over design magazines, soaking up ideas. But often when I look through magazines, I start to want things I can't afford. I have big dreams and a small pocketbook. I covet things. The problem with coveting is that it is a three-for-one kind of sin. Wanting something that isn't yours often leads to stealing, and then you lie about what you stole. Don't get me wrong. I don't steal things outright. That would be wrong. I just put them on a credit card. Which steals from my future.

Maybe you don't care about furniture, but you covet a different job or a nicer car or a better marriage. Coveting is all about being dissatisfied with what we have. We look at the life that Jesus has given us and say, "It isn't enough. I guess I will have to go out and get the life that I want for myself." This rarely pans out. The remedy for covetousness is gratitude. Jesus is the ultimate provider. In this moment, He is giving us all that we need. Mostly, what we need is Him. The other stuff is a bonus. Think of all He has provided us with: air to breathe, His love, His grace, salvation. Gratitude begets contentment, setting us up for a life of joy and fulfillment.
—SUSANNA FOTH AUGHTMON

FAITH STEP: *Take stock of your life. Take time to thank Jesus for giving you everything that you need.*

SUNDAY, AUGUST 1

The whole earth is filled with awe at your wonders; where morning dawns, where evening fades, you call forth songs of joy. Psalm 65:8 (NIV)

IN ADDITION TO OUR LOVE for Jesus, my daughter and I both love to travel. Since we share this passion, we steal away for a weekend together every year. Last summer we rented a private cottage on a Christian-owned vineyard a few hours south of home. Patios, walkways, and walls bore uplifting Scripture verses, and friendly llamas, goats, and cows dotted the neighboring pastures. Trumpeter swans glided silently across a large pond as we rested in the gazebo perched on its bank. Trails alongside the vines offered grand views of faraway hills and quiet valleys. Every minute we spent there proved a delight and a reminder of the infinite beauty of the Lord's creation.

But my favorite times of the day were sunrise and sunset. As day broke, I was blessed with the reminder that His mercies are new every morning. At dusk, as the livestock returned from the pasture, they seemed to call out to each other. Birds soared and dove, feasting on airborne bugs, their flight a graceful dance, their cries unique and stirring. As I watched the sunset, I tried to burn the memory in my mind. Jesus, in His sublime generosity, had presented us with a gift of such magnificence, and we couldn't help but smile.

Next week, we're returning to that charming cottage, and this time we're bringing our husbands along. We want to share with them the joy we experienced, to see their eyes light up and their spirits rise as ours did. Through nature's wonder, we hope not only to be blessed but also to be part of the blessing by sharing creation's song. —HEIDI GAUL

FAITH STEP: *Take a hike or walk in nature at dawn or dusk and watch creation come alive. Give thanks.*

MONDAY, AUGUST 2

Do everything without grumbling or arguing. Philippians 2:14 (NIV)

MY OLDEST SON WAS IN a summer baseball day camp a few miles away and also had nightly practices at our local park, along with several of his All-Star baseball buddies. Since all the boys live within a few miles of each other in our small town, we baseball moms wanted to carpool. Some of us work, some don't, some had other kids in other activities, some live in the same neighborhood, and some only had room in our cars for two kids. It was a little hairy sorting it out.

Of course, there are apps for this kind of thing, but we settled on hand-drawn charts and admittedly confusing text threads to shuttle the kids to and from camp, after-camp hangouts, and practice later in the day. Even with our detailed spreadsheet, our plan got derailed by forgotten cleats, oversleeping, cars breaking down, or other random life happenings. But we texted our way through the logistical changes, pitching in to make sure all the kids made it to wherever they needed to be.

I used to get stressed and annoyed with all the running we moms do, but somewhere along the way, I had a revelation inspired by this verse. I don't *have* to do this. *I get* to. This lightning-quick season of childhood and carloads of smelly raucous boys will be over before I know it. And how very wonderful that we have this supportive community of moms who work together to care for our kids and enjoy each other too. These are the moments that strung together over time make up a life well-lived. In Christ, I can do all things (Philippians 4:13) and be thankful! —ISABELLA YOSUICO

FAITH STEP: *What are you grumbling about? What seems like a thankless chore? Next time you whine about something that you have to do, think of the task as something you get to do and see if it lifts your perspective.*

TUESDAY, AUGUST 3

*The LORD is my strength and my shield; my heart trusts in him,
and he helps me. My heart leaps for joy, and with my song
I praise him. Psalm 28:7 (NIV)*

BY HER SECOND TRIP TO the pool, my little granddaughter was used to wearing floaties on her arms and felt completely at ease in the water. Lilah easily paddled across the entire length of the pool. Later that afternoon, my daughter stood in the deep end holding Lilah. "Let me go! Let me go!" Lilah repeated as she struggled to wiggle out of her mother's arms. Lilah didn't understand that she couldn't stay afloat on her own yet and that she needed to wear the inflatable floaties—the ones packed up in the tote bag on the deck chair.

Our culture promotes an independent, self-reliant spirit, the attitude that "If I believe in myself, I can do it on my own." This mindset, along with our natural pride, can keep us from understanding how desperately we need to rely on the One who is our strength and shield. If we try to fight our battles in our own strength without asking for divine help, we will fail miserably.

The psalmist explained the beauty of living in dependence on Christ's strength and power. When we ask for His help and trust Him to answer, He helps us gain victory over our difficulties and temptations. This experience fills us with joy, and we respond by praising Him. Our faith grows stronger, our Christian walk becomes more solid, and Jesus gets the glory. And it all starts with understanding how much we need His help. —DIANNE NEAL MATTHEWS

FAITH STEP: *Are you trying to tackle a problem with your own wisdom and strength? Stop right now and ask Jesus to help you with it. Then trust Him to answer, and get ready to praise Him even more.*

WEDNESDAY, AUGUST 4

*Though you have not seen him, you love him; and even though
you do not see him now, you believe in him and are filled
with an inexpressible and glorious joy. 1 Peter 1:8 (NIV)*

I HAVE A THING FOR cats. Not a crazy thing. Just a "one can never
have too many" mind-set.

This year, within six months, I said goodbye to Happy and
Puddin', both too sick to go on. That left me with only Dr. Phibes
and Pokey lolling around our huge house. I needed another fur
baby to fill my broken heart.

After several months, I was ready to add a kitten. But when I
researched the Humane Association's adoption fees, my checkbook
shrieked in alarm. I would need to save up this time, not just run to
the shelter, pick out a pretty cat, and write a small check. I set aside
five dollars a week for my New Kitty fund. After several months, I
had enough for the adoption fee.

About that time, my vet told me she had been bottle-feeding
Wally, a male kitten someone found abandoned in a ditch. When
she sent me his photo, I fell in love with him. But he wouldn't be
weaned for two weeks. I counted the days. We adopted Wally last
weekend. He was worth the long wait.

But my anticipation during the wait to meet him pales compared
to my eagerness to meet Jesus. The more I think about Him and
talk to Him, the more excited I am to be in His presence forever.
I will finally get to worship in person the One who gave His life for
me, who loves me like no one else can or ever will. I can only imagine.
—JEANETTE LEVELLIE

FAITH STEP: *Read about Jesus's return in 1 Thessalonians 4:13–18. Imagine
what you'll do when you meet Jesus face to face.*

THURSDAY, AUGUST 5

*The LORD your God is in your midst, a mighty one who will save;
he will rejoice over you with gladness; he will quiet you by his love;
he will exult over you with loud singing. Zephaniah 3:17 (ESV)*

ONE DAY I FOUND MYSELF in another rough patch because of my health. Despite my best efforts, I was losing function. Discouragement swept in like high tide. When I shared my struggle in an email to my friend Angela, she sent me a link to an online worship song. I clicked the link on my laptop. As the music began, my grandchildren tapped at my bedroom door. They'd just returned from the park—faces red and sweaty, water bottles in hand. Pausing the song, I sank to the floor, and they snuggled into my lap, full of giggles, with hair smelling of sunshine. My heart flooded with joy. I was reminded that Jesus often comforts us in the midst of ordinary moments.

We expect our Savior to strengthen our faith and rebuild our hope through spiritual means: worship music, reading Scripture, praying with a friend. We can get into a habit of seeking spiritual nourishment only on Sunday mornings or when we read a devotion during our quiet time. We may forget that He is speaking to us constantly. When we acknowledge Him, we learn that He shares His presence and His blessings through many means, including the ordinary, humble experiences of our daily lives.

Today's verse in Zephaniah reminds us that sometimes Jesus shows His love for us in mighty acts, sometimes in quiet moments, and sometimes in exultant song. Let's be alert to various ways Jesus reminds us of His love today. —SHARON HINCK

FAITH STEP: *List three ways Jesus recently showed you His love: in a mighty way, a tender way, and a jubilant way.*

FRIDAY, AUGUST 6

Weeping may tarry for the night but joy comes with the morning.
Psalm 30:5 (ESV)

HAVE YOU EVER HAD A dark night of the soul? We all have, haven't we? A day, week, year, or season that sucks the life right out of us. Perhaps it's an extended illness of our own or someone we love. It could be a time of worrying about a prodigal child, or the loss of a job and the subsequent search for what's next, while worrying about how to pay our bills in the meantime. Maybe it's a miscarriage, deep trouble with a spouse, or even a divorce. Maybe it's the betrayal of a friend.

This list, once I started making it, seems endless. There is no shortage of darkness in this world. But in Jesus we have the promise of light that overcomes darkness. He's the Morning Star—and we trust that one day He's coming back through the clouds to bring us even more joy.

Once I was in utter despair and my brother encouraged me, "Remember this will end. It feels like forever right now, but that's not true. What you're experiencing is difficult, but you'll get through it. Eventually, the night will pass, and you'll be standing in the sun." His words helped me. Sometimes it's hard to remember in the middle of our darkness that a situation isn't permanent. But keeping our eyes on Jesus helps us remember that He is our hope. Joy comes with the morning. —GWEN FORD FAULKENBERRY

FAITH STEP: *Meditate on Psalm 30:5. Acknowledge whatever it is that makes you weep today, whether with tears or just an ache in your heart. Tell Jesus how you hurt. Then take some time to dwell on the fact that joy comes with the morning. Claim it and believe joy is coming for you.*

SATURDAY, AUGUST 7

As they talked and discussed these things with each other, Jesus himself came up and walked along with them. Luke 24:15 (NIV)

WE'D FINISHED OUR BIKE RIDE, and as we loaded our bikes into our cars, my friend Laura said, "Thanks, I feel like I just had therapy."

"Me too," I said, grateful for my weekly ride with my friend.

Every time we bike, we have meaningful talks. I've discovered I connect deeply with others when I'm doing something physical. When I'm on a walk, run, or bike ride, my senses are most alive, and my heart becomes most open to sharing. Raising three boys, my husband and I had our best talks with our sons while throwing a ball back and forth, hiking, or digging in the sand. I intentionally took advantage of such times to ask them deeper questions, and they were often more likely to open up and share.

I've found I also connect deeply with Jesus when I'm active. This shouldn't be surprising as Jesus had meaningful moments with His disciples and others while doing things. He was often walking or fishing when He had incredible conversations and shared insights about Himself to those in His presence. Consider the two men on the road to Emmaus. They were walking and talking when Jesus joined them and continued on the path with them. "He explained to them what was said in all the Scriptures concerning himself" (Luke 24:27, NIV). And later they asked one another, "Were not our hearts burning within us while he talked with us on the road?" (Luke 24:32, NIV).

In quiet and contemplative times we can sense Jesus speaking to us. But I've learned to make it a habit to talk to Him as I walk, run, or ride, and listen for Him in those motion-filled moments.
—JEANNIE BLACKMER

FAITH STEP: *Take a walk or a bike ride with Jesus today and listen.*

SUNDAY, AUGUST 8

Jesus said to the man, "Get up! Pick up your mat and go on home."
The man got right up. He picked up his mat and went out while
everyone watched in amazement. They praised God and said,
"We have never seen anything like this!" Mark 2:10–12 (CEV)

I'VE ALWAYS LOVED THIS STORY where the people lower their friend through the roof so he can see Jesus and be healed. I remember making a mat out of a swatch of blue gingham and pipe cleaners and playing out the scene in Vacation Bible School as a child. I didn't remember what all those watching said though, until I recently read the story again—"We have never seen anything like this!"

My dad says that a lot when he is teasing. A jolly guy in his early seventies, he is famous in our family for quirky expressions. For instance, when a grandkid shows him something they've made or done that they're proud of, he declares, "I think it is safe to say I've never seen anything like it." Then he'll laugh from deep in his belly. But when the people praising God said that, it was no joke. They never had seen anything like it. And they never would again. There really is no one else like Jesus.

Sometimes I get so discouraged by the things I see wrong with religion, and my own faith is assailed with doubt. But I find that the words of that old hymn "Turn Your Eyes Upon Jesus" are true. When I turn my eyes upon Jesus, "the things of earth...grow strangely dim in the light of His glory and grace." Jesus is irresistible. There is nothing and no one who ever comes close. —GWEN FORD FAULKENBERRY

FAITH STEP: *Skim through the Gospels and make a word collage of things you see about Jesus. Then put it somewhere where you'll see it often and be reminded of how amazing He is.*

MONDAY, AUGUST 9

My command is this: Love each other as I have loved you.
John 15:12 *(NIV)*

"LOVE YOU," MY HUSBAND CALLED out as he left for work.

I sighed. We'd just returned from a weekend with friends at their beachfront home, where they spoiled us with their kindness. I couldn't stop smiling.

I opened my laptop to catch up on my messages.

One friend offered me some raspberries she'd picked, and another wanted to share her famous cheesecake. A neighbor had purchased a lavender plant for my yard.

Reading these words, my eyes misted. In short, each friend's email said, "I love you." So many acts of kindness, all directed toward me. Coincidence?

Then I understood. When Jesus speaks by repeating a situation over and over, He demands to be heard. Sometimes it's a warning, and other times it might be discipline, but today's message left me humbled.

It was as if the Lover of my soul yelled at the top of His lungs, "I love you!" Over and over, the phrase coursed through my soul. Now tears slipped down my cheeks.

In my heart, I hear His words: *Accept My gifts. Joy in a husband's hug. Joy in one friend's handpicked berries, and another's cake. Joy in the knowledge that you're loved by them—and by Me.*

I prayed thanks and offered my reply, *Lord, who else needs to hear You say 'I love you' today? And may I be a part of Your voice?*

I sensed the answer....

Did you hear Him? —HEIDI GAUL

FAITH STEP: *Who has Jesus used to tell you "I love you" lately? To whom has He asked you to deliver the same message?*

TUESDAY, AUGUST 10

Casting all your care upon Him, for He cares for you. 1 Peter 5:7 (NKJV)

OUR YOUNGEST GRANDSON IS OBSESSED with fishing. He can talk lures, bait, and open-face reels for hours. When we're fishing at our pond, I'm often the one taking the fish off the hook, digging through the little container to find a nice, juicy worm, and baiting his hook for him. He's learning to do these tasks himself, but because our pond is stocked with more than a few lunkers, our grandson doesn't mind my help if the fish is almost bigger than he is.

With fish on my mind, I'm looking at 1 Peter 5:7 in a new way. The heart of Jesus shows up in the words, "Cast all your care upon Him, for He cares for you." When a friend was dealt a tough blow with her son's medical diagnosis, I shared this verse with her. And I explained it was first written to an entire New Testament church. "So, the *you* is plural," I told my friend. "He cares for you *and* those you love. Jesus invites us to cast on Him the cares your son is bearing (knowingly and unknowingly), plus yours, plus the rest of your family's, plus the cares of those who love you, including us."

The word *casting* sometimes is interpreted as "giving." Give all your cares to Jesus to carry. Some suggest it means to "roll" our burdens onto Him. But when something is cast in bronze, it moves from liquid to solid. When a fisherman casts her lure or casts a net, she has to *fling* it—using wrist action. Yes, we can "drop" a line into the water, but we'll only catch the fish who aren't scared by the plop.

My faith grew when encouraging my friend by saying, "I pray Jesus will make your peace cast-iron strong!" —CYNTHIA RUCHTI

FAITH STEP: *Who could use someone to pray cast-iron words of faith for them? Now's a good time.*

WEDNESDAY, AUGUST 11

Here is the sea, great and wide, which teems with creatures innumerable, living things both small and great. There go the ships, and Leviathan, which you formed to play in it. Psalm 104:25–26 (ESV)

LAST SUMMER WE WENT ON vacation with friends who have four children ranging in ages from five to thirteen years old. We rented paddleboards for them to go out on a mountain lake and explore. I sat on the shore watching the family goof around, splash each other, tip the paddleboards over into the frigid water, and paddle across a section of the lake to explore the little pine-tree-covered island. When they came back to the shore, they skipped rocks and waded in the shallow water, searching for little fish. At one point they found wet slimy grass they threw at each other. They were muddy, wet, and cold and having a blast.

Children sure know how to play. Jesus mentioned we should be like them (Matthew 18:2-4). I always thought this meant in terms of trust and faith, but I think He meant more than that. As I watched our friends frolic from the shore, I decided to stop observing. *You never outgrow play.* So the second time they went, I grabbed a paddleboard and joined them on the island. I threw rocks into the lake and played tag. We even all waded into the lake, counted to three, and submerged ourselves in the icy water. The cold took my breath away. I gasped for air and realized I felt so alive! God created all living things and put into everything a desire for playfulness—even the creatures in the sea and even you and me. —JEANNIE BLACKMER

FAITH STEP: *Make the opportunity for yourself today to do something playful. Wade barefoot in a nearby river, take a child out for ice cream, or play a game with your family.*

THURSDAY, AUGUST 12

For the Spirit God gave us does not make us timid, but gives us power, love and self-discipline. 2 Timothy 1:7 (NIV)

EARL WAS THE HARDEST-WORKING MAN I'd ever seen. Each morning, bright and early, he arrived at our neighbors' house in his old pickup truck and unloaded his equipment. All day he worked on landscaping the yard or on a building project for his employers. He was there, rain or shine, regular as clockwork, and I considered how proud Jesus must be of this faithful, earnest man.

One sweltering day, I saw Earl weeding the neighbors' yard, sweat pouring down his face. I decided I'd bring him an ice-cold bottled water and a plate of the brownies I'd made. I'd never formally met Earl, but we always waved to each other and my husband had spoken with him. I got a bottled water out of the fridge and piled six brownies on a plate. I was almost out the door when I reconsidered. Would Earl think I was weird? Too forward? Would he tell me he had his own water? Probably. And the brownies. What if he hated chocolate? These brownies had walnuts in them. What if he had a nut allergy and went into anaphylactic shock? Too many unknowns. I wouldn't risk it.

Did Jesus hesitate before He fed the multitudes? Before He turned the water into wine at Cana? Before He cleansed the lepers? I thought not. If a person tries to do a kind thing, can it be wrong? I felt a nudge from Jesus. *Do it!* So I got the bottled water out of the fridge, grabbed the plate of brownies, and walked out to greet Earl. The big grin on his face told me I'd done the right thing.
—PAT BUTLER DYSON

FAITH STEP: *Ask Jesus to remind you that a kind deed is never wrong.*

FRIDAY, AUGUST 13

But let all who take refuge in you rejoice; let them ever sing for joy, and spread your protection over them, that those who love your name may exult in you. Psalm 5:11 (ESV)

I CAME ACROSS THIS VERSE the other day. I've read it many times before, but something new jumped out at me this time: joy. I think I normally read the verse as if it was just a directive for believers to rejoice in the Lord and sing for joy. And it is, but it's not *just* that. The believers it addresses are the ones who take refuge in *Him*. It even states, "spread your protection over them, that those who love your name may exult in you."

Refuge is a place we go for safety. I have students who were refugees in Thailand before they came to America. They ran from Myanmar— for their lives—fleeing dangers that read like horror stories. I can only imagine what it was like for them. One, who is currently twenty years old, lived in a refugee camp for seventeen years.

When we take refuge in Jesus, it's because we're afraid or experiencing emotional or spiritual danger, and He is our safe place. The promise and beauty of Psalm 5:11 is that when we run to *Him*, we'll find joy.

I don't usually think of running for my life, whether physically or emotionally, as a joyful experience. But I'm learning that there's joy in running to Jesus and finding refuge in Him, because when we're resting in His kind, strong, and loving arms, our hearts are safe.
—GWEN FORD FAULKENBERRY

FAITH STEP: *Imagine yourself running into Jesus's arms. He wraps His arms around you and covers you with His cloak. You are completely safe. Hold this idea in your imagination today and find joy.*

SATURDAY, AUGUST 14

"Because he loves me," says the LORD, "I will rescue him; I will protect him, for he acknowledges my name." Psalm 91:14 (NIV)

I REALLY *LOVE* WALKING AROUND barefoot. Without shoes, padding around the backyard, I feel the warm grass underfoot. The sensation of sand between my toes at the beach is unsurpassed. At home, I kick off my shoes as soon as I walk through the door. There is just one small problem. I have this weird habit of hurting my feet. I have broken multiple toes. My baby toes suffer the most, finding themselves caught on the legs of furniture. I have even stepped on small shards of glass, earrings, and a random pushpin. The hard truth is that I need the protection of a sturdy pair of sneakers... or possibly some steel toe boots. My toes can't seem to sense the small dangers lurking in the carpet. My husband, Scott, an avid sock wearer, looks at me and shakes his head, asking, "When are you going to learn to put on shoes?" Slowly but surely, I am realizing I need more foot protection. And I need other protection as well.

As we walk through life, we can tend to be unguarded. We may feel safe, but we often expose ourselves to temptation or spiritual harm when we are taking in the pleasures of the moment. Jesus knows we are fallible and have weaknesses and blind spots. In our moments of weakness, He offers us protection from ourselves. Using His Word, the nudging of His Holy Spirit, and the wisdom of others, He invites us to follow Him. Jesus keeps us close to His heart, held within the immense power of His love.
—SUSANNA FOTH AUGHTMON

FAITH STEP: *Is there a weakness you're struggling with? Ask Jesus to protect you, guarding your heart and mind and keeping you close to His heart.*

SUNDAY, AUGUST 15

---

*Moreover David said, "The LORD, who delivered me from the paw
of the lion and from the paw of the bear, He will deliver me from
the hand of this Philistine." And Saul said to David, "Go, and the
LORD be with you!" 1 Samuel 17:37 (NKJV)*

IN THIS SCRIPTURE PASSAGE, A teenage boy had the courage to battle
a gigantic warrior when no one else in his village would dare try. He
was seen as insignificant—a sheep herder, the youngest and smallest of his tall, handsome brothers. But what the folks around him
didn't realize was that back in the hills where no one could see,
David had been conversing with God and singing His praise daily.
He experienced hardship out there—being attacked by a lion and
a bear—and watched the Lord rescue him. Those smaller victories
were written on David's heart. When it was time for the battle with
Goliath, he was ready for the challenge (even ran toward it!) because
he knew God had his back.

Too often, when Jesus delivers me from a difficulty, I don't pause
long enough to truly honor Him and reflect on His awesomeness.
That isn't how David lived. He probably wrote a new song or a
psalm each time God rescued him! Some urban missionary friends
remind themselves of God's faithfulness by keeping two glass bowls
with small, decorative stones on their coffee table. When they pray
for something, they write one or two words related to the request
on a stone, and when the prayer is answered, they move the stone
to the other bowl. Today their big bowl of answered prayer stones is
a constant visual reminder of God's kindness to them and to their
children. —PAMELA TOUSSAINT HOWARD

FAITH STEP: *Reflect on the last problem Jesus delivered you from and allow it
to boost your faith for today's battles. Consider doing something meaningful to
commemorate each victory.*

MONDAY, AUGUST 16

---

*Set a guard over my mouth, LORD; keep watch over the
door of my lips. Psalm 141:3 (NIV)*

WHEN GENE AND I FELL upon an opportunity to buy a piece of
lakefront property saddled with a derelict house, some folks said,
"Go for it! This is a smart investment." Others tried to dissuade us,
saying, "You might live to regret it."

We ignored the naysayers and listened to those who encouraged us
to pursue our dream of owning waterfront property. The fire department used the house as a practice burn, and then we built a new one
in its place. We put a ton of work into it, but it was worth it.

Never underestimate the power of words. They carry the ability to
bless, encourage, and revive hope. They also carry the ability to do
the opposite—curse, discourage, and crush hope.

Perhaps "crushed" describes how Jairus, a local synagogue leader,
felt. He'd asked Jesus to heal his sick daughter, but before Jesus
did so, messengers arrived bearing sad news: "Your daughter is
dead.... Why bother the teacher anymore?" (Mark 5:35, NIV).

They spoke truth about the girl's death, but the manner in which
they presented those words seemed heartless, and their comment
about Jairus bothering Jesus was completely skewed. Their words
crushed his hope.

Thankfully the story didn't end there: "Overhearing what they
said, Jesus told him, 'Don't be afraid; just believe'" (Mark 5:36, NIV).
Jesus's words, kind and well-chosen, revived Jairus's hope.

Words carry weight. Before opening our mouths, let's ask ourselves
if the words on our tongue will bless and encourage the hearer. If
not, let's either remain silent or change them. —GRACE FOX

FAITH STEP: *Make today's verse your prayer today.*

TUESDAY, AUGUST 17

*You are saturated with an ecstatic joy. . . . For you are reaping
the harvest of your faith—the full salvation promised
you—your souls' victory. 1 Peter 1:8–9 (TPT)*

OUR BLUEBERRY BUSHES OUTDID THEMSELVES this year. As with many fruit trees and bushes, they didn't produce any fruit the first year they were planted. We'd been instructed to wait another year or two before harvesting any berries. We watered and made sure the soil at their feet was acidic, as instructed. And we waited.

For the past several years, they've produced more than enough for blueberry jam, muffins, pancakes, and just eating them straight off the bush. There's nothing like homegrown blueberries.

Also as instructed, we'd planted three varieties, having been told they'd draw strength from one another and eventually produce berries better than any of the individual varieties alone. True to form, this year's berries aren't tiny, small, and large—instead, they're large, medium, and extra-large with a common level of sweetness.

The same often happens with what we harvest in life. Spiritually speaking, we may not produce enough to give away until our faith has a chance to mature. If we hang out with Jesus and with people whose gifts and strengths differ from our own, eventually we take on some of their characteristics until we're better together than we would have been alone. This happens in marriage, in friendships, and with our brothers and sisters in Christ…

In 1 Peter 1:9, we're told joy is often the result of "reaping the harvest of your faith" (TPT). As I grab my basket and head to the patch, I understand more clearly that reaping a harvest of faith is a reason to rejoice! —CYNTHIA RUCHTI

FAITH STEP: *Is your life producing a harvest this year that's sweeter than the last?*

WEDNESDAY, AUGUST 18

LORD, you alone are my portion and my cup; you make my lot secure.
The boundary lines have fallen for me in pleasant places; surely
I have a delightful inheritance. Psalm 16:5–6 (NIV)

THIS MORNING I SAT IN my comfy chair, wrapped in a soft blanket, and looked out the window. The pond beyond our backyard rippled in the light breeze. A brilliant white egret waded in search of breakfast. Flowers dotted the garden with pink and yellow, and the sky stretched above blue and joyous.

When I read Psalm 16, my heart connected quickly to the words. *Jesus, You have indeed set me in a pleasant place, and I'm so grateful.*

But as I turned away from the window, I headed to my pillbox and the medications helping me function. My body throbbed and reminded me of its daily challenges. Scribbled notes on my desk demanded my attention. A family member was battling illness, and I was working to sort out needed care. Decisions and phone calls and paperwork loomed. My lot didn't feel very secure at all—in fact I felt like I was drowning. Not everything in life felt pleasant.

That's when I took another look at Psalm 16. Jesus has indeed set each of us in places where we might spot delightful blessings—as I did outside the window. But the true place of blessing is anywhere that Jesus is. He is our portion—not our house, our work, or even our dearest friends. Even when our boundary lines include pain and struggle, we can embrace our situation because He is there. The deeper truth in the Psalm is that even in places that don't seem so pleasant, there is beauty because Jesus is with us. —SHARON HINCK

FAITH STEP: *Ask Jesus to illuminate the beauty possible, even in one of the unpleasant situations in your life.*

THURSDAY, AUGUST 19

Jesus Christ is the same yesterday and today and forever. Hebrews 13:8 (NIV)

WHEN WE INTRODUCED OUR NEW kitten, Wally, to the older two cats, they were unimpressed. Pokey and Dr. Phibes hissed, growled, and watched every move of the wee intruder. Those first few days, we rescued Wally several times from angry claws swiping at his face. Apparently, the adult cats resented the change we'd forced on them. How dare we?

Dr. Phibes quit jumping on our bed to cuddle in the wee hours. Pokey refused to sit next to me on the loveseat when I read my Bible each morning. Kevin and I did our best to reassure them that Wally was no threat and just wanted to make friends. We made sure to give them extra pampering. But we couldn't convince them we were on their side.

Life often thrusts unwelcome changes upon us. Our spouse takes a job across the country, and we must say goodbye to dear friends. Our company closes, and we are forced to find new employment. Our church splits. Our marriage ends. We might be tempted to blame the Lord and say or think, *How dare You?*

Jesus understands our angst. He's not angry when we question life's upsets. In every unwanted change, He remains faithful. He walks closely beside us, guiding our steps through all the new, scary experiences. In the end, the most important change takes place in our hearts. We realize His love for us hasn't wavered, and our faith in Him grows two sizes larger.

At last, Dr. Phibes and Pokey accepted Wally into the family. Just as we have Jesus's faithful caring, they realized our care for them hadn't changed. —JEANETTE LEVELLIE

FAITH STEP: *Recall the most traumatic change in your life. Think of how Jesus helped you through it. Write Him a note, thanking Him for His faithfulness.*

FRIDAY, AUGUST 20

But God chose the foolish things of the world to shame the wise; God chose the weak things of the world to shame the strong. God chose the lowly things of this world and the despised things—and the things that are not—to nullify the things that are, so that no one may boast before him. 1 Corinthians 1:27–29 (NIV)

EVERY BOAT THAT MOTORS DOWN our river comes equipped with a smaller boat. Sometimes they hang suspended at the stern of the vessel. Often they're towed with ropes and bounce along in the larger boat's wake. That's the case with ours. We tow a gray rubber dinghy with oars and a small gasoline-powered engine.

Friends with no marine experience visited for a few days. They watched with interest as Gene checked the dinghy's tow ropes and air pressure before we left the dock. "What are you doing?" one asked. Gene said he was ensuring the dinghy was in proper working condition.

They then asked, "Why does it matter?" Gene explained it was our means of transportation to island shores. More important, it would be our lifesaver if our boat engine died. Our guests expressed surprise. "It looks so insignificant. Who would have thought it could save our lives?"

The Jews felt the same way about Jesus. Isaiah 53:2 says, "He had no beauty or majesty to attract us to him, nothing in his appearance that we should desire him" (NIV). As a newborn, He depended on His parents for survival. He grew up as a carpenter's son, assumed the form of a servant, and died a criminal's death. Jesus appears insignificant by human terms, but let's not underestimate His importance. His name is Savior for a reason: He's the only one who can save our lives. —GRACE FOX

FAITH STEP: *List three things from which Jesus has saved you. Thank Him.*

SATURDAY, AUGUST 21

In My Father's house are many mansions; if it were not so, I would have told you. I go to prepare a place for you. And if I go and prepare a place for you, I will come again and receive you to Myself; that where I am, there you may be also. John 14:2–3 (NKJV)

I LOVE BIRDS AND SEVERAL birdhouses are scattered around our yard. Every year a pair chooses one just out of view. Though I'm happy to offer refuge for these little creatures, I wish they'd pick one more visible so I could see them at work.

This year my prayer was answered. As I sat on my porch rocker, I sensed movement from the corner of my eye and turned to look. There, at our newest birdhouse, a female sparrow perched, dry grass clenched in her beak. She cocked her head at me as if asking permission to continue. I smiled, wondering if that's how I appear as I seek God's guidance. Then she entered her tiny abode.

Throughout the coming days, she and her mate spent all their time building a home for their soon-to-be family, gathering nesting materials and making it just right. As I wondered at their diligence, I considered the heavenly home Jesus is preparing for me. Even here on earth, He was a carpenter. He knows the desires of my heart and how I can use them to bring Him glory. He—and everything He does—is perfect.

As I make my place here in this world, I know He's watching over me, guarding and guiding me. And He's creating a spot where I'll belong, a place I can thrive. A place in His presence. What could be better? —HEIDI GAUL

FAITH STEP: *Purchase a birdhouse and place it outside. As you watch and wait for activity, consider the home our Lord is preparing for you in heaven. As you anticipate your future home, give thanks.*

SUNDAY, AUGUST 22

Therefore, if anyone is in Christ, he is a new creation. The old has passed away; behold, the new has come. 2 Corinthians 5:17 (ESV)

A HEAT WAVE HUNG OVER Colorado. The temperatures outside were in the triple digits. The home we rented didn't have air conditioning, so the temperature inside was triple digits too. I sat in my home office, dripping with sweat, when my friend texted me. "We're going on the boat at 3:00. Want to join?" I had so much to do, but I was wilting from the heat and had a headache. "Yes!" I texted back.

I met my friend, her daughter, and her daughter's friend at the reservoir. She drove the boat to the middle of the lake because the first thing we wanted to do was dive in. We took the plunge. The cold water rushed over me from head to toe. It felt amazing. I popped my head up, and the two young girls were laughing and screaming. My headache was gone. My body temperature was comfortable, and I felt refreshed and renewed. I went under the water and came up a new person.

In the Bible, water symbolizes many things, including its role in baptism. John the Baptist stood in the Jordan River, dunking who knows how many people, even Jesus. When Jesus came up out of the water a dove landed on Him, and a voice said, "This is my Son, whom I love; with him I am well pleased" (Matthew 3:17, NIV).

Every so often when I jump in water, I'm reminded of who Jesus is and what He's done for me. I don't need to be baptized over again, but when I'm hot and grumpy and I immerse myself in water, I come out refreshed and renewed every time. —JEANNIE BLACKMER

FAITH STEP: *Find water and jump in (even if it's your bathtub)! Take notice of how your body, mind, and spirit react, and see if you sense renewal.*

MONDAY, AUGUST 23

But Jesus turning and seeing her said, "Take courage, daughter..."
Matthew 9:22 (AMP)

SOMETHING I'VE LEARNED ABOUT PAIN is that no one can really fix it except Jesus. In my life Jesus has used time, loved ones, writing, running, baking, reading, music, nature, crying, teaching, church, sleep, medicine, therapy, walking, movies, coffee, fruit, traveling, work, and dogs to heal me. But the biggest comfort is that I know He sees me. *He really sees me.*

If you do a word search you find that Jesus does a lot of seeing in the Gospels. He sees people and heals them. He sees their hunger and feeds them. He sees and has compassion, sees and gives peace, sees and rebukes, sees and forgives, sees and invites. He is the God who sees.

Glennon Doyle wrote, "We just need someone to see the pain.... To say: Yes. I see this. This is real.... We just need a witness." I think we need to know that someone gets it. That we are not alone. I imagine that when Jesus turned and fixed His eyes on the lady who touched the hem of His garment, she felt Him. She knew He understood. "Take courage, daughter." I am here. I see you.

The people who have helped me the most in my painful times are the ones who saw me and understood. They're the ones who babysat my kids, brought me meals, sent cards, came to my house, and prayed with me. The ones who got me out of bed to walk, who listened over coffee, who did my laundry. The ones who let me know I was not alone. —GWEN FORD FAULKENBERRY

FAITH STEP: *Among the people you know, who do you see in pain? Or maybe it's a stranger. Do something practical today to meet someone's need. Let this person know he or she is not alone.*

TUESDAY, AUGUST 24

*Look carefully then how you walk, not as unwise but as wise, making the best
use of the time, because the days are evil. Ephesians 5:15–16 (ESV)*

WHILE I WAS GROWING UP, a huge cottonwood tree stood near our
house. In the summer, little white tufts with seed inside constantly
floated through the air. Sometimes it got so thick it covered our
window screens. One day I wondered if the cotton from the tree
was the same as the cotton my dad planted in the fields—the fields
that we chopped weeds in during the hot summer and that we
picked cotton in the fall and piled in a trailer to be taken to the gin.

  Hmm, I thought, *this cotton floating through the air is like free
money! All we need to do is reach out and grab it.* I pulled the small
tea strainer from the kitchen drawer and headed outside to make
my fortune. As I chased after the white floating puffs, it didn't take
me long to understand that getting enough to make a bale of cotton
would probably not be possible.

  When we're young, we don't think much about wasting time.
But the older we get, the more we realize how precious and limited
our time is. I can't imagine a more valuable use of our time than
obeying Jesus's leading. He has already planned works for us to
do and people for us to speak with on His behalf. We miss out on
the joy of being used by Him if we crowd our agenda with personal projects and the pursuit of pleasure. We might feel a sense of
accomplishment from our work, but if it's not Christ's will, then it's
like chasing after the wind (Ecclesiastes 2:11)—or puffs of cotton.
—DIANNE NEAL MATTHEWS

FAITH STEP: *Develop the daily habit of praying over your to-do list, always
asking Jesus to reveal what He wants you to accomplish.*

WEDNESDAY, AUGUST 25

He laid his right hand on me, saying, "Fear not, I am the first and the last, and the living one. I died, and behold I am alive forevermore . . ." Revelation 1:17–18 (ESV)

LAST SUMMER WE WENT TO Colorado and followed the path of the Arkansas River. We live in Arkansas on its biggest bend. But it starts as a trickle from a melting glacier in the mountains near Leadville, Colorado. About Salida, it turns into this great mountain stream where you can whitewater raft some fun rapids—but not near as wicked as it gets at the bottom of the Royal Gorge.

Since we have no rafting skills to speak of, we geared up for a trip down the river with a guide. It was exciting but also a little ominous when he told us, "If you fall out, do not be afraid. I will get you." He was so capable and strong-looking that I felt safe—until we encountered some crazy water. Then I did not feel safe, but it was too late. There was nothing to do but trust him. And even though I got wet, I never fell out of the boat. Our guide got us to our destination successfully, and it was a beautiful place.

This experience turned out to be a good metaphor of the Christian life. Jesus has promised He will never leave us and commanded us to not fear. But if I'm honest I don't always feel safe. In fact, a great deal of the time I feel vulnerable and afraid, but I've made my commitment. I'm in His hands. And His promise isn't based on how I feel. It's based on who He is. We are safe with Jesus.
—GWEN FORD FAULKENBERRY

FAITH STEP: *Do a word search and find out how many times "fear not" appears in the Bible. Let that sink in, and next time you're afraid, let His perfect love cast out your fear.*

THURSDAY, AUGUST 26

For as the body without the spirit is dead, so faith without works is dead also. James 2:26 (NKJV)

WHEN JESUS WANTS ME TO do something big, it always requires stepping off a cliff (or so it seems), trusting for a safe landing. Once, it was laying hands on a neighbor I hardly knew; another time it was moving across the country, with only a week's notice, to attend Bible College. Both times I was afraid of failing and, admittedly, afraid of looking dumb. Knowing Jesus was with me, and that He had sent me, was the only thing that propelled me to act.

Sometimes we think we are waiting on God to move, but He's usually waiting for us. The day I decided to enroll in school I was fed up. I told Jesus that I'd do anything He wanted me to do that day—anything. I knew something had to change. I went to church and listened to the announcements for an opportunity. Nothing. I fellowshipped with friends afterward and expected someone to ask me to go on a missions adventure. Still nothing. At 6:00 PM I got upset and said, *Lord, I said I'd do anything You asked me to do today, and today is almost over.* I heard Him answer, *But it's not over* yet. Sitting at my desk minutes later, I looked up and saw the Charis Bible College brochure I'd had for months. This was the day to act on it! One week later, I was in Colorado Springs, sitting in class. It was one of the best decisions of my life and set me on course to receive blessing upon blessing.

Think about the man in Luke 6:10 whom Jesus told, "Stretch out your hand." He received his healing only as "he did so" (NKJV).
—PAMELA TOUSSAINT HOWARD

FAITH STEP: *Take a step forward in faith on something you've gotten God's direction for, and see His provision as you go!*

FRIDAY, AUGUST 27

This is my commandment, that you love one another as I have loved you. Greater love has no one than this, that someone lay down his life for his friends. John 15:12–13 (ESV)

MY PALMS WERE SWEATY, AND my heart pounded. I adjusted the microphone and double-checked my notes. I was teaching a multi-session class at a writers' conference, and I'd spent months preparing. I longed to offer encouragement and tools to the attendees.

My first two sessions, I covered my prepared material. Polite laughter met my humorous anecdotes. Smiles and nods responded to advice I shared. I relaxed a little. To be honest, although I wanted to serve the attendees, my selfish side had a second agenda. I also wanted to be accepted and respected, and be seen as knowledgeable, useful, or valuable to others.

Before the final session, I was resting in my hotel room and praying. Jesus gave me that gentle nudge we sometimes sense. It was time to set aside my striving to impress and just be real. I grappled in prayer. I didn't want to talk about my struggles. I didn't want to admit my fears and doubts. I didn't want to be vulnerable.

But as I began the third session, I pushed aside my script and spoke from my heart. Afterward, the writers shared that mine was the talk in which Jesus spoke to them most powerfully.

When Jesus talked of laying down His life, it was something He was literally about to do. Most of us aren't confronted with dying to save another person. But when we share our experiences, when we are authentic, when we show up for others even though we feel inadequate—that is a way of laying down our life for others. —SHARON HINCK

FAITH STEP: *Today, be vulnerable and available to someone in a way that takes courage or sacrifice.*

SATURDAY, AUGUST 28

Therefore, do not worry about tomorrow, for tomorrow will worry about itself. Each day has enough trouble of its own. Matthew 6:34 (NIV)

I HUNG UP THE PHONE with a realtor after making an appointment to see a house. I leaned back in my chair, took a deep breath, and wondered, *Where are we going to live?* A few years ago, we sold our home and gave away most of our belongings, only keeping the items we loved. Our three adult sons were living on their own, and we wanted to simplify our life, experience more financial freedom, and start our empty-nest life as an adventure.

The past few years, not tethered to a house, had been great. But now I longed for a home again—my own nest. I thought this nesting instinct usually affected younger women starting their families, so I was surprised that I still had this desire. Worrying about it was definitely stealing my joy.

Then, I was reminded of Jesus's words giving us an anecdote to worry. He said, "Look at the birds of the air; they do not sow or reap or store away in barns, and yet your heavenly Father feeds them. Are you not much more valuable than they?" (Matthew 6:26, NIV). The answer is yes. The process of learning to trust God to take care of us is a lifelong practice, not just with where we live but in every area of life. Here I am again, turning my worry into trust. I still don't know where my next nest will be, but I'll take Jesus at His words and remember how He provides for the birds in the air and how much more He will provide for me. —JEANNIE BLACKMER

FAITH STEP: *Write down something you are worried about. Take a walk outside and observe birds. Remember how much God loves and provides for them and all the more so for you.*

SUNDAY, AUGUST 29

A thousand may fall at your side, and ten thousand at your right hand; but it shall not come near you. Psalm 91:7 (NKJV)

YOU TURN ON THE TV, and the commercial suggests that you may need to be treated for an ailment. Open a magazine and see that you need this pill if you're over forty, or find out you have a one in a thousand chance of succeeding at something. Negativity is all around us, making us wonder if our outcome will be any different from those who don't trust Jesus.

Personally, this is when I must rehearse—out loud—that I am chosen and appointed to bear lasting fruit (John 15:16), despite what is happening to the other ten thousand, especially when it comes to health. The previous verses of Psalm 91 talk about sickness, disease, and sudden destruction. But we can have confidence that if we have made Jesus our refuge, these things shall not consume us. Do you believe that? One simple way I practice this is to stand in resistance against things said about health that are contrary to the Word. When allergy season comes around, I speak to my body and tell it to block unnecessary histamines, no matter the outcome. Like Elizabeth and Sarah in the Bible, I'm believing Jesus for the strength to conceive a baby even though I'm middle-aged. The world is filled with a tremendous amount of messages saying no, but I believe the Word gives me good reason to say yes! (The amazing stories of Elizabeth and Sarah are in Luke 1 and Genesis 18–20, respectively.) To stand out from the crowd, I have to train my mind to believe what the Word says instead of what the world says. —PAMELA TOUSSAINT HOWARD

FAITH STEP: *Read Psalm 91 each day this week and watch your faith muscles grow.*

MONDAY, AUGUST 30

I am counting on the Lord; yes, I am counting on him. I have put my hope in his word. Psalm 130:5 (NLT)

LIVING IN A MARINA MAKES me track the weather forecast more intently than when living in a house. For instance, I plan my laundry day based on whether the sun will shine. That's because walking a city block to and from the laundromat while carrying a hamper filled with clothes feels like pleasant exercise on a sunny day. Not so much in the pouring rain.

I count on the weatherman, and you probably do too. He's often right, but occasionally he misses the mark. We wake expecting sunshine, but then rain rolls in and forces us to either change our plans or grin and bear it.

Some of us count on our adult kids to help with occasional tasks. Maybe we count on a friend to listen when we need to talk. Or we count on our employer to give us a check on payday.

Unfortunately, not everyone in whom we place confidence meets our expectations at all times. They might let us down because circumstances beyond their control enter their lives and hinder them from keeping a promise they've made. But we can always count on the Lord to be there for us and to help us.

We can count on Jesus to give us wisdom when we're perplexed. To forgive us when we confess our sins. To grant joy when we obey Him. Best of all, we can count on His unending presence.

"And be sure of this: I am with you always, even to the end of the age," Jesus told His disciples (Matthew 28:20 NLT). It's encouraging to know that Jesus is with us today too. We can count on His faithful promises, and He will never disappoint. —GRACE FOX

FAITH STEP: *For what are you counting on Jesus today? Praise Him for being fully reliable.*

TUESDAY, AUGUST 31

I am not saying this because I am in need, for I have learned to be content whatever the circumstances. Philippians 4:11 (NIV)

ON A RECENT FAMILY BEACH vacation, we watched hermit crabs swap shells. Several hermit crabs were crawling around, so we lined them up near an empty shell, biggest to smallest. Sure enough, the largest hermit crab, first in line, started checking out the empty shell. He must have liked it because suddenly he popped out of his shell and stuck his worm-like rear-end into the new shell. He found something bigger and better. This started a chain reaction. Each hermit crab crept out of its current home and plopped into the empty shell in front of it.

We're not that different from hermit crabs. We live in a culture that encourages bigger and better. Whether it's a job, home, vacation, car, or mountain to climb, we spend enormous amounts of time, money, and energy looking for what's bigger and better. I have. We moved from a small apartment to bigger homes. I wrote books, hoping each one would outsell the last. We planned vacations, seeking bigger and better experiences. It's an exhausting, vicious cycle.

Paul wrote incredible wisdom about this empty desire, while in a dank, dark prison. He had learned the secret to contentment: knowing Jesus. Paul experienced wealth and poverty. He knew without a doubt that nothing brings the lasting satisfaction we crave except knowing Jesus. He closed this chapter in Philippians with the promise, "And my God will meet all your needs according to the riches of his glory in Christ Jesus" (v. 19, NIV). Let's stop struggling for more and discover true contentment found only in Jesus. —JEANNIE BLACKMER

FAITH STEP: *Read Philippians 4. Meditate on it and find contentment in Jesus.*

WEDNESDAY, SEPTEMBER 1

Children are a heritage from the LORD, offspring a reward from Him. Psalm 127:3 (NIV)

CLEAN CLOTHES COVERED EVERY SURFACE in my daughter Melissa's house. "Just have a seat anywhere, Mom," Melissa joked. "I wash and I dry, but somehow I never have time to fold and put away." Melissa had a husband, a nine-year old son, and a newborn baby boy. "It's hard to keep up with housework when you're nursing every two hours," Melissa said. It had been years since I'd had babies, but not so long ago that I'd forgotten.

"That's what I'm here for," I said. So for the next hour, Melissa and I folded. As baby Jameson drowsed in his swing, Melissa poured her heart out to me: worry about how her older son was adjusting to his brother, concern about whether Jameson was getting enough to eat, doubts about her adequacy as a mother, anxiety about how her husband was handling a full-time job and college, fear that something might happen to Jameson, worry over a stubborn rash the baby had, and wondering, Would she ever get any sleep?

Much as I enjoy giving advice, Jesus whispered in my ear, *Shh,* and I just listened. Melissa's tears dampened some of the clean clothes, but they survived. I made her a cup of tea and vacuumed her house while she fed the baby. I'd brought a casserole for the family's dinner, so I preheated the oven. I told Melissa what a good mother she was, and that I'd be back in a few days to help fold clothes, bring their supper, and do anything she needed me to do. She thanked me over and over, and I thanked Jesus for the joy of being a mother and a grandmother. —PAT BUTLER DYSON

FAITH STEP: *Thank Jesus for the gift of children. Pray for the children in your life, one by one.*

THURSDAY, SEPTEMBER 2

Cast all your anxiety on him because he cares for you. 1 Peter 5:7 (NIV)

GOD ANSWERED A SIXTEEN-YEAR-LONG PRAYER when our daughter announced that her family would be moving to our hometown. Ever since our oldest granddaughter, Jenessa, was born, Kevin and I had longed to have them near us, rather than a day's drive away. When her siblings Daniel and Grace came along, our desire intensified. But neither us nor them were able to relocate. Until now.

I was elated. "My family is moving six miles away!"

A few weeks later, worry attacked. When the kids were little, they adored us. We filled our visits with ice-cream dates, trips to the "widawary" (Jen's word for library), and outings in the park. When they'd visited us, we baked cookies, read books, and watched *Mr. Rogers' Neighborhood*.

Now that they were teenagers and we'd see them often, would we lose the special place in their hearts? My mind filled with worst-case scenarios which, I am happy to say, never happened.

We no longer play Candyland, sing "The Clean Up Song," or order Happy Meals. But we have as much fun with our teenage grandkids as we had when they were toddlers—it's just a different kind of fun. Now we relate to them on a grown-up level and do grown-up activities. That's gratifying for them (and expensive for us).

You'd think by now I would've learned that worry is as useless as Bermuda shorts on a penguin. Yet every so often, Jesus has to reteach me the same lesson: I have to trust Him to take care of my loved ones. Someday I'll finally realize: He has it all figured out.
—JEANETTE LEVELLIE

FAITH STEP: *Cast your cares at Jesus's feet. Leave them there.*

FRIDAY, SEPTEMBER 3

Let your light so shine before men, that they may see your good works, and glorify your Father which is in heaven. Matthew 5:16 (KJV)

THE WIND TORE LEAVES, LIMBS, and power lines. The storm raised rivers and felled giant maples. Winds toppled so many power poles that it will be days before power, phone service, and the internet are restored.

Because we live far from the nearest town, we have a generator we can run for short stretches to keep food in the freezer from spoiling. But the generator can't handle normal electrical usage, so we've limited ourselves to only necessary electrical draws.

It's natural to assume that with the power out, we would catch up on reading. There's a reason pioneers' and pilgrims' eyes went bad reading by candle glow. We've propped flashlights so their circle beams land on the page we're reading. But as frugal as we are to save the hard-working generator, I caught myself looking at the lamp on my desk and, reminiscent of a Dickens character, internally asking, "Please, sir, could I have this one small light?"

If you're like me, you often feel that your influence to make a difference for others is no more influential than one small light in an otherwise pitch-black world. Little difference? Switch it off for a moment, and you'll realize that its influence is much more significant than you imagine. People crave something that will help illuminate the mess they're in and send the darkness fleeing. Jesus is that Light. We serve as His reflections. Jesus is asking, "Could I have your one small light?" It does make a difference. —CYNTHIA RUCHTI

FAITH STEP: *Let your light shine brightly today, and before the day's end, make sure someone who needs hope sees it in and hears it from you.*

SATURDAY, SEPTEMBER 4

Give praise to the LORD, proclaim his name; make known among the nations what he has done. Sing to him, sing praise to him; tell of all his wonderful acts. . . . Remember the wonders he has done, his miracles, and the judgments he pronounced. 1 Chronicles 16:8–9, 12 (NIV)

LAST NIGHT, WE GOT TOGETHER with our good friends the Couches. My husband, Scott, and I have known Shane and Marty since college. We couldn't help remembering our early days of friendship. Those were formative days of growth and joy. In college, Shane and I became friends performing in lip-sync battles together. We took our fun seriously. Scott and Shane took a statistics class together off-campus. Their struggle with high math established their friendship. Marty and I got to know each other after she and Shane got married. We had our kids during the same season, and our third babies were born only days apart. While launching their counseling ministry, Shane and Marty attended our church plant. It was a huge encouragement for us to have them there. As our kids grew, we celebrated and had parties with dancing and board games. Through the years, we have also supported each other through surgeries, emotional struggles, and career moves.

Remembering is a way we honor our friendship. In our relationship with Jesus, looking back can help us move forward. Remembering all that He has done for us builds up our faith. By naming those moments when Jesus intervened on our behalf delivers us from darkness and sets our feet on a path of healing, we cement our bond with Him. He loves us. There is no reason to doubt Him. Look at all He has done for us. —SUSANNA FOTH AUGHTMON

FAITH STEP: *Remember all that Jesus has done for you. Make a time line of the moments that He has come through for you and thank Him for each one.*

SUNDAY, SEPTEMBER 5

I will ask the Father, and He will give you another Helper (Comforter, Advocate, Intercessor—Counselor, Strengthener, Standby), to be with you forever. John 14:16 (AMP)

I BELIEVE THAT INSIDE ME and every believer is the powerful Holy Spirit who strengthens, comforts, and counsels us in every life situation. No app can do that! Like any of the provisions Jesus has put in place for us, we'll benefit from the Holy Spirit's guidance as we acknowledge Him.

I know firsthand how the Comforter ministers to pain in ways no person can. When my beloved mom, Gloria, was diagnosed with pancreatic cancer, I vowed to fight the good fight of faith and see her healed. She was the one who taught me about faith, and this was my chance to agree with her in prayer. One day she called me to her bedside and said excitedly, "Pamela, Jesus is waiting for me! I won't be with you much longer." This was not what I wanted to hear! I cried a million tears and told her she was wrong. But Jesus showed me that it was true and right. At eighty-six, my mom had more than lived out her days and was ready to see her Father. After that declaration, no amount of cheering up, healing prayer, or worship music soothed her. She died in my arms one month later. Only the constant voice of the Holy Spirit telling me, "She's with Me now. Don't worry," kept me from bawling. Several times I even heard in my heart Jesus say, "She loves it here!" What a comfort that was. Now whenever I feel overwhelmed, I know that if I can stay quiet and listen, I will receive His strength. —PAMELA TOUSSAINT HOWARD

FAITH STEP: *Meditate on John 14:16 in the Amplified version above and ask the Lord for revelation.*

LABOR DAY, MONDAY, SEPTEMBER 6

Very truly I tell you, the Son can do nothing by himself; he can do only what he sees his Father doing, because whatever the Father does the Son also does. John 5:19 (NIV)

LORD, I'M TOO BUSY, I whined. *I'll never find the time to do everything.*

Jesus's sweet, strong voice resonated in my heart: *Jeanette, you're too busy because you're doing things I never asked you to do.* I knew He was right. With my Irish enthusiasm, I frequently added tasks and volunteered for causes without bothering to pray. Then I found myself in a state of panic or exhaustion, causing stress not only to myself but also to my husband, Kevin.

Earlier this year I signed up for a line-dancing class, giddy with anticipation. I love to dance; Kevin doesn't. Since I won't dance with another man, dancing solo in this class seemed like the perfect solution. I learned the steps quickly. I met several new friends. But after four weeks, the realization dawned: I'd spread myself too thin. I needed to spend time elsewhere—with my aging mom, with my husband, or simply relaxing.

When Jesus was here, He did only those things He saw His Father do. He never veered off the course God set for Him, dipping His toe in a hobby or cause on a whim. I'm convinced Jesus had plenty of fun; He attended a wedding, so He must have danced! But He knew His life was not His own. Jesus was here on a mission—to show us God and to die in our place. How grateful I am He accomplished His assignment.

I hope someday to declare as Jesus did, "I do only what I see my Father do," not only for God's glory but also for my—and Kevin's—sanity. —JEANETTE LEVELLIE

FAITH STEP: *Ask Jesus for His grace to eliminate everything from your schedule that He hasn't told you to do.*

TUESDAY, SEPTEMBER 7

The thief comes only to steal and kill and destroy; I have come that they may have life, and have it to the full. John 10:10 (NIV)

I BRUSH MY RESCUE CAT, Milo, and I'm not sure which of us enjoys it more. Bringing his luxuriant fur to a sleek shine, as his paws knead the air, makes me smile. His trust is complete, and his peace is contagious.

We first rescued this black and white tuxedo cat as a kitten, scrawny as the stuffed mice he now plays with. But at the farm where he'd been born, he couldn't keep his paws off the chickens, which is why he had to go.

To see Milo today, you might question the validity of the hen-chasing stories. I've yet to see him hunt for anything but food dishes and patches of sunlight to flop in. This furball is the happiest creature I've ever met. He purrs even in his slumber. When he spots me across the room, he'll blink his eyes slowly as if to say, "I love you." Milo appreciates his life, and his gratefulness is lavish.

If this cat had a human twin, it would be me. As a teenager, I couldn't stay out of trouble. My lips and hands remained sticky with forbidden fruit, and no amount of washing removed the stain—or the hunger for more. But just as we rescued Milo, Jesus rescued me. He pulled me from the dangerous existence I'd chosen and gave me sanctuary in Him. The emptiness of my early life amplifies the abundance of the one I now lead. Grateful, I can rest in His peace. I've found my spot in the Son. My hunt is done. —HEIDI GAUL

FAITH STEP: *Curl up in a patch of sunlight with your Bible. Meditate on verses that focus on peace and gratitude. Close your eyes and say, "I love You, Jesus."*

WEDNESDAY, SEPTEMBER 8

Beginning with Moses and all the Prophets, he interpreted to them in all the Scriptures the things concerning himself. Luke 24:27 (ESV)

EACH TIME I JOIN A new Bible study, I hear similar comments as the ladies introduce themselves. The women express how much they enjoy the fellowship and how much they learn from the workbook and videos. Eventually someone will say that when she tries to read the Bible on her own, she doesn't understand it, and others agree. And that always makes me sad.

Don't get me wrong—I love gathering with others to study the Word. I need the fellowship and encouragement, and the discussions can be stimulating. But in my opinion, there's nothing more exciting than reading the Scriptures on my own and having the Holy Spirit open my eyes to see something new. Sometimes I gain a deeper understanding of a passage, or I glean a specific way to apply a verse or principle in my life.

The Gospels show that Jesus loved teaching people about Scripture. Whether speaking with crowds, privately with individuals, or even with the hardhearted religious leaders, Jesus often explained how the Old Testament revealed God's will for how we should live. One of the first things He did after rising from the dead was interpret the Scriptures about Himself to travelers on the road to Emmaus.

I believe that Jesus still wants to teach His followers about the Bible, so I've developed the habit of pausing after I open it and praying what the prophet Eli advised young Samuel to say in 1 Samuel 3:9: "Speak, LORD, for your servant is listening" (NIV). And He always speaks. —DIANNE NEAL MATTHEWS

FAITH STEP: *Each time you open your Bible say, "Speak, Lord, I'm listening."*

THURSDAY, SEPTEMBER 9

Here I am! I stand at the door and knock. If anyone hears my voice and opens the door, I will come in and eat with that person, and they with me. Revelation 3:20 (NIV)

MATTHEW 8:28–34 TELLS THE STORY of Jesus healing two demon-possessed men who were so violent that the villagers had to avoid them. Jesus granted the demons' plea to send them into a herd of pigs, and then the pigs plunged off a cliff into the lake. Someone ran to spread the news, and a crowd came to see Jesus. Luke's account adds that they saw one of the men dressed and sitting peacefully at Jesus's feet. A threat to their neighborhood had been removed and two men had been given a new chance at life, and how did the onlookers react? They begged Jesus to leave their area.

Maybe these people had a superstitious fear of Jesus's power. Perhaps they were concerned about further loss of livestock. In any case, it's sad to think about how much they missed by asking Jesus to leave them alone. It's also sad when we call ourselves His followers but don't welcome His presence and power into our daily lives. How much do we miss by focusing on our personal agenda while avoiding the One we call our Master?

In Revelation, Jesus pictured Himself knocking on the door of our heart, waiting for us to invite Him in for fellowship. Each day we make the choice either to shut Him out of our personal life or to keep the door always open by praying, reading the Word, and keeping our mind fixed on Him. When we choose the latter, He infuses our life with joy, peace, and power. —DIANNE NEAL MATTHEWS

FAITH STEP: *Have you been welcoming Jesus into your daily life or avoiding Him? Think about how you can throw the door wide open today.*

FRIDAY, SEPTEMBER 10

These things I have spoken to you, that in Me you may have peace. In the world you will have tribulation; but be of good cheer, I have overcome the world. John 16:33 (NKJV)

IT SEEMS THE NEWS HEADLINES grow more negative every day. The problems within our society and beyond are so incredibly huge that we can't even pretend to fix them.

Drug overdoses, terrorist attacks, shootings, human trafficking, and persecution of believers cause suffering and death to more than we'll ever know. And that list doesn't include those victimized by domestic violence or those struggling with homelessness, mental health issues, or chronic illnesses. The list seems endless.

I'm not trying to be a Debbie Downer. I'm just saying that mankind isn't doing so well right now. We shouldn't be shocked. Jesus guaranteed trouble when He said, "You will have tribulation." He was right—as always. Every day around the globe, people experience a measure of trouble. It's not a matter of *if* we'll encounter difficulty; it's a matter of *when*.

Now comes the good part. Jesus didn't promise tribulation and end His sentence there. He continued with "but" and promised something that infuses hope into the headlines: "I have overcome the world." Whatever tribulation we face, Jesus is bigger. Whatever pain we suffer, Jesus heals. Whatever battle we fight, Jesus wins.

The enemy wants us to wring our hands and run for cover, but he can't scam us. We belong to Jesus, and we know how the story ends. We are people of hope because we belong to Jesus. Let's reflect that hope to those around us who don't yet know Him. —GRACE FOX

FAITH STEP: *Spread hope through a kind word or deed today.*

SATURDAY, SEPTEMBER 11

The joy of the LORD is your strength. Nehemiah 8:10 (NIV)

TODAY'S VERSE IS A FAMILIAR biblical truth we cling to when we lack strength or face a tough challenge.

What intrigues me about this verse is that it was originally spoken to people who'd been drained of all kinds of strength—physical, mental, emotional, relational.

Refugees from captivity in Babylon worked feverishly, day and night, against innumerable odds, to restore the protective wall around Jerusalem, their literal and symbolic home. Without the wall, the city would remain vulnerable to future attack. Without the wall, the city could not reclaim its former glory or position of respect. The wall was the city's first defense and its symbol of safety.

The task was gargantuan. Some labeled it impossible. I'm not building a stone wall around a city, but some of the tasks I face and some of the heartbreak of those around me seems gargantuan—impossible. But we're not told that our muscles will be our strength or that our engineering degrees (or inventing the perfect answer to our children's or grandchildren's or friend's or church family's needs) will be the source of our strength. Our power to survive, to conquer, and to stand strong in the face of insurmountable odds comes from the joy of the Lord.

Joy isn't butterfly-wing thin. It's not fragile or fleeting like soap bubbles and rainbows. The joy of the Lord is equated with steel, iron, stone—it's impenetrable. With courage, we can go on, no matter how daunting the circumstances. I needed this reminder today. Did you? —CYNTHIA RUCHTI

FAITH STEP: *Some count to ten before reacting to a stressful situation. What if we adopted the practice of reciting "The joy of the Lord is my strength" when faced with depleted energies or discouraging circumstances? I'm in. Are you?*

GRANDPARENTS' DAY,
SUNDAY, SEPTEMBER 12

People brought little children to Jesus for him to place his hands on them and pray for them. But the disciples rebuked them. Jesus said, "Let the little children come to me, and do not hinder them, for the kingdom of heaven belongs to such as these." Matthew 19:13–14 (NIV)

THE NIGHT OF THE ANNUAL Sunday school program had finally arrived. Parents and grandparents sought prime seats so they could take pictures of their little people for memory's sake. Gene and I were there too—in the front row, camera in hand.

About two dozen kids filed onto the stage. Many scanned the audience, seeking a reassuring smile or nod from their personal cheerleaders. Music signaled the start, and the choir burst into song. Actors and singers performed their parts with gusto. The message of Jesus being the reason for the season came through loud and clear.

As the program concluded, a three-year-old girl dressed in a white robe and crowned with gold tinsel took her place on center stage. The director placed a mic in her hands and the toddler began to sing a birthday song to Jesus. She ended with four words: "I love you, Jesus."

From the mouth of babes, right? I'm glad I always carry tissue.

A frequent prayer for my grandchildren is: *Jesus, teach them to love You with all their heart, soul, mind, and strength.* If this first and greatest commandment is fulfilled, then everything else will fall into place. They'll make choices that honor Him, enjoy reading His Word, grow to know Him intimately, and receive His blessings.

Jesus loves the little children. May they learn to love Him in return. —GRACE FOX

FAITH STEP: *Send a fun note that says "Jesus loves you!" to a little person in your life.*

MONDAY, SEPTEMBER 13

And be kind to one another, tenderhearted, forgiving one another,
even as God in Christ forgave you. Ephesians 4:32 (NKJV)

I DASHED INTO THE GROCERY store, grabbed a bag of chocolate chips, and hurried home. I would have just enough time to bake a batch of chocolate chip cookies for my twenty-five-year-old daughter Brooke, a teacher in Houston, before my husband Jeff needed to leave for his meeting in Houston. I could visualize Brooke's face when she got a surprise visit from her dad, enhanced by that tin of her favorite cookies. *Thank You, Jesus, for the close, loving relationship Brooke has with her dad.*

That night after Jeff got home, I asked what Brooke had said about the cookies. I could tell by his crestfallen expression that something was wrong.

"I'm so sorry, Pat, but I forgot to give Brooke the cookies. Please forgive me. I knew you'd be mad." He was right about that. I *was* mad! Unkind words sprang up inside me. I wanted to remind him of how much trouble I'd gone to, how happy Brooke would have been, how disappointed I was. But then I looked into the dear face of my husband of thirty-eight years, who'd been by my side through the best and worst of times and who'd forgiven me for much worse things than forgotten cookies. There was no question in my mind what Jesus would do.

"Of course I forgive you, Jeff," I said. "They're just cookies. More for us! Now tell me about your visit with Brooke."

Jeff enveloped me in a big hug, and once again I thanked Jesus for the father of my children. —PAT BUTLER DYSON

FAITH STEP: *Have you been holding a grudge toward someone? Forgive him or her right now, on the spot. Jesus forgives you every day.*

TUESDAY, SEPTEMBER 14

---

*Then a voice came from heaven, "You are My beloved Son,
in whom I am well pleased." Mark 1:11 (NKJV)*

DID YOU KNOW THAT WE are pleasing to the Lord just the way we are? In the passage above, God the Father declared to the world that He loved His Son. It was a message about Jesus, but also *for* Jesus. Sometimes we need that, and Jesus was no exception. He had just been baptized and had not yet embarked on His life's work of preaching, teaching, and healing. He was still a ministry newbie. Yet, the Father wanted Jesus to know He was already pleased, before Jesus taught one sermon or performed one miracle. The Father was just pleased with His Son.

I struggled with this because I'm more like the biblical character Martha than Mary. I love to do, to research, to get things ready, to pull off the event with gusto. But if you're familiar with the story in Luke 10, Martha's sister Mary was the one who sat with Jesus and listened to Him. Martha was busy setting out the matching china and polishing the good forks (just my imagination). Jesus loved them both, but He commended Mary—and Martha, well, not so much. Why? Mary had sensed that Jesus wanted fellowship with her and wanted to lavish His love on her, not watch her work.

The idea that God is already pleased with me was a hard truth for me to accept. I'm always eager to work for the Lord, and I am surrounded by opportunities to serve. But I want to remain mindful not to attach my value as His child to my service. Today, I'm mindful that I'm pleasing to the Lord just because I'm His.
—PAMELA TOUSSAINT HOWARD

FAITH STEP: *Spend a few minutes laughing with the Lord today—let Him enjoy your company.*

WEDNESDAY, SEPTEMBER 15

He has delivered us from the power of darkness and conveyed us into the kingdom of the Son of His love, in whom we have redemption through His blood, the forgiveness of sins. Colossians 1:13–14 (NKJV)

ON A RECENT VISIT TO my mom's house, we were talking quietly one evening when the dogs started barking. I looked out the window and felt amazed to see how the security light illuminated so much of the yard. Quite a contrast to my childhood memories. Growing up, we didn't have a single light outside. With no other houses nearby, the nights were pitch-black except for the moon and the stars scattered across the sky. On evenings when a cow started bawling or our dog howled, my dad always went outside to look around. Meanwhile, my mom sat nervously waiting for him to come back, and I was thankful I wasn't the one who had to go out in the darkness.

As an adult, I still feel intimidated by the dark sometimes—but instead of being in the yard, this darkness tries to infiltrate my mind. Darkness comes when I don't understand what's happening around me, when the future seems so uncertain, when I face decisions that confuse me, or when circumstances tempt me to doubt the certainty of God's love and care. That's when I need to remember that Jesus has rescued me from the power of darkness. Every kind of darkness.

Once we belong to Jesus's kingdom, He illuminates our life with His forgiveness, love, and protection. We can trust Him to go out to meet any danger that threatens us and to chase any darkness away. Our Savior is better than any security light; after all, He is the Light of the world. —DIANNE NEAL MATTHEWS

FAITH STEP: *Ask Jesus to shine His light on any area of your life that seems dark and frightening to you.*

THURSDAY, SEPTEMBER 16

Surely your goodness and love will follow me all the days of my life, and I will dwell in the house of the LORD forever. Psalm 23:6 (NIV)

MY DEAR FRIEND GAYLE PASSED away recently after a tough battle with cancer. Some of the world's goodness left with her. Authentic, hilarious, and caring, she was one of my favorite people. She mentored me in college and then became an amazing elementary school teacher, beloved by both her students and coworkers. She loved her people like crazy. When I found out I was going to be teaching middle school two years ago, I called her. I was more than a little apprehensive. She encouraged me, saying, "You can do this. We will get you through it." She sent me a teacher emergency kit containing a travel toothbrush and toothpaste, deodorant, vitamin C, antacids, and a small vial of air freshener. When I had asked her about the air freshener, she told me, "Every teacher gets sick to their stomach on the first day of school. It's a given." We couldn't stop laughing.

Yesterday, I found the emergency kit. As I opened it, I began to cry. Gayle loved me in the tiniest details. I felt it in her encouragement, her thoughtfulness, and our shared joy. Goodness and love followed her wherever she went. I was blessed to be one of her people. We are blessed to be Jesus' people. His goodness and love spill out onto everyone who follows Him. His love for us is unfathomable, unending, and precise. He loves us in the tiniest details. He cares for our hearts and minds, surrounds us with hope, and lets His bright mercy intersect our daily lives. —SUSANNA FOTH AUGHTMON

FAITH STEP: *Put together a small care package for a friend who needs encouragement. Let her know that Jesus loves her and so do you . . . down to the tiniest detail.*

FRIDAY, SEPTEMBER 17

Therefore do not worry about tomorrow, for tomorrow will worry about itself. Each day has enough trouble of its own. Matthew 6:34 (NIV)

THERE ARE SOME THINGS YOU can only fully appreciate and understand when you don't have them anymore. We usually think of the good things we've lost that we took for granted. But I've been thinking about the bad things Jesus has enabled me to shed.

I recently dropped my older son off at a friend's house, and the friend's mom and I started to chat. My younger son got in the mix and begged me to stay. Fifteen minutes turned into two hours, leisurely chatting at the poolside on a beautifully balmy Florida evening. Laundry and deadlines were delayed to another day. On a weightier note, I was awaiting a final step in a long legal process and haven't heard from my lawyer in a few days. I hadn't felt compelled to follow up and was perfectly peaceful waiting. One day or one moment, at a time, resting in Jesus. Just being present.

"So what?" you may ask. I used to be downright incapable of spontaneous leisure or letting matters unfold naturally. On this side of faith-filled rest, I feel sad about the many years I spent fretting, questioning, and twirling inside and out. I see how my anxious ways hurt me and others. Though I must concede, those anxious years are exactly what drove me closer and closer to Jesus and what compelled me finally to submit to His easy yoke.

I can't undo the past, but I can enjoy the rewards of finally trusting that God has all well in hand. Day by day, I can enjoy the abundant and peace-filled life Jesus promised from the very start.
—ISABELLA YOSUICO

FAITH STEP: *Next time you feel anxiously compelled to act or have a chance to have some spontaneous fun, try the way of faith over fear, and simply do it.*

SATURDAY, SEPTEMBER 18

Do you not remember the five loaves for the five thousand, and how many baskets you gathered? Matthew 16:9 (ESV)

MY FRIEND WENDY AND I met at a trailhead near my home for a quick hike. When she got out of her car, she said, "Can I put my keys in your car so I don't have to carry them?"

"Sure," I replied. "That's a good idea. I'll put mine in your car."

We locked our cars, and went on our hike. When we got back to our cars, I had a sinking feeling as I realized what we had done. Neither of us could open our car doors because our keys were safely locked inside each other's vehicles.

If Jesus ever rolled His eyes at His followers, I imagined He would have rolled His eyes at our ridiculous situation. Just as I imagine He might have had to refrain Himself from chuckling at His disciples sometimes, such as the time when they crossed the lake, just after witnessing Jesus miraculously feed thousands of people bread and fish—twice. When they arrived on the other side, Jesus warned them not to follow the teaching of the Sadducees and Pharisees, using the leaven in bread as an example. Once He mentioned bread all they could think about was how they forgot to bring any and fret over this mistake (Matthew 16:5–12). It seems ridiculous that they would forget what Jesus can do, especially after seeing Him perform those miracles and gathering baskets full of leftovers.

We are similar to the disciples and forget what Jesus has done, just as easily as we can forgetfully lock our keys in our cars. The Bible frequently reminds us to remember His miracles to boost our faith. Thankfully we serve a God who has a sense of humor. —JEANNIE BLACKMER

FAITH STEP: *Write down a miracle you remember Jesus did in your life. Next time you have a forgetful moment, read your note.*

SUNDAY, SEPTEMBER 19

*No one puts new wine into old wineskins; otherwise the
[fermenting] wine will [expand and] burst the skins, and
the wine is lost as well as the wineskins. But new wine
must be put into new wineskins. Mark 2:22 (AMP)*

I HAVE ALWAYS WONDERED WHAT Jesus meant when He said this.
And I still don't know for sure. But I think it has something to do
with becoming. In *The Velveteen Rabbit*, the rabbit asks the Skin
Horse how to be real. He answers, "You become." He goes on to
explain the transformation process by which everything changes:
your hair gets loved off, your eyes drop out, and on the whole you
look shabbier. When you become, you're not the same as you were.

My own process of becoming has been painful at times. But when
God makes something new out of us, many times we don't fit in our
old lives anymore. Whether we're aging our rough edges away like
the rabbit, or becoming something more beautiful like a caterpillar
transforms into a butterfly, the point is we're becoming different—
new wine. And we don't fit in our old wineskins.

What this looks like may be different from person to person.
Sometimes it means we have to find a new job, home, or church.
Sometimes friends and neighbors change. Sometimes it's just an
idea that doesn't fit anymore, like that shirt you loved but grew out
of. Your favorite jeans that got too tight. It's hard and scary to leave
behind old wineskins. But we must when they cannot contain us
anymore. —GWEN FORD FAULKENBERRY

FAITH STEP: *Is there a person, place, thing, or idea you've outgrown? Something
you need to leave behind in order to move into greater joy? Clean out your closet
or desk or a drawer and get rid of that clutter. Let the action galvanize you to
clean out the spiritual clutter too.*

MONDAY, SEPTEMBER 20

When they saw him, they worshiped him; but some doubted.
Matthew 28:17 (NIV)

TODAY'S KEY VERSE HAS OFTEN baffled me. How could the disciples both worship Jesus and doubt Him at the same time? I decided to research its meaning, and what I found surprised me.

In the original Greek language, the word used for "doubted" is *distazo*. It implies hesitation or uncertainty about how to respond. It's not to be confused with unbelief. In this context, eleven disciples met with Jesus shortly before His ascension. They worshiped Him as the risen Savior, but they doubted—they were unsure of how to respond to Him. Should they bow on their faces? Should they throw their arms around His neck and give Him giant hugs? Should they engage in dialogue or remain silent in His presence?

Understanding the meaning of this verse has helped me. I try to be intentional about daily living, but occasionally I doubt too. Sometimes I'm unsure about how to respond when my prayers aren't answered as quickly as I wish. Should I keep asking or reword my requests and try again? Am I missing the mark completely? Is there something I should know or change before pursuing this prayer request any longer?

I once thought that worship and doubt could not abide in the same heart. Now I understand that doubt—*distazo*—is part of our faith journey. Let's be honest with Jesus when we're uncertain about how to respond to Him. He knows our hearts anyway—we can't hide from Him. Honesty with Him deepens intimacy with Him.
—GRACE FOX

FAITH STEP: *Is there something you don't understand? Tell Jesus.*

TUESDAY, SEPTEMBER 21

Can a mother forget the baby at her breast and have no compassion on the child she has borne? Though she may forget, I will not forget you! See, I have engraved you on the palms of my hands...
Isaiah 49:15–16 (NIV)

SEVERAL YEARS AGO, WHEN A loan officer called me "Jennifer," I smiled and gently corrected her. But when she said Jennifer was the name she had in her head for me and that's what she was going to call me, I was a little annoyed. On the way home, I reminded my husband what the famous motivational speaker Dale Carnegie had said, "A person's name is the sweetest and most important sound to them."

During my elementary school years, Mom taught me fun tricks for recalling names, tricks I've used for fifty years. As a pastor's wife and public speaker, I used to feel smug about my ability to remember names. Then something happened.

The older I got, the harder it was to make Mom's tricks work. I found myself too often saying, "I apologize that I forgot your name." And when I answered the phone at work during a stressful day and forgot my own name, I laughed till I cried. My only comfort is that I know the One who always remembers.

The moment we surrender our hearts to Jesus, He writes our name in His Book of Life. We belong to Him. He can't forget us. Out of millions of Marys, Jesus has memorized all that makes us unique. He knows if we love pecans or chocolate. He knows the wounds of our souls. He doesn't need Mom's tricks to remember who we are. His love makes Him remember. —JEANETTE LEVELLIE

FAITH STEP: *Ask Jesus to tell you how your name reflects His deep love for you.*

WEDNESDAY, SEPTEMBER 22

I pray that the eyes of your heart may be enlightened in order that you may know the hope to which he has called you, the riches of his glorious inheritance in his holy people, and his incomparably great power for us who believe. That power is the same as the mighty strength he exerted when he raised Christ from the dead and seated him at his right hand in the heavenly realms. Ephesians 1:18–20 (NIV)

TO SAVE A LITTLE ON our car insurance, my husband and I signed up for an online driver's safety course. Some parts were a good review. Other parts were tedious. One message was repeated several times: "As you age, you are more frail and more likely to die in a car accident." Frail? My husband and I bristled at the description. First of all, we don't think of ourselves as old. Second, we don't see ourselves as weak. But whatever our age, our bodies do grow weak eventually. In small and large ways, we are forced to acknowledge our mortality.

That's why I'm grateful for these verses in Ephesians. Because of Jesus, we will one day rise in glory. Not only that, but He lives in us right now. In the day to day of our lives, His resurrection power is at work in us. He empowers, enlightens, and renews our hope. That is a whole lot of mighty strength! Our bodies may become frail, but it doesn't hinder His will and His work. In fact, Jesus told the apostle Paul, "My power is made perfect in weakness" (2 Corinthians 12:9, ESV).

If we feel daunted by the tasks ahead of us today, let's ask Jesus to help us see His power at work. —SHARON HINCK

FAITH STEP: *Take a deep breath. Invite Jesus to live through you and bring His love to others while you still have breath in your body.*

THURSDAY, SEPTEMBER 23

Be joyful in hope, patient in affliction, faithful in prayer.
Romans 12:12 (NIV)

HOPE: HAVE ONLY POSITIVE EXPECTATIONS. Something inside me bucks up against this maxim. After all, not every story has a happy ending. Or does it? I can easily think of several lasting benefits that have come from some of the hardest things in my life. More than making lemonade out of lemons, certain "afflictions" have produced results I now enjoy every day.

My childhood was very broken—mentally ill and alcoholic parents, painful isolation from our family in Italy, both fleeting wealth and poverty, and the tragic death of a brother, among other things. But brought to Him, Jesus has used every smidgen of it to deepen my dependence on Him, increasing my faith, patience, and joy manifold. Verses such as James 1:2–8 repeats this theme of "count it all joy" (v. 2, ESV) when we face hardship.

I've also experienced peace and joy that aren't attached to circumstances. Plus, I get the added perk of sharing that with others facing "trials of various kinds" (v. 2, ESV).

This kind of hope, transcendant HOPE is the result of counting on Someone loving and all-powerful, the One able to make the sweetest lemonade out of the sourest lemons. Beyond the fruit (pardon the Galatians 5:22–23 pun) I can have here on earth, I have the assurance that my "momentary troubles" will ultimately give way to an eternal glory I can't fathom (2 Corinthians 4:17–18). My true hope is heaven. —ISABELLA YOSUICO

FAITH STEP: *Allow yourself to imagine heaven and its healing.*

FRIDAY, SEPTEMBER 24

Finally, be strong in the Lord and in his mighty power. Ephesians 6:10 *(NIV)*

THE WEEK HAS BEEN INTENSE. I've spent thirty-six hours in a hospital waiting room as my youngest daughter, Kim, labored to deliver her first child. The baby came during the same week that she and her husband had planned to move into a different apartment, so Gene and I immediately shifted our focus from welcoming our new granddaughter to unpacking boxes and bringing order to their place before the hospital discharged them.

Then came the five-hour drive home through the mountains—in separate cars. Darkness fell as we stopped at a gas station on the outskirts of the city. "Buy something to eat to keep yourself awake," Gene said. Snack options included chocolate bars, candy, salted peanuts, and potato chips. The latter are my favorite, so choosing was easy. As I deliberated about what flavor to buy, a thought came to mind: *On what are you relying for strength to drive home—potato chips or Jesus?*

The answer convicted me, but I bought two bags anyway. I'll admit not feeling proud about my decision, but the experience gave me a spiritual "aha" moment.

For years I'd believed the lie that junk food could fuel me with energy when my body felt taxed. That night Jesus challenged me to think differently. Eating these foods in moderation was not sin, but loving them more than Him and trusting their power over His to strengthen me was akin to making them an idol.

I still enjoy chips, but I no longer rely on them for energy. Jesus is my go-to. When I'm weary, He's just a prayer away.
—GRACE FOX

FAITH STEP: *Do you turn to food for solace when you're tired or stressed? If so, ask Jesus to help you turn to Him instead.*

SATURDAY, SEPTEMBER 25

Consider it pure joy, my brothers and sisters, whenever you face trials of many kinds. James 1:2 (NIV)

THE NEWS COULDN'T HAVE BEEN worse: our flight from Nashville to Houston had been canceled due to weather. In fact, *all* flights had been scrapped until the following morning. My heart sank. I wanted to go home.

Four days before, I'd flown with my husband, Jeff, to Nashville for a fun-filled retreat for board members and their spouses. Four days was over my limit for time away from home. I had two grand-babies due in the near future, and I missed my cat.

Larry, Beverly, and Linda had traveled with us, so we were all stuck. Larry had a doctor's appointment the next day. Jeff had a college class to teach. When someone mentioned renting a car and driving home, I said, "Let's do it!" We rented a Suburban around noon and set off with Jeff driving. We were facing a twelve-and-a-half-hour drive if conditions were perfect. Radar showed we were heading into storms. I beseeched Jesus to get us home safely.

For the first six hours, cheer reigned with the passengers, but morale plummeted as darkness fell. We ran out of snacks. Conversation ceased. Slipping down the dark hole of despair, I forced myself to thank Jesus for having the means to rent a car, for the good driver who was getting us home, for the soft bed I'd be crawling into. Heavy rains and strong winds forced Jeff to slow to a crawl. I was praying nonstop by then, and I think everyone in the car was doing the same. When we finally emerged from the bad weather, Larry said, "Thank you, Jesus!" Hungry, tired, and cramped as we were, joy filled the car. —PAT BUTLER DYSON

FAITH STEP: *Ask Jesus to remind you that even in the worst of times, you still have Him. And that fact brings joy!*

SUNDAY, SEPTEMBER 26

When he drew near and saw the city, he wept over it, saying, "Would that you, even you, had known on this day the things that make for peace! But now they are hidden from your eyes." Luke 19:41–42 (ESV)

THIS PRECIOUS GLIMPSE OF JESUS'S heartfelt cry is an important example for me. He longs for people to know Him and accept His salvation, and He hurts for those He loves who are blind to His grace. His tears give me permission to let my own tears flow. I have family members and friends who are not walking with Him, and sometimes it hurts even to pray for them. There is so much potential for a life in service to Jesus—so much joy in living in relationship with Him. He longs for us to be in fellowship with Him, and I long for that for each of my family and friends.

There are times I stop praying for a while because I'm discouraged and because when I pray from my heart, the yearning hurts and brings me to tears. But Jesus didn't hold back from compassion. He gave vent to His fierce longing for the best for His people.

I'm using these verses in Luke 19 to give me new courage in my prayers. Because Jesus is praying with me. Even those who ignored Him in Jerusalem were the focus of His love. And my dear ones are also the focus of His love—and His action on their behalf. He is not giving up, and neither will I.

As I pray, and sometimes weep, I'll also watch in faith for the ways He will work in the souls of those I love and pray for.
—SHARON HINCK

FAITH STEP: *Do you have a family member or loved one who doesn't know the truth? Pray with bold faith today, knowing Jesus is at work.*

MONDAY, SEPTEMBER 27

Oh, the depth of the riches of the wisdom and knowledge of God!
How unsearchable his judgments, and his paths beyond
tracing out! Romans 11:33 (NIV)

MY PARENTS BOTH HAD DOCTORATES. I attribute several personal strengths and weaknesses to my deep academic legacy. Two of my personal favorites (*not*) are analysis paralysis and needing to know why—both perils of my hyperanalytical mind. It's not so bad when I'm trying to evaluate cell-phone carriers but pretty futile and foolish when trying to understand God's ways.

Before and after placing my faith in Jesus, I've wasted a lot of time analyzing situations, reviewing "data"—in my head and in conversation with others—weighing pros and cons, reading, journaling and stressing about information as though the fate of humanity rested on my perfect understanding.

I've speculated endlessly. Why was I saddled with so many childhood challenges? Why was my son Isaac born with Down syndrome? Why didn't that relationship or job work out?

Thanks to Jesus's continued work in me (Philippians 1:6), I no longer need to exhaust myself with supporting data to make a decision or to know why. I still seek to understand and still have questions, but in Christ, I know the One who has all the answers. Now I rest, trusting that He'll reveal them to me at the right time.
—ISABELLA YOSUICO

FAITH STEP: *Take one persistent question and ask Jesus for the grace to surrender the "why" to Him!*

TUESDAY, SEPTEMBER 28

Then Jesus said, "Let's go off by ourselves to a quiet place and rest awhile." Mark 6:31 (NLT)

YEARS AGO, MY HUSBAND HAD a job assignment in northern Minnesota. When I flew out to see him, we decided to visit a nearby wolf sanctuary. Richard had a phone call on the way, so he pulled off the tree-lined highway and stepped out of the car to get a better signal. I got out to stretch my legs and strolled toward a separate stand of trees up a slight incline. Just ahead I spotted a small clearing, lit by slanting rays of sunlight. It drew me like a magnet and soon I found myself standing in an open space surrounded by tall trees. I stood, looking up as though mesmerized, vaguely aware of the muffled sounds of cars passing down the highway—yet at the same time enveloped in the quietness of the woods.

I've never forgotten that moment that seemed almost magical. It reminds me of how God has designed us with a built-in need to commune with Him. We live in a noisy, hectic world. Even Jesus needed time away for rest and renewal. It isn't always easy to find that "quiet place," especially for parents. Even if we live alone, it can be hard to get away from the noisiness and chaos in our mind.

I find it easy to connect with God through His creation, but right now, I live in a city subdivision. So I have created a quiet place in my home for my prayer time. I sit in a certain spot with my Bible, journal, and favorite pen. Nearby is a scented candle that I find soothing. These are "spiritual magnets" that draw me in to a place where I can find rest in Jesus. —DIANNE NEAL MATTHEWS

FAITH STEP: *If you don't have a consistent routine for quiet time, ask Jesus to help you prepare a special place with spiritual magnets of your own.*

WEDNESDAY, SEPTEMBER 29

Yes, there's a right time and way for everything, even though, unfortunately, we miss it for the most part. Ecclesiastes 8:6 (MSG)

TODAY'S SCRIPTURE VERSE FROM THE Message translation really captures how easily we can do things outside of God's timing. It can be the right thing—directed by God—but done at the wrong time. A ministry friend dabbled in the stock market for a while and was successful in doubling the value of his portfolio. He wasn't a broker and didn't have a degree in finance. He simply asked the Holy Spirit which stocks to buy and when. There were times he wanted to buy, but the Lord said "sell" or "wait." As he followed God's leading and resisted his own natural instincts, his stocks prospered. But as he grew in his own understanding of market trends and analytics, he got away from relying on the Spirit's timing and began buying and selling without counsel. Of course, the portfolio tanked. Timing is crucial.

For many years, I was an avid league tennis player. Being successful in tennis is hugely dependent on correct timing when you hit the ball. I learned from watching career champions like Venus and Serena Williams, and Maria Sharapova how important it is to swing your racquet back early so you are prepared to hit the ball accurately. Often the Lord will have us wait on something so we can be prepared to hit a home run (I know, mixed sports metaphors, but you get it). On several occasions, Jesus told His mother, Mary, and the disciples that His time had not yet come (John 2:4; 7:6, 8). He knew timing was key to success in His assignment.
—PAMELA TOUSSAINT HOWARD

FAITH STEP: *Ask the Lord, When should I pursue _____? Fill in the blank and listen for a response.*

THURSDAY, SEPTEMBER 30

I remain confident of this: I will see the goodness of the LORD in the land of the living. Psalm 27:13 (NIV)

DO YOU EVER FEEL OVERWHELMED with bad news? In the last few years, I've had tough circumstances touch my life. A good friend got breast cancer, my husband had hip-replacement surgery, one of my sons had his heart broken, and several friends shared with me their children's addiction struggles. My spirit was heavy.

Then I read Psalm 27:13. David's confident words of faith, "I will see the goodness of the LORD in the land of the living," sparked hope in me. David was fleeing his enemies when he wrote those words. As Jesus faced betrayal, rejection, and crucifixion, His faith in what was about to happen strengthened His resolve, for He is the One "who for the joy that was set before Him endured the cross, despising the shame, and has sat down at the right hand of the throne of God" (Hebrews 12:2, NKJV). With Jesus's hopeful perspective, we're able to see goodness in the midst of discouraging circumstances. I needed a hopeful outlook so my joy wouldn't be swallowed up by despair.

I started repeating this verse to myself and began looking for the goodness of the Lord, in the here and now. When I saw a tragic news story, I looked for goodness and focused on those brave people running to help others. Concerning my husband, son, and friends, I watched the Lord tenderly touch each of their lives in their challenges and restore their hope.

Now, I look for the goodness of Jesus, and I see it.
—JEANNIE BLACKMER

FAITH STEP: *Start a joy journal and log God's goodness daily.*

FRIDAY, OCTOBER 1

The centurion replied, "Lord, I do not deserve to have you come under my roof. But just say the word, and my servant will be healed. . . ." When Jesus heard this, he was amazed and said to those following him, "Truly I tell you, I have not found anyone in Israel with such great faith." Matthew 8:8, 10 (NIV)

I'M CONSTANTLY A CHILD AT heart and easily amazed. Whether it's a friend's generosity, roses exploding in bloom, or the smile in my husband's eyes, I get caught up in the grandness of life. The same happened with the disciples as they watched Jesus's miracles and ministry.

Not so with Jesus. Since He can do anything and created everything, he isn't so easily amazed. According to the Bible, it only happened a few times. Jesus was amazed once by the centurion's faith in a sight-unseen healing (Matthew 8:5–10, Luke 7:1–10) and once by his family and townsfolk's lack of faith (Mark 6:6). I desire to amaze Jesus with my devotion, not the lack of it.

This week, I've been put to the test. A medical diagnosis frightened me, shaking my world. Questions that had no business in my thoughts circled like vultures. Will I be okay? How does this story end? As a believer, I'm to think on things that are true, noble, right, pure, lovely, admirable, excellent and praiseworthy (Philippians 4:8). Nowhere does it say to live in terror or forget the Savior's love for us.

I might not have a choice about my health. But He does.

I want to have faith like the centurion, believing that if Jesus deems me healed, I am. I need to trust that whatever His decision, it's best, because He doesn't—can't—make mistakes. Beyond that, there's a simpler reason. I need to always be amazed, especially by Him. —HEIDI GAUL

FAITH STEP: *What have you hoped for but not dared to pray for? Amaze Jesus with your faith. Let Him amaze you.*

SATURDAY, OCTOBER 2

*May the God of hope fill you with all joy and peace as you trust
in him, so that you may overflow with hope by the power
of the Holy Spirit. Romans 15:13 (NIV)*

MY FRIEND RITA WAS CONCERNED about her upcoming mammogram. With a family history of breast cancer and having endured multiple biopsies, Rita wondered when her number would be up. This time it was. *Infiltrating lobular carcinoma,* she texted me. *Stan and the kids are wrecks, but I'm okay.*

I was with Stan and the kids! I panicked about the dire diagnosis for my dearest childhood friend. But through every step of the long process, Rita remained optimistic. The cancer was determined to be Stage 1 and surgery revealed it was not in her lymph nodes. *Good news!* The pathology report revealed some cancer had spread to the margins, but it was easily removed. *Piece of cake.* No chemo would be necessary. *Hooray!* Only four weeks of radiation, five times a week. *And the day I finish radiation, my kids and grandkids from Boston will be here for their summer visit. I'm so happy,* Rita texted me.

Happy in the face of all she'd been through? How did Rita do it? She told me that her faith in Jesus and His steadfast love got her through. She rejected negative thoughts. She trusted that whatever happened, Jesus would help her handle it. And she just refused to worry.

Refuse to worry? That was an alien concept to me. But Rita reminded me that worry did nothing to change the final results. *I choose joy,* she told me. *Try it, Pat!* What an example for me to follow. And with Jesus's help, I'll do just that! —PAT BUTLER DYSON

FAITH STEP: *Start each day thinking of one thing that gives you joy. No matter what the day brings, remind yourself of that one joyful thing.*

SUNDAY, OCTOBER 3

The Spirit of the Lord is on Me, because He has anointed Me to preach good news to the poor. He has sent Me to proclaim freedom to the captives and recovery of sight to the blind, to set free the oppressed. Luke 4:18 (HCSB)

WE SING A SONG IN church that combines the old hymn "Amazing Grace" with the chorus "My chains are gone." From the piano, I look out at the people singing, who are caught up in a moment of gratitude because at some point they heard the good news, stepped from darkness into light, and began to see. We enjoy the freedom Jesus came to proclaim. The question that haunts me sometimes is whether we adequately follow Jesus as liberators.

We Christians don't perceive ourselves as oppressors. But the truth is that we all have the capacity to be liberators or oppressors, and how we perceive ourselves is not always how others see us. When life becomes a checklist of things we do because it's expected, we're actually oppressing ourselves. And when we take on the role of moral police, we begin to lock people up in—or out of—our communities of faith.

Maybe instead of wearing bracelets that say "WWJD?" we need ones that say "WWJND?"—what would Jesus *not* do? That seems equally important. We never see Him cast the first stone or shy away from sinners. We never see Him require someone to change before they could be loved. Jesus seemed to recognize that giving people access to Him was what eventually brought about change. By listening to people, feeding them, letting them touch Him, and touching them back, He was acting as a liberator and leading them into the freedom of His love. —GWEN FORD FAULKENBERRY

FAITH STEP: *Take some time to examine the way you treat people outside of your belief system. Do you have the heart of a liberator? If not, ask Jesus to give you one.*

MONDAY, OCTOBER 4

*An angel from the Lord spoke to Philip, "At noon, take the road that leads
from Jerusalem to Gaza."... Meanwhile, an Ethiopian man was on his way
home from Jerusalem, where he had come to worship.... The Spirit told
Philip, "Approach this carriage and stay with it." Acts 8:26–27, 29 (CEB)*

PEOPLE OFTEN SAY HOW WONDERFUL it is to be self-employed
because you're your own boss. Personally, I find being a self-
employed writer difficult because—I'm my own boss. Besides all
the hours I spend on writing, marketing, business correspondence,
education, and record-keeping, I also put in a lot of time wondering
what I should be doing. My mind flits between projects and ideas,
unsure of which one to pursue. Sometimes I'm overwhelmed by
the staggering number of available opportunities and resources. I
often wish God would put Post-It notes on my computer each day,
outlining how I should arrange my schedule.

Maybe that's why I love passages in the Bible when a person receives
specific instructions. As the early apostles worked to spread the good
news about Jesus, God directed Philip to take the road toward Gaza.
Philip's obedience led him to the right place and the right person at
just the right time. The eunuch was reading a passage of Scripture,
and once Philip explained its meaning, the man became a Christ
follower. He joyfully returned home, carrying the gospel with him.

We may or may not receive specific instructions regarding life decisions, but Jesus does tell us which direction to go. When He called His
first disciples, He told them, "Follow me" (John 1:43, NIV). As long as
we're doing our best to follow His will, we'll always find ourselves in
the right place at the right time. —DIANNE NEAL MATTHEWS

FAITH STEP: *Are you struggling to discern which direction to go in about a decision?
Ask Jesus to guide you in His will, then renew your commitment to follow Him.*

TUESDAY, OCTOBER 5

The fruit of the Spirit is love, joy, peace, patience, kindness, goodness, faithfulness, gentleness, self-control . . . Galatians 5:22–23 (ESV)

I HAVE NO SELF-CONTROL WHEN it comes to Nutella. The hazelnut-chocolate spread is so delicious that I can't take just one bite. When I have too much, I feel awful. Isn't that always the result of no self-control?

Thankfully, with the indwelling Holy Spirit, Paul says that we can possess the fruit of the Spirit—all those qualities that are essential in the life of Christians, including self-control. As I read this Scripture, I was struck with how these virtues are enmeshed. Paul uses the singular word *fruit*, not the plural word *fruits*. Together, these character traits are like an orange: composed of different sections, sweet and delicious on their own but fused under one thick skin.

Jesus is the perfect example to us of bearing all the fruit. For example, Jesus practiced self-control when Judas betrayed Him and He was arrested. Jesus showed love, goodness, and kindness countless times when He healed the sick. Jesus's example is aspirational because we have the same Spirit in us.

When we cooperate with God's Spirit in one of these areas, all the fruit of the Spirit is more evident in our lives. When I'm more self-controlled, I'm more loving, more peaceful, and more joyful because they are all cohesive. Each fruit is crucial, but I want to take ahold of the whole orange and live the most fruitful life possible.
—JEANNIE BLACKMER

FAITH STEP: *Which fruit of the Spirit is most evident in your life? Which fruit of the Spirit would you like to experience more? Watch for opportunities today to experience the fruit of the Holy Spirit.*

WEDNESDAY, OCTOBER 6

When the priests withdrew from the Holy Place, the cloud filled the temple of the LORD. And the priests could not perform their service because of the cloud, for the glory of the LORD filled his temple. 1 Kings 8:10–11 (NIV)

HAVE YOU EXPERIENCED A MOMENT when God's presence was so tangible, so strong, and so sweet that your heart nearly burst with gratitude and joy? That's how I imagine the priests felt when the Lord's glory filled the temple. I experienced a wee taste of it while spending time with Lexi, my one-month-old granddaughter.

Lexi's dad had to be away for a week, so I'd asked my daughter Kim if she wanted me to stay with her during that time. Her yes delighted me. I planned to help by cooking meals and doing house-work, and I hoped to enjoy lots of snuggle time with Lexi.

Reality exceeded my expectations. Every morning around 6:00 AM, Kim handed the newborn to me and returned to bed until Lexi's next meal. I basked in the solitude and silence of those hours, cradling the baby close to my heart. I rocked her, prayed over her, and told her of Jesus's love for her.

Jesus's presence filled the room and inhabited every nook and corner. I sensed His smile and songs of delight. Just as I wrapped Lexi in a soft swaddling blanket, so He wraps me—us—in His love. Every morning in that place, a picture of Jesus holding a child close to His heart came to my mind. I knew that child was me.

Friday arrived too soon and I had to return home. My morning snuggles with Lexi sadly came to an end, but the memories of those moments spent cradling her and being cradled by Jesus will remain in my heart forever. —GRACE FOX

FAITH STEP: *Look up the lyrics to "Jesus Loves Me." Sing them to yourself, believing every word.*

THURSDAY, OCTOBER 7

For this people's heart has grown dull, and with their ears they can barely hear, and their eyes they have closed, lest they should see with their eyes and hear with their ears and understand with their heart and turn, and I would heal them. Matthew 13:15 (ESV)

LAST YEAR DURING AN EYE exam, the doctor shined a searing bright light into my dilated pupils, which caused sharp pain. This time she used the same light, but I didn't feel anything. You'd think that was a good thing, yet it was actually a clue of bad news. The cataracts that were developing had worsened. They don't need surgery yet, but my vision is getting cloudier. My eyes didn't react to the brilliant light the way they should.

I also struggle with something I call "spiritual cataracts." God's glory shines in our world every day. His power is revealed in nature. His grace is unveiled in Scripture. His love is manifest through the church universal. Yet my sinful nature sometimes clouds my ability to see Him at work. My eyes are dimmed by the cares of the world. Doubts and fears blur my vision.

Like cataracts, this dullness can develop gradually. As my time in the Word slips away, my mind fills with the lies of the world instead of the truth of my Savior. I neglect worship and fellowship and begin to feel alone. I slide into habits of complaining instead of praise, and suddenly, my soul is in shadows. Little by little, the world looks darker.

Jesus healed the blind physically while He walked on earth. He also offers healing from spiritual blindness to all of us. Jesus restores our vision so we can see the light of God with more vibrancy.
—SHARON HINCK

FAITH STEP: *Ask Jesus to open the eyes of your heart to better see the glory of God's grace.*

FRIDAY, OCTOBER 8

Judge not, and you shall not be judged. Condemn not, and you shall not be condemned. Forgive, and you will be forgiven. Luke 6:37 (NKJV)

As I WALKED INTO THE crowded restaurant, I spotted the friends I was meeting, who were already seated at a table. The path was blocked by a large party that was surrounding the hostess stand. In order to slip through, I lightly tapped the shoulder of a woman in an orange dress, excusing myself as I did. Imagine my shock when the woman shrieked, "Don't touch me! How dare you touch me!" Everyone in line and in most of the restaurant stopped what they were doing and stared. Mortified, I apologized profusely to the glaring woman and slunk over to the table to join my friends.

Embarrassed and shaken, I noted where the woman and her party were sitting. I briefly considered going over there and confronting the woman in the orange dress, demanding, "How dare you yell at me?" Then I stopped myself. I wondered, *What would Jesus do?* Not that.

My friends speculated that the woman either had emotional problems or was having an exceedingly bad day. My friend Janie suggested we all pray for her. I had calmed down by then and agreed with Janie's idea. Whatever had caused the woman to strike out at a stranger was the symptom of a bigger problem. What I needed to feel for her was compassion rather than contempt. Later in my car on the way home, I prayed again and asked Jesus to help the woman in the orange dress and to forgive me for judging one of His kids.
—PAT BUTLER DYSON

FAITH STEP: *Ask Jesus to help you feel what it would be like to walk in another's shoes. Try on someone else's shoes. What does it feel like? Now imagine walking in another's shoes spiritually.*

SATURDAY, OCTOBER 9

As the heavens are higher than the earth, so are my ways higher than your ways and my thoughts higher than your thoughts. Isaiah 55:9 (NIV)

"I'M SORRY I SCHEDULED THIS book signing, Beth. I guess people don't come to a library to spend money." After two hours, my coauthor and I had sold only three books. We'd set a goal of selling ten books that night and asked God to help us reach our goal. Was it even worth all the time spent, not to mention the goody basket we'd given away?

Beth reassured me she'd had fun during our evening at the library. The librarian had stationed us directly outside the children's room—the perfect spot. Beth and I relived childhood memories of exciting trips to the library when we'd loaded our little arms with as many books as we could carry. We met a fascinating gentleman who stood at our table for over an hour, delighting us with stories about his various careers. And best of all, the three people who bought our books had a chance to discover Jesus's love in a deeper way. The book signing wasn't a waste at all—just a different result than we'd planned.

We plan and set goals—for our ministries, our careers, our families, and our retirement. There's nothing wrong with our desire for success. Studies show that people who write their objectives down earn more money than those who keep goals only in their minds. And there's nothing wrong with earning money either.

However, Jesus has higher thoughts and better plans. He sees the big picture of our lives. He knows what we need (and those we touch) better than we do. Our goals may help us succeed in this life, but Jesus's plans prepare us for eternity. —JEANETTE LEVELLIE

FAITH STEP: *Write down three goals for your day or your life. Invite Jesus to enlarge them.*

SUNDAY, OCTOBER 10

Christ in you, the hope of glory. Colossians 1:27 (NKJV)

I HAD LUNCH THIS WEEK with a young woman who is battling anxiety issues that appeared and intensified when she disappeared from church. I imagined myself as an ambassador tasked by Jesus to love the young woman and listen as He would have—as He still does.

It seems every decision she's making these days takes her farther and farther from what Jesus would want for her. It's heartbreaking, but His love won't walk away from her. Neither will mine.

During the meal, she said something that startled me but also drove me to my internal knees in prayer. She said, "I wish I were like you." Though she didn't say it, I think what she meant was that she wished she could have what I have—a soul at peace, a safe place to dispose of my guilt (on Jesus's shoulders), joy that doesn't get rattled by circumstances, freedom from fear, confidence that I am held by One who loves, cares, protects, and provides. She wishes she could have—in a word—Jesus.

And she can. He wants the same for her too. His arms are laden with an abundant supply of all she lacks, and He can't wait to shower them on her. What she saw in me that day that she longed for wasn't *me*. It was Him.

My prayer is that she starts to see Jesus and stops resisting that truth. I'll be here, praying for her, listening to her, and letting her know that what she seeks is hers for the asking. —CYNTHIA RUCHTI

FAITH STEP: *Who first talked to you about Jesus? Find a way today to say thank you to the person who introduced you to the source of joy and hope.*

MONDAY, OCTOBER 11

---

*He said to them, "Whatever house you go into, stay there until you leave
that town. Whoever does not take you in or listen to you, when you
leave there, shake the dust off your feet . . ." Mark 6:10–11 (NLV)*

I WAS BLESSED TO HAVE great parents who taught me the important
principle of not quitting. Mom and Dad talked about it, I'm sure;
but I remember their example most. I never saw either of them
quit a job. They never quit taking care of my brother and me. They
never quit on each other. They're just not quitters—and neither am
I. It's a value I hope I've also instilled in my children.

In my adult life, though, I've learned that sometimes quitting
has its place. And I believe Jesus taught that concept when He sent
out the twelve. When He gave them instructions about where to
stay, it's with the assumption there would be a time to leave. They
weren't obligated to stay anywhere forever. And if they encountered
strong resistance or were rejected, He advised them, "Shake the dust
off your feet."

Vince Lombardi, said "Winners never quit." He got the idea
from Winston Churchill, who said, "Never, never, never give in!"
Until recently, I didn't know what Churchill added, ". . . . except to
conditions of honor and good sense." It's a caveat we'd do well to
remember. Perhaps there is third option to consider. Rather than the
false dichotomy of being a winner or a quitter, one might actually be
both. Wisdom is often like that—somewhere in the messy middle,
where we must listen to His voice. —GWEN FORD FAULKENBERRY

FAITH STEP: *Take a look at your life. Are there things that have dried up? Are
there literal locations, relationships, or places of the heart you need to leave? Do
you have habits—whether considered good or bad—you need to quit? Formulate
your exit plan.*

TUESDAY, OCTOBER 12

In their hearts humans plan their course, but the LORD establishes their steps. Proverbs 16:9 (NIV)

MY LONGTIME FRIEND BEV, WITH whom I'd recently reconnected, called to let me know her husband, Wiley, had died and asked me to attend his funeral in Houston. I promised I'd be there.

Driving two hours to Houston was grueling. Houston drivers were aggressive. If you missed your exit, you were toast. With those things in mind, I programmed my trusty GPS with the church's address and hit the road early, asking Jesus's blessing for a safe trip. I was feeling confident as I rolled along at the speed limit—no construction, no wrecks, and almost thirty minutes ahead of schedule.

Then I got jammed up. The exit my GPS told me to take was blocked, due to construction. I took the next exit, and tried to get back where I was supposed to be, but my GPS seemed as confused as I was. *Recalculating, recalculating.* I kept driving, searching for a landmark. Found it! The same blocked exit. I'd been driving in circles.

My thirty-minute cushion disappeared and the start-time for the funeral loomed ever closer. I was desperate and hopelessly lost. I considered heading home, but I'd made a promise. *Lord, help!*

I rushed into a Whataburger and asked a woman in line if she could direct me to the Katy Freeway. "Honey, you're just three blocks away. You've got it made." Sure enough, I got to the church just as the funeral began. With Jesus riding along, you're never really lost!
—PAT BUTLER DYSON

FAITH STEP: *Practice surrendering your plans to Him. Let Jesus be your GPS.*

WEDNESDAY, OCTOBER 13

"Have you understood all these things?" They said to him, "Yes." And he said to them, "Therefore every scribe who has been trained for the kingdom of heaven is like a master of a house, who brings out of his treasure what is new and what is old." Matthew 13:51–52 (ESV)

DO YOU EVER FIND YOUR eyes glazing over as you read familiar stories in the Bible? Recently I was reading through some of Jesus's parables, and my brain tuned out. I've heard or read the stories a hundred times. Then I reached verse 52 and blinked. I felt as if Jesus was reminding me that whether an insight is new to me or is old and familiar, it has value. Both new and old bring spiritual treasure into my life.

When I was younger, I chafed at the formal liturgy of our congregation. Repeating the same Scripture-based lyrics each week seemed tedious. Yet set to melody, that repetition of Scripture settled deep into my memory and my heart and often hums through my mind even today. Later, I attended churches with new music and cutting-edge worship styles. I found new treasure as I explored different ways to pray, to fellowship, and to praise.

The same truth applies to our reading of the Bible. No matter how old and familiar the chapters are, Jesus often gives us fresh insights. A verse that spoke about one issue a year ago may take on deeper meaning after our recent experiences. I'm learning to stay more alert as I read the Bible.

God's Word is a storehouse full of treasures. Some are old and familiar, but each time we dig in, Jesus can bring us fresh grace and truth. —SHARON HINCK

FAITH STEP: *Read one of your favorite chapters of the Bible. Ask Jesus to help you glean one new treasure from the familiar words.*

THURSDAY, OCTOBER 14

"Return home and tell how much God has done for you."
So the man went away and told all over town how much
Jesus had done for him. Luke 8:39 (ESV)

AS A WRITER, I'VE HAD the honor of interviewing people after they survived incredible events, such as surviving an avalanche, being lost in a snowstorm for a week, experiencing a heart attack while saving others from drowning, to name a few. I love talking with people at such moments in their lives because they are—understandably—sincerely grateful to be alive. I've also noticed that survivors delight in sharing their stories with others, not to build themselves up but to spread hope.

This reminds me of the demon-possessed, naked man who lived in a graveyard whom Jesus healed. Jesus had compassion on the man and wanted to free him from the demons, who didn't want to leave. Jesus looked around and saw a herd of pigs. He commanded the hundreds of demons to depart from the man, and He sent them into the pigs, who rushed down a steep bank into a lake and drowned. This man was so grateful he wanted to stay with Jesus, but Jesus told him to go tell everyone he knows how much God had done for him.

Jesus wants to do miracles in our lives, and He wants us to share these testimonies so hope spreads. I'm thankful for the stories I get to write because selfishly I experience infectious gratitude as people tell me their stories. And I know when I pass them along, they continue to bring hope to those who read or hear them.
—JEANNIE BLACKMER

FAITH STEP: *Share a hope-building story or testimony with someone today!*

FRIDAY, OCTOBER 15

And the Child grew and became strong in spirit, filled with wisdom; and the grace of God was upon Him. Luke 2:40 (NKJV)

AT A LOCAL LIBRARY, I used to run into a sweet young woman who is clearly gifted in ministry. I've heard her conversations with others and can attest to how good she is at encouraging people with the Word. As I got to know her better, I saw that her life seemed very unstable. She was estranged from her husband, had young children in foster care, and barely knew where she would lay her head each night. When I suggested she focus on improving her living situation and perhaps get under the covering of her pastors, she balked and said, "We are all ministers."

I blessed her with a gift and wished her well, but today's Scripture verse shows us that even Jesus had to spend time growing strong and gaining wisdom before He launched into ministry. This applies to stepping out into any venture, whether it's a missions trip or a new career.

When my mom and I applied for a loan to start a catering business, we couldn't just walk into a bank with our great idea—we had to show a good track record and provide a detailed business plan. Moses had his forty-year prep time in the Midian desert before his heart was ready to receive the call (Acts 7:29–30). And a little known fact about the apostle Paul is that he spent three years in Arabia after his conversion before joining the disciples in ministry (Galatians 1:17–18). Look how successful they were—two of the greatest Christians in history! If Jesus, Moses, and Paul had to prepare for success, I do too. —PAMELA TOUSSAINT HOWARD

FAITH STEP: *Begin writing down steps to accomplish each day to move toward your goal or vision. Resist rushing ahead of the plan.*

SATURDAY, OCTOBER 16

*Precisely because they have misled my people, saying, "Peace,"
when there is no peace. . . . Ezekiel 13:10 (ESV)*

THOUGH I'VE LIVED MOST OF my life in the Northwoods of
Wisconsin, I'm a fan of southern expressions. To describe the string
of high temps lately—the heat dramatically out of character for this
area—I might say the day is hot enough to sell ice cubes to a polar
bear. Of a savvy salesman, I'd say, "He's so good at it, he could sell
wool socks to a lifeguard."

I've been thinking about catch phrases like that lately because of
the pervasive air of sadness and gloom that's as close to us as the evening news or a social media thread. I'm glad I'm not joy's marketing
strategist. How do you market joy to a joyless, peaceless culture?
What enticements could anyone offer a world that's noted for its
perpetually sour mood, its quickness to complain, its daily evidence
of hatred, and its deeply embedded despair disorder?

Wait. I *am* on the joy-marketing strategy team by virtue of my
relationship with the Joy-Giver, Jesus. It's part of my calling to
promote what He promotes. I'm a carrier—a joy-carrier. It's in the
DNA He gave me when I gave Him my life.

My marketing bullet points are: demonstrate what real joy looks
like; show that real joy is found in Jesus, despite circumstances; and
keep joy vibrant and visible even when life is hard.

Like selling wool socks to a lifeguard, right? No. It's like selling a concept to a world that is already hungering and thirsting for it: "Come
and get your joy! Joy for the taking. No minimum age or height require-
ments. It's all here in Jesus, waiting for you." —CYNTHIA RUCHTI

FAITH STEP: *Expose your joy to the sunlight today. Someone watching may need
to catch a glimpse of Jesus in you.*

SUNDAY, OCTOBER 17

God causes all things to work together for good to those who love
God, to those who are called according to His purpose. For those
whom He foreknew, He also predestined to become conformed
to the image of His Son . . . Romans 8:28–29 (NASB)

LAST SUNDAY, A COUPLE VISITED our church and led the music. This gave me the day off from leading it myself, so I sat in the pew along with the others and listened. There was a lady sitting beside me with her husband and three kids. One of the kids, her eight-year-old son, sat between us with a scar shaped like a lightning bolt on the back of his head. A recent biopsy confirmed a grade three astrocytoma. Clear surgical glue matted his dark, spiky hair. He looked at a Spiderman book as his mother trailed her fingertips back and forth across his narrow shoulders.

At some point the worship leaders sang a song that repeated the words "You are good." A common complaint I hear about contemporary praise music is that it says the same things over and over. I thought that myself as they kept singing it: "You are good, you are good, Jesus, you are good." Distracted, I looked over at the mother of the little boy and saw tears streaming down her cheeks. Her hands were clasped in front of her as in prayer, face forward set like flint. Her lips moved over the words as though she was drinking each one.

Sometimes Jesus doesn't need our praise as much as we need to remind ourselves of what's true. And sometimes we have to keep speaking that truth, over and over, till we believe it ourselves.
—GWEN FORD FAULKENBERRY

FAITH STEP: *Are you struggling with difficult news or just the ongoing difficulty of life in a fallen world? Tell Jesus He is good. Tell Him again and again till you believe it.*

MONDAY, OCTOBER 18

Each of you should use whatever gift you have received to serve others, as faithful stewards of God's grace in its various forms. 1 Peter 4:10 (NIV)

IN A RECENT CONVERSATION WITH a friend, I told her how much I enjoyed her writing. Her reply startled me. After thanking me, she said she'd never considered herself a writer. My response was automatic, and speedy: "I think you *are* a writer. You just don't know it yet." My words rang true.

Sometimes we don't notice our God-given talents. Or maybe they don't match our ideas of service to Jesus or how we see ourselves.

For decades I worked in the optometric field. I excelled at what I did, but it took years to reach my skill level. It wasn't a natural talent. When Jesus called me to writing, I realized the ability to put words on paper was a gift He'd equipped me with even as a child. Yet, I'd never paid any attention to it. There are so many different skills, and being a writer didn't match my plans for the future. Without wanting to, I'd ignored His wishes.

But Jesus can't be denied. When He provides a gift, He expects us to use it for His kingdom. Following this calling has been a leap of faith, a time of discovery, and a chance to use a new craft in obedience to the Lord. I've never been happier.

As I sit at my desk, tapping out sentences, I wonder how long it will be before my friend surrenders to His will. She'll be glad she did. —HEIDI GAUL

FAITH STEP: *Jesus has given you many gifts. Identify a new one you can use to bring Him honor. Be prepared to reap the blessings.*

TUESDAY, OCTOBER 19

*May the God of endurance and encouragement grant you to live
in such harmony with one another, in accord with Christ Jesus,
that together you may with one voice glorify the God and
Father of our Lord Jesus Christ. Romans 15:5–6 (ESV)*

MY HUSBAND AND I RECENTLY had our fortieth wedding anniversary. We joked that we married when we were ten, since we don't feel old enough to have celebrated such an anniversary. Indeed, we did get married fairly young.

Through the years, harmony was occasionally challenging to find. On personality tests, we score very opposite. Ted is quiet and I'm a chatterbox. He's patient and easygoing. I'm extroverted and more tightly wound. Each of our qualities hold strengths and weaknesses, and we've learned how our traits can affect each other. We've worked to adapt, to view situations through the other's perspective, and to show love in the way the other appreciates it.

If we had spent forty years focusing solely on harmony with each other, we would have hit more sour notes. From the time we committed to walking through life together, it was a three-fold commitment. A powerful phrase is buried in today's verses from Romans: "in accord with Christ Jesus." As both of us focused on turning our hearts toward Jesus, we found it easier to resonate with each other.

The same is true with other relationships in the body of Christ. It's hard to find unity when we're singing from different sheet music. But when we align our hearts with Jesus, we find that, despite our many differences, we are able to glorify God with one voice along with our fellow believers. And that's a song Jesus sings with us. —SHARON HINCK

FAITH STEP: *Sing a song with someone else today and find a harmony. Ask Jesus to bring harmony to one key relationship in your life.*

WEDNESDAY, OCTOBER 20

Because of the LORD's great love we are not consumed, for his compassions never fail. They are new every morning; great is your faithfulness. Lamentations 3:22–23 (NIV)

I WAS HIKING WITH A friend who had recently survived a battle with breast cancer. She had chosen to have a mastectomy. About the same time, doctors discovered abnormal cells in her uterus, so she also needed a hysterectomy. The recovery from both surgeries was brutal.

"I'm so thankful all that is behind you," I said.

She paused and with a heaviness in her voice she said, "Me too. Last year was rough and I was hoping this year would be better but…" she choked back tears and told me about her adult son's health issues that involved multiple trips to urgent care and eventually a diagnosis of a lifelong autoimmune disease.

She continued to talk about how hard life is sometimes. She'd had hard things happen, one after another, and it felt like more than she could handle. I had no words of comfort. As I listened, I silently prayed, *Please Jesus, give her a break.* When she paused, I asked her, "How are *you* doing? How are you making it through each day?"

"Every morning I watch the sunrise. The sky turns beautiful colors as the sun peeks over the horizon. It's God's way of faithfully greeting me, and this puts a little joy in my heart to start the day," she said.

I had prayed for her to have a break, but God was already doing that. Every morning at daybreak, He reminded her of His great love, compassion and faithfulness with each sunrise that she enjoyed.
—JEANNIE BLACKMER

FAITH STEP: *What is an action you can take today, such as watching the sunrise, to remember Jesus's great love for you?*

THURSDAY, OCTOBER 21

Keep your life free from love of money, and be content with what you have, for he has said, "I will never leave you nor forsake you." Hebrews 13:5 (ESV)

MY EIGHTY-SIX-YEAR-OLD MOM DECIDED THE time had come to downsize from the seniors' condo in which she lived. The facility she considered a good option to move into would provide her with a small apartment that included a sitting room, an ensuite bedroom, and a tiny kitchen.

Mom had downsized twelve years prior to move into her current residence. The thought of doing it again seemed overwhelming, so we tackled it together. We sorted clothes, dishes, books, and furniture. When feeling hesitant about a specific item, she'd remember the size of the apartment and its limited space. That helped her decide whether she truly wanted or needed it.

Mom gave a few treasured pieces to me and my siblings and her grandchildren. She donated nearly everything else to a faith-based thrift store. She gave her sofa and chair to a single mother. I watched her shed the occasional tear as she let go of things that obviously triggered happy memories. One morning she came to the breakfast table carrying her wedding gown in a box. "It's time to let this go too," she said. That's when I shed a tear.

Downsizing isn't easy, and I'm proud of Mom for doing it well. She'd never base her happiness on money or material possessions, but letting go was like signaling the beginning of the end of her independence. That was a huge step. I believe her faith in Jesus gave her the courage to take it.

Mom knew her possessions couldn't accompany her and she was okay with that. She was content knowing Jesus would move with her. For her, Jesus's presence was enough. —GRACE FOX

FAITH STEP: *Give a treasured belonging away as an act of worship to Jesus.*

FRIDAY, OCTOBER 22

My dear brothers and sisters, take note of this: Everyone should be quick to listen, slow to speak and slow to become angry. James 1:19 (NIV)

LAST FRIDAY—OUR DAY OFF—MY HUSBAND, Kevin, and I sat in our living room. We look forward all week to these quiet times of chatting over coffee. When Kev mentioned a musician he liked, I asked him to tell me more. Kevin loves to share little-known facts about his favorite topics. As he compared and contrasted the artist's work with others, detailing the man's background, I listened—fascinated. I don't mind that half of what I learned will be forgotten by Sunday. It's the joy of my changed heart that matters.

Three decades ago, after hearing a lengthy explanation from Kevin about something that bored me, I sighed and said, "I'm going to pray that Jesus sends you friends who like to listen."

"Why don't you pray for more patience?" Kev asked.

I told him I didn't want to learn patience—I wanted him to talk to someone else.

Jesus answered my prayer. Soon afterward, Kevin discovered a men's Bible study where he made several close friends—men who encouraged him to share his heart. He came home each week, elated that his thoughts and words were important to someone. That's when I realized how I'd passed up too many opportunities to encourage Kev. So I prayed a new prayer: *Lord, please change me into a listener.* Again, Jesus answered. I won't lie and say I'm always patient with detailed accounts and descriptions. But the smile on Kev's face when I listen is everything! —JEANETTE LEVELLIE

FAITH STEP: *If you, like me, find listening a challenge, see how long you can listen next time you have a conversation. If listening comes easy to you, thank Jesus. If it doesn't, ask Him to help you.*

SATURDAY, OCTOBER 23

Oh, the depth of the riches of the wisdom and knowledge of God!
How unsearchable his judgments, and his paths beyond tracing out!
Romans 11:33 *(NIV)*

WHEN I ASKED MY FRIEND Beth to collaborate with me on a book, my motives were 90 percent selfish. After publishing four books in five years, I was drained. Yet, I believed God was asking me to write about how women need to see themselves as beautiful—not based on society's definition of "pretty" or messages from their broken pasts but through Jesus's eyes of love. What I did not realize was how God planned to change both Beth and me in the process.

Although I'm outgoing and chatty, I often wrestle with self-doubt and condemnation. Beth, a born introvert, struggles with shyness and fear. As we wrote stories from our own lives, sharing how Jesus helped us overcome our insecurities, we began to see a greater purpose in the project. Jesus didn't want only the women who read *Hello, Beautiful!* to change their self-image from "less than" to lovely. He also longed for Beth and me to believe His bottomless love.

During the process of writing the manuscript, whenever one of us started to berate ourselves, the other would laugh and say, "Go back and read the book." Along with our laughter came the realization that we needed to trust what Jesus said about us more than we trusted our fickle feelings.

Sometimes we think we know what God has in mind when He calls us to a particular task. Yet, His plans are always greater and deeper than our imagination. His work in us is never finished. He loves us that much. —JEANETTE LEVELLIE

FAITH STEP: *Ask Jesus to show you how much He not only loves but likes you. List three things you like about yourself, and thank Him for His grace.*

SUNDAY, OCTOBER 24

Jesus was in the stern, sleeping on a cushion. The disciples woke him and said to him, "Teacher, don't you care if we drown?" Mark 4:38 (NIV)

GENE STUDIED THE WEATHER FORECAST and tide charts for days prior to an overnight sailing trip. We left the dock and motored ninety minutes on the Fraser River until we reached its mouth. That's when wind, tide, and current combined, creating waves bigger than we'd bargained for.

Our boat rocked and heaved. Waves splashed over the stern into the cockpit where Gene stood at the helm. I sat white-knuckled and wide-eyed. I glanced inside the boat and saw apples and oranges rolling back and forth across the floor. The minifridge's door swung open and spilled eggs, milk, and yogurt onto the rug.

I crawled inside to retrieve the runaway food and positioned myself beside the fridge to hold its door closed. Nausea hit me within a minute. Suddenly I understood the disciples' fear during storms at sea.

Over time I've pondered their scary sailing trip. Circumstances frightened them, but fear compounded because they doubted Jesus's intent toward them. I understand that thinking. Maybe you do too. Perhaps you've thought, *Jesus, don't You care that we're almost broke? That I'm lonely? That my marriage has ended?*

The truth is, Jesus cares deeply for us just as He cared for His disciples. He knew the storm was coming their way, so He climbed into their boat in advance (Mark 4:36). Friends, He's already in our boats too. Sooner or later the winds will rise and the waves will rock us, but let's remember that He's with us. His intent is not that we panic but that we experience His power and His peace. —GRACE FOX

FAITH STEP: *Complete this sentence, filling in the blank with whatever concerns you at this time: I choose to believe that Jesus cares about _____.*

MONDAY, OCTOBER 25

When Jesus had spoken these words, he lifted up his eyes to heaven, and said, "Father, the hour has come; glorify your Son that the Son may glorify you. John 17:1 (ESV)

I RECENTLY TURNED TO JESUS's prayer recorded in the Gospel of John. After the Last Supper, and before He was arrested, Jesus prayed a heartfelt and powerful prayer—for His ordained work, for His disciples, and for all of us who would one day know Him. Today, as I read the introduction to the prayer, I was struck by John's point that Jesus "lifted up his eyes to heaven."

Another tragedy had recently hit the news. People who were interviewed murmured things such as, "Our thoughts and prayers are with the victims." But those words can sound hollow. Our thoughts do little to change painful situations for those who are suffering. As followers of Jesus, we can follow His example. He turned His gaze toward His Father in heaven. He had a specific focus for His prayer. He directed His loving requests to the One who created and sustains our world, whose heavenly kingdom had come and will come.

We don't have to murmur prayers to the universe or offer vague wishes into the ether. We can lift our eyes confidently to our loving Father and our Savior, who is seated at His right hand. Like Jesus, we know where to look for help. Jesus was about to face unimaginable suffering, so He lifted His eyes to heaven. When our loved ones suffer and we bring our broken hearts to Jesus on their behalf, we do the same, lifting our eyes to heaven. —SHARON HINCK

FAITH STEP: *Today, if you catch yourself wishing or hoping for something, stop and lift your eyes to heaven and turn those thoughts into a prayer.*

TUESDAY, OCTOBER 26

Blessed are those who mourn, for they will be comforted. Matthew 5:4 (NIV)

I APPRECIATE THE IRONY OF applying the term "empty-nest syn-drome" to cat owners. But after the unexpected loss of our two aged felines within a month of each other, my husband and I couldn't deny the void in our hearts.

When a series of coincidences landed us at the local humane society, we decided to investigate the cats available for adoption. A ten-year-old tabby named Julie caught our attention, but we hesitated. How could we take on a new pet while still mourning the others? Surely someone else would choose her.

A week passed with Julie crowding my thoughts daily. After returning to the pet sanctuary, we requested details about her past. We learned Julie's world had been turned upside-down when one of her human parents died and the other had entered a memory care facility. Her level of mourning eclipsed ours. This tiny cat had lost everything she'd ever known.

We brought her home that day. She's mended our hearts with laughter, surprising us with a joy we didn't think possible. I think of this verse: "A time to weep and a time to laugh, a time to mourn and a time to dance..." (Ecclesiastes 3:4, NIV). Who knew those feelings could overlap? Jesus knows what we need to heal and grow in Him. He provides us opportunities to help others—even four-legged ones—as they suffer challenges similar to our own.

Rescue-pet owners often question who really did the rescuing, the owner or the animal. But the answer is Jesus. —HEIDI GAUL

FAITH STEP: *Are you in mourning? Visit a pet sanctuary and replace mourning with gladness.*

WEDNESDAY, OCTOBER 27

"Blessed is the man that trusteth in the LORD, and whose hope the LORD is." Jeremiah 17:7 (KJV)

THE MEDICAL PROCEDURE WASN'T SUPPOSED to take long. But because they needed me to be relaxed and calm, the medical team told me they'd give me a little "happy medicine." It didn't kick in until after the procedure was over. The happy medicine was a disappointment.

Anything we use to "medicate" happiness usually is.

Take this three times a day. Rub this ointment on affected joints as needed. Drink more water. Eliminate sugar and nightshade vegetables from your diet. Strip your home of anything and anyone that doesn't spark joy.

And next week, there will be new so-called remedies for what ails us, saddens us, or makes us anxious. Even in Jesus's time, people tried to find their own versions of happy medicine to numb their pain and introduce artificial joy. All failed them, because there is no "joy medicine." It's found in a person (Jesus) and a lifestyle (living for Him).

Artificial means of conjuring joy bear a bad aftertaste: regret. Like the happy medicine that didn't kick in until after my medical procedure was over, anything we use as a substitute for what only Jesus can give, will often—no, always—disappoint.

"Nothing is strong enough to cover my current pain," you say? Increasing the dosage, switching from generic to more expensive, and changing to a new "family" of drugs won't help. But there's One who knows your pain, sympathizes with it, and can cover you until the pain subsides—better and stronger than anything on the market, with no negative side effects. *Jesus.* —CYNTHIA RUCHTI

FAITH STEP: *Accustomed as you may be to thanking Jesus for your meals, make it a habit also to ask Him for the "joy medicine" He provides your heart.*

THURSDAY, OCTOBER 28

So go to the street corners and invite to the banquet anyone you find.
Matthew 22:9 (NIV)

AS MY BIRTHDAY APPROACHES, I look forward to dinner out with my husband—and the gifts. I do enjoy gifts. But I don't relish them as much as I did as a selfish little kid.

When I was planning my seventh birthday party, my penchant for presents led to trouble. Because my friend Jenny couldn't afford to bring a gift to my party, I uninvited her. She ran down our driveway toward her house, sobbing. Mom asked me—in that *way* parents have—why Jenny went home crying.

I was too young to have honed my lying methods. I opened my eyes as large as I could and squeaked, "I have no idea." Mom wasn't fooled. When I confessed my greedy act, she told me I could either march down to Jenny's and re-invite her to my party, or there wouldn't be one. She said, "Parties aren't for presents, anyway. They're for celebrating our friends, and you won't have any friends left if you keep that selfish attitude."

Now it was my turn to cry. How could I face Jenny and admit that my self-centeredness had gone too far? Lying was out; I saw how well that worked. So I trudged the half block down the street and rang the bell. I gulped back my tears, and told Jenny she was welcome to attend my party, and of course, I didn't expect a gift. Thankfully, she accepted.

I love to think of the party Jesus is planning for us that's mentioned in Matthew 22. I'm sure it will be one huge celebration, with everyone there receiving the best gift possible—eternity with Jesus.
—JEANETTE LEVELLIE

FAITH STEP: *Find something you treasure. Wrap it in pretty paper, then give it to someone who needs to experience Jesus's love.*

FRIDAY, OCTOBER 29

I can do all things through Christ who strengthens me.
Philippians 4:13 (NKJV)

OUR DAUGHTER MELISSA, HER HUSBAND, Daniel, and their eight-year-old son, Winston, unexpectedly visited my husband, Jeff, and me one night, and Winston handed me a wrapped package. Puzzled, I unwrapped the gift to find a photo of Winston jumping in the air. "Look at his shirt, Mom," Melissa said. On the shirt were the words, *Promoted to Big Brother!* We were going to have another grandchild!

Less than a month later, our son Brent and his wife, Erin, announced that they, too, were expecting a baby. Overwhelmed with joy, Jeff and I thanked Jesus for the gift of these new lives.

As the reality of the situation set in, my joy was tempered by self-doubt. Was I up to the challenge ahead of me? Winston was our youngest grandchild; it had been eight years since I'd even *held* a new baby. Since both expectant families lived locally, I knew I'd be frequently called on to help. That made me happy, but I wondered if I could summon the strength and the stamina needed to help care for two infants. I would want to cook and clean as well as tend to the babies. Could I do it all? I was healthy. I exercised daily. I volunteered and continued to do freelance writing. But what I needed most was reassurance from the One who holds my life in His hands.

I got down on my knees and prayed, *Jesus, please give me the strength I'm going to need to help with these new little ones.* And deep in my heart, I knew He would. —PAT BUTLER DYSON

FAITH STEP: *Make a list of five strengths you possess. Rejoice in the gifts God's given you and give Him praise!*

SATURDAY, OCTOBER 30

For His anger endureth but a moment; in his favour is life: weeping may endure for a night, but joy cometh in the morning. Psalm 30:5 (KJV)

"IT'S A GIRL!" THE WORDS brought cheers from the crowd waiting outside the hospital birthing room. Ecstatic, my husband, Jeff, and I thanked Jesus for the safe arrival of our granddaughter. Our son Brent and his wife, Erin, had elected not to find out the gender of their child before birth, and they hadn't shared any potential names for the baby. Three days had passed, and it was time for Erin and the as-yet-unnamed little girl to go home.

"Mom and Dad," Brent said, "if it's okay with you, we'd like to name her Blake." Tears filled my eyes and I couldn't speak, but Jeff answered, "That would be great!"

Over thirty years ago, our youngest son, Blake, had died from a sudden illness at age three. With Blake's death, our lives changed forever. Jeff and I struggled to maintain some semblance of a normal family life for Brent and his older brother Scott, but our grief was profound. In the five years following Blake's death, we adopted two little girls into our family. We moved ahead with life, but we never stopped missing our little blond dynamo.

We spoke of Blake on his birthday and occasionally at other times, but mostly, saying his name made us sad. Now we would be saying "Blake" every day! Could I do it? Only with Jesus's help. It was such an honor, such a tribute for Brent and Erin to name their baby after our beloved little boy. This Blake is a girl and her hair is red! I couldn't imagine the joy she would bring to our family. Yes, I could call her Blake! —PAT BUTLER DYSON

FAITH STEP: *Where in your life do you need to thank Jesus for bringing joy out of sadness? Praise Him!*

SUNDAY, OCTOBER 31

There is no fear in love. But perfect love drives out fear, because fear has to do with punishment. The one who fears is not made perfect in love. 1 John 4:18 (NIV)

MY BOYS LOVE TO SCARE me. The other night, I was walking into my room when Addison, my thirteen-year-old, jumped out from behind the door and yelled, "Boo!" I screamed and lurched to the side, my hands immediately closing into fists. Addie jumped back, knowing my response would be to strike at whatever had just scared me. He couldn't stop laughing. I was irritated and said, "What in the world?" Addie laughed and said, "Mom, you look so funny when you are scared." I wasn't laughing. My heart was racing. I was scared, ready to fight.

I tend to collect fears: fear of spiders, fear of heights, fear of giant children jumping out from behind doors. But fear wasn't a part of Jesus's original plan. There is no reason for fear when you are surrounded by perfect love. The moment Adam and Eve stepped out of that love to shape their own destiny—fear rushed in. Hence, we all have that heart-pounding response toward anything beyond our control or understanding. Fear sucks the joy out of life.

Jesus said, "I have come that they may have life, and have it to the full" (John 10:10, NIV). It is hard to live life to the full when we are freaking out. Jesus came into this world to forgive our sins, to restore us, and to help us share His love with others. When we invite Jesus to shape our destiny, He begins to cast out every fear, surrounding us with His perfect love—joy in its fullest form.
—SUSANNA FOTH AUGHTMON

FAITH STEP: *What are you afraid of? Tell Jesus about it. Believe that you are hemmed in by His perfect love. Step out today and live unafraid.*

MONDAY, NOVEMBER 1

Can a mother forget the baby at her breast and have no compassion on the child she has borne? Though she may forget, I will not forget you! See, I have engraved you on the palms of my hands . . . Isaiah 49:15–16 (NIV)

MY MOM RECENTLY GAVE ONE of my books to a new member at her church, and the man excitedly told her he thought he had a niece who went to school with me. The next time I visited, Mom introduced us. The man pumped my hand and asked if I knew his niece. Her name seemed familiar, but I couldn't visualize her face—which wasn't surprising since I'd moved away right after college. I fumbled, not wanting to lie but feeling bad. Suddenly, the man said, "She says she doesn't remember you at all."

As a young adult, I felt like the most forgettable person on the planet. So many people simply did not remember me. When I worked at a hospital, one intern introduced himself to me three different times in the elevator. In those days, I never forgot a face and usually remembered names and details about a person. I assumed some people didn't care enough to make an effort.

In Israel, the high priest's garment had shoulder pieces with the names of the tribes engraved on onyx stones. When the exiled Israelites wondered if God had forgotten them, He assured them He had them engraved on His hands. The nail prints engraved on Jesus's hands remind us that He died in our place. We can be sure He will never forget us, even if everyone on earth does.
—DIANNE NEAL MATTHEWS

FAITH STEP: *Create or buy a pretty card and write Jesus on it. Place it in a spot where you'll see it every day. Each time you look at the card, tell Jesus why His name fills you with joy.*

TUESDAY, NOVEMBER 2

Carry each other's burdens, and in this way you will fulfill the law of Christ. Galatians 6:2 (NIV)

HAVE YOU EVER HAD THE feeling it would be a bad day, even before your feet touched the floor? Having overslept, I was already running behind for my dentist's appointment two hours away in Houston. And my sweet little SUV that drove like a dream? It was in the shop, so I'd be wrangling my husband Jeff's gigantic new pickup truck. Frazzled from fighting traffic, I wheeled into the parking space at a crooked angle—fine in the front but too close to the rear of the car next to me. I prayed it would be a clunker. Not even close. I'd shimmied up next to a shiny new Mercedes Benz.

Jesus, please let that Mercedes be gone when I'm done, I prayed. But when I returned to the parking lot, it was still there. I climbed into Jeff's truck, started it up, then turned off the engine, convinced if I tried to back up, I'd scrape the truck *and* the Mercedes. I had no choice. I'd have to ask for help, my least favorite thing to do *ever*.

I went back up to the dentist's office and explained my situation to the receptionist. Just then a policeman came to the checkout. "I bet Jason will help you," she said. Cringing, I told Jason what I needed, and he said he'd be glad to help me. I handed him the keys and he expertly backed out the truck, without scraping the car.

"How can I thank you?" I asked. "May I pay you?" He shook his head and said, "It's always my pleasure to help someone, ma'am." I felt a nudge from Jesus. Like Jason, I delighted in helping. Was I depriving others of that joy by not asking for help myself?
—PAT BUTLER DYSON

FAITH STEP: *Ask Jesus to teach you how to ask for help.*

WEDNESDAY, NOVEMBER 3

Delight yourself in the LORD, and he will give you the desires of your heart. Psalm 37:4 (ESV)

FOR THE PAST YEAR I'VE had a monthly phone call with a spiritual director. I reached out to her because I was feeling unclear about God's purpose for me in this empty-nest season. She is not a counselor or therapist; her purpose is to continually draw me deeper into my relationship with Jesus and listen to what He's saying to me.

As we talked, she frequently asked, "What do *you* want?" I hadn't considered that question for myself in a very long time. It's an important question and one that even Jesus asked. For example, in Matthew 20:29–34, two blind men cried out to Jesus as He walked past. The crowd told them to be quiet, but they shouted louder. Jesus stopped and asked them, "What is it you want?" They said, "We want to see." He touched their eyes, and they could see.

We have to be careful when we seek our desires to not become self-consumed. One sure way to avoid this selfishness is to continually delight ourselves in the Lord. As today's Psalm promises, if we delight in Him, He will give us the desires of our hearts. We show our delight in Jesus through close connection with Him.

After time spent in conversations with my spiritual director, prayer, and journaling, I've articulated the desires of my heart: meaningful work, community and connection, vibrant healthy relationships with Jesus, others, and myself, and to lead and live wholeheartedly. Like the blind men, I'm excited to see how Jesus will respond as I honestly express my desires, because He delights in giving. —JEANNIE BLACKMER

FAITH STEP: *Tell Jesus all about your heart's desires.*

THURSDAY, NOVEMBER 4

So he got up and went to his father. But while he was still a long way off, his father saw him and was filled with compassion for him; he ran to his son, threw his arms around him and kissed him. Luke 15:20 (NIV)

ONE OF OUR ORGANIZATION'S MINISTRIES serves Romanian children and youth living with HIV and AIDS. Their society treats them like modern-day lepers, so it's difficult for them to understand their worth to Jesus. We assure them of His love, but words aren't enough.

In this situation, demonstrating love through appropriate human touch is one of the most meaningful things we can do. A warm, respectful hug is the opposite of the neglect or abusive touches they've known most of their lives, so it speaks volumes. We also spend time making crafts, playing games, enjoying silly skits, and worshiping the Lord together. The message we communicate through actions is far different from the message they receive when others recoil in disgust or fear upon learning of their disease.

Scripture tells us that Jesus hurts with those who hurt and that He does something about it. On one occasion, He encountered a funeral procession mourning a widow's only son. His heart overflowed with compassion, so He raised the boy to life and gave him back to his mother (Luke 7:11–15). On another occasion, He felt compassion for the crowds that seemed lost, that were like sheep without a shepherd. He responded by teaching them and providing dinner for them (Mark 6:34–44). And then there was the day a leper begged for healing—Jesus touched the untouchable and restored his health (Mark 1:40–42).

Jesus's compassion for those who hurt moved Him to action. We represent Him well when we do likewise. Even a cup of cold water given in His name makes a difference. —GRACE FOX

FAITH STEP: *Buy a gift card from a local restaurant. Give it to a homeless person.*

FRIDAY, NOVEMBER 5

She comforts, encourages, and does him only good and not evil all the days of her life. Proverbs 31:12 (AMP)

SOMETIMES I HAVE TO REMEMBER that one of my God-ordained jobs is to build my husband up with my words and to comfort him. We have fun together and joke around a lot in our relationship, but I know I have a sarcastic streak that can give something I say innocently a sharp edge. He may not say anything to me about it, but that doesn't mean what I said didn't sting. One of the ways to do someone "only good" all the days of our lives is to make conscious efforts to use our mouths only to edify, not to nag or put down. Any wife who has practiced praising her husband knows it usually has immediate and amazing results! Despite an often tough exterior, the men in our lives feed on our verbal affirmation.

I had the opportunity to comfort my husband recently when his mother passed away. It was the first time I saw him tear up in the four years of our relationship, and it touched me to the core. Being there beside him in that moment and through the funeral and being available later to talk about it has ministered comfort to his heart. Sometimes simply being present with someone is comforting— physically there and not tethered to a cell phone. Provide a safe space to talk. Of course, there are a thousand other ways to do your husband good and not evil—from being smart with your shared resources (i.e., shopping!) and telling him the truth about things large and small. But using your mouth for good when talking with him *or about him* goes a long way. —PAMELA TOUSSAINT HOWARD

FAITH STEP: *Make a point of sharing an encouraging word today and every day.*

SATURDAY, NOVEMBER 6

Being confident of this, that he who began a good work in you will carry it on to completion until the day of Christ Jesus. Philippians 1:6 (NIV)

THERE ARE A COUPLE OF things I really like about this verse. First, it says I can be sure that *God* started a good work in me and He will complete it, and I don't have to strive or struggle in my own strength. I only have to comply, and He'll produce lasting change in me! That's good news indeed, because on my own, I've failed miserably to change my faults or shortcomings, no matter how hard I've tried and prayed.

I also really like that the scripture suggests my evolution happens over time—maybe even a long time. I may want instant results, especially when it comes to some troublesome traits, but God's not rushing. His timing is different than mine, and He knows best.

While I'm busy fretting to fix myself in a hurry, it's the gentle Jesus in me who affects true change. I take great comfort in this verse and others (like 2 Corinthians 3:18) that assure me that God is changing me slowly but surely. Meanwhile, Jesus stands in the gap between who I am, and who I'll be in eternity. While He empowers me to change, I am unconditionally loved and accepted, just as I am. —ISABELLA YOSUICO

FAITH STEP: *Reflect on a shortcoming that you can't seem to change and write a prayer to Jesus to help you enjoy the promise of today's verse.*

SUNDAY, NOVEMBER 7

---

*I have trusted in your steadfast love; my heart shall rejoice
in your salvation. Psalm 13:5 (ESV)*

THE WORST THING THAT HAS ever happened to me happened this
year. My mother had a stroke. I was afraid she was going to die. It's
the most out-of-control I have ever felt in my life. Completely out
of my area of expertise, completely dependent on doctors, and completely powerless to stop the deterioration of the body that gave birth
to me and houses my heart. We were completely at the mercy of God.

I didn't know how to pray. But I don't know how not to. So I
just stayed by her bed, holding her hand and crying, *Jesus, Son of
God, have mercy on us.* I didn't feel much of anything. Looking back
now, I guess there was an underlying peace; there always is. In the
moment, I just felt numb. I'd like to be a person who experiences
great signs and wonders, but that's not me. Whatever is spiritual in
me sat like a rock in my gut for days.

I cannot say I knew what would happen or that I had any sense
or assurance of healing. I didn't. I was on the edge of the abyss with
no tree or rope to hang onto. But I had the Rock under my feet; my
only hope was Jesus's love. Fragments of Scripture came to mind.
"Nothing can separate us from His love." "Greater love has no one
than this." "We have this hope as an anchor for the soul." I planted
my feet on the Rock that is Jesus, and willed my soul to trust, even
as my mind gaped into the waiting dark.

This time we got to keep her. I don't know why and I don't know
what will happen next. But I do know I can trust Jesus's love.
—GWEN FORD FAULKENBERRY

FAITH STEP: *Place your trust in Jesus—completely at His mercy is where you
want to be.*

MONDAY, NOVEMBER 8

Now godliness with contentment is great gain. For we brought nothing into this world, and it is certain we can carry nothing out.
1 Timothy 6:6–7 *(NKJV)*

MY HUSBAND AND I ALWAYS thought that by the time we reached our mid-to-late sixties, we'd be living on a few acres of land in a rural setting. But Richard is still working, and our last relocation a few years ago brought us to a manufacturing area. The landscape around the corner of our house is filled with industrial factories, plants, towers—all things metal as far as the eye can see. Fortunately, the golf course in our neighborhood has some trees and grass.

Each time I walked by the small wooded area along our subdivision's entrance, I prayed, *Lord, thank You that at least I have this.* The deep shade provided a momentary respite from the heat and humidity. I loved hearing the leaves rustle, the insects chirping, and the birds singing. Occasionally I saw a rabbit nibbling grass.

Then one day we returned from a trip to find the trees uprooted. Eventually, construction began on a new development of houses. At first I felt shocked at the loss of what I considered a blessing. But I sheepishly remembered Jonah, who pouted after God destroyed a plant that had shaded him. Jonah's selfish reaction showed that he was more concerned about his own comfort than God's plans for the city of Nineveh.

When we lose a blessing, it sometimes has nothing to do with us. Other times, it may be a reminder that if we know Jesus, we already have all we need to be content—even for a country girl living in a metal and concrete world. —DIANNE NEAL MATTHEWS

FAITH STEP: *Have you recently lost a blessing or despaired of never receiving something you've wanted? Each time you think about that, tell Jesus why He is all you really need.*

TUESDAY, NOVEMBER 9

So if the Son sets you free, you will be free indeed. John 8:36 (NIV)

MY FAMILY AND I RECENTLY visited a new restaurant. After we were seated, I asked for directions to the restroom. I followed them carefully, retracing my steps, and searching for the red door. Locating it, I entered. The instant the door clicked shut, I knew I'd made a mistake. I turned the knob to leave. It was locked. I was trapped. This was no bathroom but was a dank warehouse. Broken antiques and cobwebs cluttered the space. Water puddled beneath the leaky roof.

No problem. I'd knock, and someone would hear and let me out. But the solid metal door reduced my knocking to a dull thud. I yelled. And I prayed. Jesus's presence calmed me.

Ten minutes passed, then twenty. The loading-dock doors were padlocked, and some were rusted shut. Spotting an exit sign, I hurried there, only to find it blocked by shelving. Back at the red door, I rapped with my rubber-soled shoes, but they were quieter than my bruised knuckles. I screamed louder and prayed harder.

Outside, my family had split up, searching the building's perimeter and grounds, while one stayed inside with my belongings. When that failed, my daughter asked a server to join the search. After thirty minutes, they found me.

At last, I was free! The joy I felt was immeasurable and the relief immense. It was as if I'd been imprisoned and just received a pardon.

My mind flashed back to the day I realized the immense freedom I found in Jesus. Freedom from all the junk piled up in my past, the brokenness, the loneliness, the sin. I walked outside into the light, free indeed. And grateful. —HEIDI GAUL

FAITH STEP: *What keeps you from the freedom found in Jesus? String a key onto a chain and wear it as a reminder that you have been freed from everything that imprisons you.*

WEDNESDAY, NOVEMBER 10

He sighed deeply in His spirit, and said, "Why does this generation seek a sign? Assuredly, I say to you, no sign shall be given to this generation." Mark 8:12 (NKJV)

IF IT WERE POSSIBLE, WE would probably exhaust Jesus by constantly asking for outward signs before we act. He never asks us to do anything contrary to His Word. And even though we have the Bible available in hundreds of translations, we often still ask for a sign from a person or through a circumstance.

Fear can be a reason why we seek outward signs. Decades ago, my uncle Jerry was preparing to ask my aunt Agnes out on a date. He had heard clearly in his spirit that she was the one God had for him: she was a godly, faithful, country girl whom he had gotten to know through youth choir. Yet, he needed a sign from God to approach her, largely because of a tough breakup he had experienced the year before. He didn't want to make another mistake. I, too, asked for a sign when I first met my husband-to-be because I had been wrong several times before! But in today's verse, the Pharisees (religious folks) *constantly demanded* signs and miracles from Jesus because of their spiritual blindness and opposing spirits. Even His death and resurrection couldn't convince them He was the promised Messiah. Many still remain unconvinced today.

I'm grateful that as a Christian, I have "a better covenant, which was established on better promises" than Old Testament believers did (Hebrews 8:6), and I want to walk boldly toward the things I know He has called me to do, be, and believe, without needing a sign before every step. —PAMELA TOUSSAINT HOWARD

FAITH STEP: *Walk confidently in your calling today, guided by Jesus.*

THURSDAY, NOVEMBER 11

Take delight in the Lord, and he will give you the desires of your heart. Psalm 37:4 (NIV)

"LORD, PLEASE GIVE JEANETTE HER house," Betty prayed. The ladies in my Sunday school class knew I wanted a home of my own. Kevin and I appreciated the lovely house that the rural congregation we pastored had provided for us. But I knew someday we'd either retire or take a new ministry. For twenty years, my faithful friends agreed with me in prayer that Jesus would grant my heart's desire—a home in the country, surrounded by trees and wildlife.

Even when I despaired that we would never have enough money to purchase our own place, I continued to ask. One day a few months ago, Jesus surprised me.

As I looked out the dining room window of my home, I noticed the maples and dogwoods bordering our yard were in full leaf. Chickadees, cardinals, and finches perched on feeders hanging from the eaves. Chipmunks skittered across the porch. Overhead, squirrels chased each other from branch to branch.

As insight flashed, and I put my hand over my mouth, happy tears brimmed and spilled down my face. "Lord, You answered—you gave me my heart's desire—and I didn't even realize it." We had lived in this country house for twenty years, surrounded by trees and critters. We didn't own it, but Jesus had fulfilled my dream anyway. He simply answered my prayer in a different way than I'd expected.

How many times have I asked Jesus to do something for me and then told Him how to accomplish it? I forget that He is smarter than I am. He has a million of ways up His sleeve for getting me what I need and even sometimes what I want. —JEANETTE LEVELLIE

FAITH STEP: *Think of a long-held desire. Has Jesus given it to you in a different way than you expected? If so, thank Him for His creativity.*

FRIDAY, NOVEMBER 12

*I am persuaded that neither death nor life, nor angels nor principalities
nor powers, nor things present nor things to come, nor height nor depth,
nor any other created thing, shall be able to separate us from the love
of God which is in Christ Jesus our Lord. Romans 8:38–39 (NKJV)*

DOGS HAVE HELPED PEOPLE FOR a long time. Luke tells us how
they came and licked the beggar's sores. I often marvel at how mine
minister to me. As I believe everything is spiritual and all truth is
God's truth, it is not far-fetched to say that animals manifest the
love of Jesus toward us.

One example is when I was forty years old and pregnant. The
pregnancy was welcome but unexpected, and it was difficult because
I was older, more out of shape, and working full-time as well as
tending to my other three young children. I had migraines every
day. My doctor's suggestion was to take medicine, lie down when I
got home from work, and try to sleep them off.

The only room in our house I could make completely dark was
my son Harper's. I would go in, shut the door, pack pillows around
my head, and try to sleep. And every day our dog Dot would go
with me. Even though she'd been home alone all day and was surely
ready to get outside and play, she followed me to the bed, curled up
at the small of my back, and stayed beside me, for however long it
took for me to fall asleep.

This is such a picture of Jesus. He sticks to us like glue. There is
nothing and no one able to separate us from His love; He wouldn't
rather be somewhere else. His love is faithful no matter what
happens, no matter where we are. —GWEN FORD FAULKENBERRY

FAITH STEP: *Send someone a text with today's verse to remind her that she's
never forgotten and is always loved.*

SATURDAY, NOVEMBER 13

The LORD is close to the brokenhearted and saves those who are crushed in spirit. Psalm 34:18 (NIV)

WE LOST HIM, PAT. THE text from my classmate Janie shocked and crushed me. Janie's grown son Stephen had been battling pneumonia in a hospital. Many class members were praying for Stephen's recovery. I was certain he would be all right and had told Janie that often. *Jesus, please help me comfort my friend.*

Over thirty years ago when my three-year-old son Blake died, there was nothing anyone could say to comfort me. My grief paralyzed me. I was lost. Then one day, several months after Blake died, I read in the newspaper about a car accident that had taken the life of the teenaged daughter of a man who'd been a football star at my high school. Jesus led me to set aside my sorrow and sit down and write a note to Billy, telling him that I, too, had lost a child and that if he ever needed to talk, I was here. I never heard from Billy, but this was the first step in *my* healing—reaching out to another brokenhearted parent.

Over the years, I've written notes to many people whose children have died. In the note, after telling the parents how sorry I am for their loss, that I understand because I've been there, that I am available to talk, I write something such as, "Let me offer you hope. It *does* get better. Your life will never be quite the same and you will never stop missing your child, but you can find joy again." At the time I lost Blake, what I needed more than anything was hope. I found that hope the nearer I drew to Jesus. —PAT BUTLER DYSON

FAITH STEP: *Write a note to someone with a broken heart.*

SUNDAY, NOVEMBER 14

See what great love the Father has lavished on us, that we should be called children of God! And that is what we are! The reason the world does not know us is that it did not know him. 1 John 3:1 (NIV)

LIKE A LOT OF WOMEN, I've wrestled with "impostor syndrome," questioning whether I was worthy of a position or promotion. This sometimes caused near crippling anxiety—once so bad it caused me to quit a great job. At best, I had persistent low-level insecurity and self-doubt that didn't help my performance one bit.

In my journey as a Christian, I've felt something similar. I've realized that I've missed out on some of God's rich blessings or at least failed to fully enjoy them because I just didn't understand my worth in Christ. Despite the plain truth of the gospel, I sometimes didn't believe I had fully received God's unconditional love. Saved by grace through faith, of which I can't boast (Ephesians 2:8–9), I have the righteousness of Christ (2 Corinthians 5:21) and am the adopted daughter of the King (Romans 8:15).

In Christ, the only qualification for God's love, mercy, and blessing is trusting Him. Ephesians affirms the truth of our rich spiritual blessings "in Christ," a phrase which appears nearly thirty times in that one book alone.

The Bible is clear that I can't do anything to make my Father love me more or less.

If I don't accept my high value in Jesus, I not only deny myself but also minimize the cross. Far from a spiritual impostor, I wear the royal mantle of the risen King, and carry my head high, confident of my standing. —ISABELLA YOSUICO

FAITH STEP: *List some of the ways you feel like a spiritual impostor and find verses that contradict that.*

MONDAY, NOVEMBER 15

Therefore encourage one another and build each other up, just as in fact you are doing. 1 Thessalonians 5:11 (NIV)

I RECENTLY BOUGHT A SMALL gift book for my son Jack who is getting ready to leave for college in a couple months. It is called *Letters to Open When...: Write Now. Read Later. Treasure Forever.* It is a small, rectangular book in the shape of an envelope. Inside are empty letter templates that have different titles instructing the reader what each letter is about and when it should be opened: "Open when you are looking for inspiration." "Open when you need courage." "Open when you need a laugh." This summer I am going to have my family and Jack's friends fill out the letters. When he feels alone at school, he can open a letter and find the encouraging words of those who love him most. In this season, I want Jack surrounded by hope and peace.

Words of encouragement can change our lives. When we encourage each other, we are following in the footsteps of the One who loves us the most. When Jesus walked the dusty hills of Nazareth and the sandy beaches of Galilee, He used His words to heal and restore. His words offered hope to the desperate, fulfillment to the love-starved, and redemption to the broken. His words transformed His followers, inviting them to change the world. We can do the same. With encouragement, we speak to each other's hearts with love, truth, and hope. Encouragement builds out grace and mercy in the lives of those around us, recognizing them for who they are—the beloved of Jesus. Our encouragement can surround people with hope and peace. —SUSANNA FOTH AUGHTMON

FAITH STEP: *Write a letter to someone in your life today. Following in Jesus's footsteps, use your encouraging words to build her up and surround her with love.*

TUESDAY, NOVEMBER 16

When he arrived and saw this evidence of God's blessing, he was filled with joy, and he encouraged the believers to stay true to the Lord. Acts 11:23 (NLT)

WHEN THE GOSPEL WAS PREACHED in Antioch, large numbers of Gentiles listened and chose to follow Jesus. News of their conversions spread, and the believers in Jerusalem sent Barnabas to check out the reports. Barnabas saw the rapid church growth as evidence of God's favor, as the gospel was carried throughout the world, making relationship with God possible—through Jesus—for every race and nation.

Occasionally we're privileged to see extraordinary proof of God's favor spiritually, physically, and materially. Such experiences create excitement and joy and make us feel loved in a tangible way. I'm grateful for those times, but I'm also thankful for both seen and unseen evidence of God's blessing that surrounds us every day.

Personally, one of the greatest unseen evidences of God's blessing is the peace that comes from knowing Jesus as my Shepherd: He knows me by name. He leads me along the right paths for me. He protects me and provides rest when I need it. He is ultimately responsible for my well-being, and I can trust Him with full confidence because He has my best interest in mind.

Sometimes Jesus allows pain in my life. It's His favor in disguise— it's like a magnet that pulls me to Him and creates deeper intimacy. It's what refines me and makes me more like Him.

Evidence of God's blessing surrounds us, and we owe Him our gratitude. Barnabas was right to encourage the believers to stay true to Jesus. Jesus has done everything for us, and He deserves our loyalty in return. —GRACE FOX

FAITH STEP: *Identify three pieces of evidence of Jesus's blessing in your life.*

WEDNESDAY, NOVEMBER 17

He will take great delight in you; in his love he will no longer rebuke you,
but will rejoice over you with singing. Zephaniah 3:17 (NIV)

IN TODAY'S VERSE, WE'RE TOLD that God delights in us! I especially like this verse because it foreshadows Jesus's act of reconciliation so we're no longer subject to rebuke.

Zephaniah 3:17 includes the phrase "*great* delight" (emphasis mine) and reminds us that God is rejoicing over us with singing. Can you imagine God dancing around the heavenly realm, singing our praises, brimming with joy? Only my limited human experience of enjoying my kids can render this clear to me. I'm guessing God's delight in me is not tainted by my undone chores or back talk, the kind that leads me to reprimand my kids, usually without much delight. Because of Jesus, I never have to fear God's scolding. I much prefer feeling as if someone is delighting in me, rather than feeling as if I'm bracing for rebuke. Because of Jesus, God looks at me and sees only a perfect child, clothed in His Son's righteousness, not my own.

There are many verses, most in the New Testament, about our standing as sons and daughters—children of God. Jesus closes the giant gap between the remote, scary God of the Old Testament and the dancing-with-delight Abba Father. Wow! —ISABELLA YOSUICO

FAITH STEP: *Just sit with this notion for a while. In Christ, our heavenly Father is delighting over us with singing, not rebuke!*

THURSDAY, NOVEMBER 18

Looking unto Jesus the author and finisher of our faith; who for the joy that was set before him endured the cross, despising the shame, and is set down at the right hand of throne of God. Hebrews 12:2 (KJV)

I COULD JUST SENSE MY middle school son Pierce rolling his eyes, embarrassed, and then his laughter. I was in my usual state during worship: eyes closed, swaying, head thrown back, arms raised, lost in musical ecstasy. And singing. *Loudly.* Some readers of *Mornings with Jesus* have read about my stage fright, and how I struggled to even sing in the pews. I couldn't just relax and worship unreservedly.

Then, after mustering the courage to sing with the choir at our former church, we eventually joined a church that didn't have a choir. Instead, they have an anointed worship team that composes and sings great contemporary music. The music routinely brings me and others to tears.

Until now, I'd only attended churches where gentle swaying was the standard of worship. But at my new church, the worship is passionate and there's a cluster of believers planted at the front who are very animated in their praise, raising their hands and singing with glee. My stage fright held me back until I finally got a clear word from God: *Jesus bore my shame.* In fact, He despised it.

I think of the uninhibited way little kids dance and sing and of King David's unbridled worship, full of joy. Now I, too, despise the shame that's held me back from so many things, including worshipping my King: *Jesus.* Jesus is worthy of my praise. —ISABELLA YOSUICO

FAITH STEP: *Has shame been holding you back from being the person God created you to be? Ask Jesus to remove it.*

FRIDAY, NOVEMBER 19

Let your light so shine before men, that they may see your good works and glorify your Father in heaven. Matthew 5:16 (NKJV)

THE GLOOMY DAY PERFECTLY REFLECTED my mood. I'd barely slept the night before, tossing and turning, thinking about things I couldn't change. The rain kept me from riding my bike, so endorphins weren't flooding my body to raise my spirits. My car was in the shop, so I couldn't leave the house. I'd gotten a rejection on a story I'd worked on for days, crushing my self-esteem. And I had a pimple, the perfect accessory to wear to a pity party. *Jesus, I could use some direction here.*

What would your mother do? I had a pretty good idea. Mother was a devoted "note writer." A stickler for writing thank-you notes, Mother wrote other notes as well—a note to congratulate a friend on her son's making the honor roll, a note to wish someone luck in a golf tournament, a note offering prayers for an upcoming surgery, a note to say, "I love you, and I'm glad you're my friend."

Thanks to my mom's influence, I'm a note-writer too. I pulled out my stationery and my favorite pen and got ready to write. Who needed a cheery note from me? My neighbor Gloria, whose husband had died six months before and I hadn't seen lately. Betsy, whose last little chick had just left home for college. Jack, who was recovering from knee surgery. Kay, who was grieving the loss of her aged dog. Ted, who had a new grandbaby. With each note I wrote, I felt better. By afternoon, the sun had emerged outside, as well as in my soul. I thanked Jesus for reminding me to honor Him by doing something good for someone else. —PAT BUTLER DYSON

FAITH STEP: *Always keep a supply of stationery, pens, and stamps so you can write a quick note to someone who needs encouragement.*

SATURDAY, NOVEMBER 20

We all stumble in many ways . . . James 3:2 (NIV)

THE BOOK OF JAMES IS my least favorite book in the Bible. I know, I know—since I'm a pastor's wife, I should like them all. I do read James—occasionally. But I cringe every time I see passages about finding joy in adversity, taming my tongue, and not grumbling with others. Ouch. That's stepping on too many of my toes.

This morning, however, I came across one tiny phrase tucked in among all the reprimands and instructions. A phrase I never noticed before. One I was shocked to hear from James, this servant of God—"We all stumble in many ways." Really? You, the brother of Jesus and leader of the first century church in Jerusalem, stumbled in many ways? Ah, now I feel better about you, James.

I have a hard time forgiving myself when I lose my temper with my husband, think mean thoughts, or gossip. *You know better, Jeanette. Will you ever learn? You acted like someone who's never heard of God, let alone claims to follow Him.* If I don't catch those dark thoughts when they first sneak up on me, I quickly get depressed. I end up thinking I'm the worst hypocrite in Jesus's family.

Then James comes along with his sweet reminder that we *all* stumble in many ways. I'm not the only one who wrestles with sin and bad habits. Even pillars in the church grapple with demons. No one is exempt from stumbling. Yet Jesus is willing to use us—flawed as we are—to heal the broken, encourage the downtrodden, or even change the world by writing a book that ends up in the Bible. That's amazing grace. —JEANETTE LEVELLIE

FAITH STEP: *If you have recently stumbled (I know I have), look in a mirror and say aloud, "As Jesus forgives you, I forgive you." Now thank Him for His grace.*

SUNDAY, NOVEMBER 21

Here I am! I stand at the door and knock. If anyone hears my voice and opens the door, I will come in and eat with that person, and they with me. Revelation 3:20 (NIV)

AFTER RUNNING ERRANDS YESTERDAY, I noticed the light blinking on my voice mail. But I was tired and still had to put away the groceries. I decided to check it later. Afternoon turned to evening, and by the time I'd loaded the dinner plates into the dishwasher, I'd forgotten.

This morning, the light continued flashing. I could listen after my morning coffee. But I didn't. Instead, I went on with my day. As I stood in the basement, placing laundry in the washer, I heard knocking at the front door. I shook my head and kept loading. Whoever had come to visit would come another time, right?

When I finally stopped to clear the voice mails, what I heard upset me. I'd missed an invitation to attend the symphony the previous evening. A loved one needed to talk with me—badly. And the doctor's office had called with my test results. Yet, I'd ignored the calls and turned a deaf ear to a visitor.

I glanced at the kitchen table, where my Bible sat, unread. Had I ignored Jesus's calls as well? Had that been Him at the door earlier? "For I was hungry and you gave me something to eat, I was thirsty and you gave me something to drink, I was a stranger and you invited me in" (Matthew 25:35, NIV).

I pulled out a kitchen chair and sat. It was time to open the Bible, my heart, and my home. Because whatever I do for the least of us, I do for Him. —HEIDI GAUL

FAITH STEP: *Next time you're tempted to ignore the phone or a knock at the door, answer it. As you respond to others in need, you might be answering His call.*

MONDAY, NOVEMBER 22

Do not judge, so that you won't be judged. For you will be judged by the same standard with which you judge others, and you will be measured by the same measure you use." Matthew 7:1–2 (CSB)

THE OTHER DAY, I WAS reading *The Cost of Discipleship*, a book by Dietrich Bonhoeffer, one of my heroes, when I came across this passage: "Judging others makes us blind, whereas love is illuminating. By judging others we blind ourselves to our own evil and to the grace which others are just as entitled to as we are." It made me think about the command Jesus gave us when He said, "Do not judge." I've never thought about it just this way before, but Bonhoeffer seemed to believe the alternative to judging is showing grace. And based on all of the things Jesus said about love and how He showed us of grace, I think Bonhoeffer is right.

We teachers like to make lists. One list we make is classroom rules. Some think it's better to make rules positive, rather than negative statements. So instead of saying "Students will not be tardy," one might phrase it as "Students will be on time." If we re-imagine not judging as giving grace, it looks like this: "Give grace, so that you will get grace. For you will be given grace in the same measure as you grant it to others."

This helps me keep in perspective how much grace I need—and how much I need to give. Like Bonhoeffer said, shifting the focus from judgment to love keeps me humble as I seek to see others as Jesus does. When I stay aware of my own darkness instead of obsessed with the sins of others, I'm more willing to extend grace because I'm more keenly aware of my need. —GWEN FORD FAULKENBERRY

FAITH STEP: *Practice the posture of grace as you go throughout this day. Every time you are tempted to judge, take that thought captive and replace it with grace.*

TUESDAY, NOVEMBER 23

As for you, the anointing [the special gift, the preparation] which you received from Him remains [permanently] in you, and you have no need for anyone to teach you. But just as His anointing teaches you [giving you insight through the presence of the Holy Spirit] about all things, and is true and is not a lie, and just as His anointing has taught you, you must remain in Him [being rooted in Him, knit to Him]. 1 John 2:27 (AMP)

THIS MORNING I CONDITIONED MY butcher block cutting board. This sturdy slab of wood sits on my counter all the time. It endures the sharpest of knife cuts. It survives having cheese smeared all over it, tomatoes dripping on it, and onions and garlic scenting it when they are chopped.

But even the most faithful butcher block needs to be cared for. As I rubbed the special oil into the wood, I felt myself wishing someone would condition me. I've been feeling the knife cuts of life, the scrapes, and the mess. Where can we go to be soothed, healed, and renewed? We can turn to Jesus. We can spend time letting His Word permeate us. He can rub away the marks, scars, and dents and pour healing oil over our hearts.

The instructions on the wood conditioner say to leave it on for several hours before buffing. Those directions made me smile as I thought about the Word of Jesus. Sometimes I read a quick verse or two and jump up, ready to get on with my day. But my soul needs deep conditioning. I determined to take more time to let the Word sink into my heart, to allow Jesus to anoint me with His truth, wisdom, and healing. —SHARON HINCK

FAITH STEP: *Schedule a longer-than-usual time today to sit with Jesus, asking Him to let His Word sink in deeply and bring healing to your soul.*

WEDNESDAY, NOVEMBER 24

Carry each other's burdens, and in this way you will fulfill the law of Christ. Galatians 6:2 (NIV)

TEARS FILLED MY EYES WHEN my husband, Kevin—who's also my pastor—asked me to speak at last year's Thanksgiving service. "Can you speak about why you're thankful for our family?"

"But honey, our family isn't doing so well."

In the four years since our daughter's divorce, she'd struggled to make ends meet while raising three kids. Our grown son had wrestled with depression for over twenty years. My ninety-two-year-old widowed mom was quickly declining. What could I offer to encourage others?

Kevin reassured me that while our family isn't perfect, we always support each other. That's what keeps us going. My mind filled with thoughts of the many times we'd helped each other navigate some rough patches. "Well, when you put it that way... okay, I'll do it."

I began my remarks by confessing how reluctant I'd been to talk about our messy family, but that Kevin's insight helped me see our situation in a new light. Moist eyes, smiles, and nodding heads responded to my admission about our imperfect family. I said, "Flawlessness isn't what Jesus looks for in a family, but rather kindness and encouragement. His example of unconditional love empowers us to stand with each other during the tough times and say, 'I've got your back. I'll walk through this darkness with you.'"

Kevin told me afterward how silent the sanctuary was while I spoke. I was glad I'd listened to him. Our family will never be perfect— whose is? But Jesus has filled us with love for each other that knits our hearts together, a perfect reason to thank Him. —JEANETTE LEVELLIE

FAITH STEP: *Think of the ways you can show your gratitude for your imperfect family, from praying for them to cooking their favorite meal to sending a card that says, "I'm glad we're related."*

THANKSGIVING, THURSDAY, NOVEMBER 25

"Give thanks to the LORD, for he is good; his love endures forever." Psalm 107:1 (NIV)

I'M IMPLEMENTING A NEW PRACTICE for Thanksgiving. No, I'm not going to try to convince these Midwesterners that oysters really do belong in authentic turkey stuffing. My idea is to tweak our tradition of each naming one thing or person we're thankful for.

Today, I want to also spend time alone thanking Him for restoring joy to situations I thought held none, for seeing me through disappointments and concerns that threatened to unravel the tightly intertwined fabric of faith He created in me. Circumstances seem to work hard to poke holes in our very souls, as if those events and crises could drain every drop of joy and empty us.

It feels that way sometimes. But reflecting on them now, I'm conscious that disappointments and crises did not succeed. Some of the trials still exist, but true joy cannot be crippled or permanently disabled for the person whose hope is rooted in Jesus.

I have so much for which to be thankful. A crisis from ten years ago is resolved. Concerns that disturbed my sleep five years ago have dissipated. The hurt that stung so hard last week turned into a bridge to a deeper relationship. The "joy stealers" lying in ambush along the way of my career and family and ministry were unsuccessful in their attempts...because of Jesus.

Yes, I have much for which to be thankful. —CYNTHIA RUCHTI

FAITH STEP: *What has Jesus brought you through this past year? Decade? Lifetime? How can you turn that gratitude into an expression of thanksgiving today to the One who preserves our joy.*

FRIDAY, NOVEMBER 26

In the morning, LORD, you hear my voice; in the morning I lay my requests before you and wait expectantly. Psalm 5:3 (NIV)

I'VE HEARD IT SAID, "EXPECTATIONS are the building blocks for disappointment." True. Especially during the holidays. We are bombarded with unrealistic messages of what our meals and homes should look like, and what clothes we should wear.

One year, when my three boys were small, I was determined to get the perfect family photo for our Christmas card. My sons didn't like the matching clothes I bought, and wouldn't smile on cue. Disappointed, I gave up. Instead I wrote a humorous Christmas card about what we learned the past year ranging from "Don't hug your dog after a skunk sprays him," to "Don't shave off your eyebrows, they take a long time to grow back." I received grateful comments from friends because we didn't try to look like the perfect family.

Unrealistic expectations do lead to disappointment and steal joy. However, expectations based on knowing Jesus lead to everlasting joy. He is Immanuel, which means "God with us" (Matthew 1:23, NIV). Nothing can separate us from His love (Romans 8:38–39). He never changes (Hebrews 6:17). When we base our expectations on Jesus, He will not disappoint.

I never got the perfect family photo when my kids were little, but this year my adult sons did smile and wear the shirts I bought, but they didn't shave. Thankfully, I've stopped focusing my expectations on the unimportant, and instead I'm waiting expectantly on Jesus. —JEANNIE BLACKMER

FAITH STEP: *What's one unrealistic expectation you have today? Let it go!*

SATURDAY, NOVEMBER 27

And he said to them, "Take care, and be on your guard against all covetousness, for one's life does not consist in the abundance of his possessions." Luke 12:15 (ESV)

MINIMALISM HAS BEEN A POPULAR topic in recent years. Adventurous folk are moving into tiny houses. Others are tidying their belongings with religious fervor. Many fight to stem the tide of materialism in their lives.

Throughout our married life, my hubby and I made an effort to keep our possessions under control. This was challenging when grandparents showered our children with gifts, or coupons from the local craft store tempted me to stock up on supplies each week. A tight budget didn't make a difference. We still managed to accumulate clothes and books from yard sales and thrift stores.

This past year, Ted and I dove into sorting and simplifying. My husband admits he is a "better keep it just in case" guy. But he isn't the only one. As we emptied closets, I was amazed at how many things I had carried with me through the years—and forgotten about. We set a goal to get rid of about a quarter of everything. Each decision challenged us to trust that if we ever again needed the "just in case" items, Jesus would provide. We weren't using many of the items we owned, but they brought us a sense of security. However, we've found great joy in letting things go and a new gratitude for all He has granted, and we've determined to be better stewards of those items that remain.

The words of Jesus in Luke aren't a call to deprivation and suffering but are a joyful invitation to focus on what really matters in life: loving Him and loving others. —SHARON HINCK

FAITH STEP: *Rummage in the back of a closet or cupboard. Choose items to give away, praying they will bless others.*

FIRST SUNDAY OF ADVENT, NOVEMBER 28

Now faith is confidence in what we hope for and assurance about what we do not see. This is what the ancients were commended for. Hebrews 11:1–2 (NIV)

FOR AS LONG AS I can remember, I have harbored huge dreams. With the passage of time, they change. As a young woman, I dreamed of finding a funny, handsome man to love who would love me back. After I was married to my funny, handsome husband, Scott, I dreamed of following my passion of storytelling. This was coupled with my dream of raising a family of beautiful boys with hearts for Jesus. Today, Scott and I realized another dream. We picked up the keys to our first home: a dream we had thought would never come true. It was too big, too grandiose, too unreal to hope for, yet . . . here we are. In a miraculous turn of events, with the hand of Jesus, the help of parents, and the prayers of friends, we are seeing the impossible become possible.

This is the currency that Jesus deals in. Prayers. Dreams. Promises. Possibilities. He is a Savior without limits. He out-blesses us, out-gives us, and out-loves us at every turn. He knows a little something about hopes and dreams. For thousands of years, the Israelites waited in hope, believing in the face of unfathomable odds that the heavenly Father would keep His promise and send a Savior: His one and only Son. We can dream, standing in that same hope and rock-solid place of faith, knowing that Jesus, the hope of heaven, has come and will come again. That is more than a dream come true.

In this Advent season, revel in that great hope.

—SUSANNA FOTH AUGHTMON

FAITH STEPS: *Journal about your dreams, adding dates for future reference. Know that Jesus is the One who deals in the impossible and is moving on your behalf even now.*

MONDAY, NOVEMBER 29

A woman in that town who lived a sinful life learned that Jesus was eating at the Pharisee's house, so she came there with an alabaster jar of perfume. As she stood behind him at his feet weeping, she began to wet his feet with her tears. Then she wiped them with her hair, kissed them and poured perfume on them. Luke 7:37–38 (NIV)

DESPERATE. EXHAUSTED. HOPELESS. THAT'S HOW the woman felt the night she sought Jesus when He dined with the Pharisees. Wearied from the weight of sin, she wept tears of remorse mingled with worship for the Savior. He alone could cleanse her and remove her shackles of shame. Only He could set her free and give her a fresh start.

She didn't care what others thought of her actions. Their snide comments, criticism, and judgment didn't matter. Her only concern was of Jesus and His thoughts about her.

She opened the alabaster jar filled with expensive perfume. She poured it onto Jesus's feet and, as she did, she gave Him all the pain of her past. *Every single drop.* "Your sins are forgiven," Jesus said. "Your faith has saved you; go in peace" (Luke 7:48, 50, NIV).

Numerous women have shared their secrets with me. Their stories of abuse and shattered dreams break my heart. Shame and pain break theirs. But inner freedom and joy come when they entrust their deepest pain to Jesus. *Every single drop.* He forgives, affirms, and restores them as He did the woman with the alabaster jar.

Do you have an alabaster jar too? Open it, and pour out your pain onto Jesus's feet. Worship Him. Trust Him. He will forgive, affirm, and restore you, dear one. —GRACE FOX

FAITH STEP: *Pour out a drop of perfume or scented oil. Inhale, and thank Jesus for forgiveness and the freedom it brings.*

TUESDAY, NOVEMBER 30

*I keep my eyes always on the LORD. With him at my right hand,
I will not be shaken. Psalm 16:8 (NIV)*

"I NEVER FIGURED OUT WHAT that noise was last night, even after I went outside," I told my husband, Jeff, over breakfast. Jeff's reaction shocked me. He was horrified that I went outside at night without him! He made me promise I'd never do that again. I didn't understand what the big deal was. We live in a snug little house in a nice, quiet neighborhood. I'm not afraid of anything, except maybe snakes. We live near woods, so a coyote might have grabbed me but not without a fight. Besides, I feel secure knowing that Jesus is with me.

I'm reminded of a hymn I love called "Leaning on the Everlasting Arms." I especially like the words from the refrain: "Safe and secure from all alarms." That's how I feel about my relationship with Jesus.

A. J. Showalter, who in 1887 penned the lyrics to "Leaning on the Everlasting Arms," had received letters from two of his former students, telling him their wives had died. Attempting to write condolence letters to his students, Showalter found inspiration in a phrase in Deuteronomy 33:27: "The eternal God is thy refuge, and underneath are the everlasting arms" (KJV). What could be more comforting than resting in the arms of Jesus?

I'm not foolish. I know I need to be careful in the world I live in today. We lock our doors. We have an alarm system that we set when we leave the house and when we settle down for the night. I don't leave my keys or purse in the car. Safety precautions are necessary, but I refuse to live in fear. I choose to believe that Jesus's everlasting arms will keep me from harm. —PAT BUTLER DYSON

FAITH STEP: *Imagine yourself in Jesus's arms.*

WEDNESDAY, DECEMBER 1

But the Lord answered her, "Martha, Martha, you are anxious and troubled about many things, but one thing is necessary. Mary has chosen the good portion, which will not be taken away from her." Luke 10:41–42 (ESV)

SOMETIMES AN UNWANTED BUT FAMILIAR guest shows up in my home for the holidays. Her name is Anxiety. And she just doesn't show up in my home. Recent research shows an increase in anxiety, especially for women, during the holidays. This is because women usually bear the burden of shopping, cooking, decorating the home, entertaining, and all the other demanding details required to create a meaningful experience for our friends and families. I sure do.

Most of us are familiar with the story of Mary and Martha (Luke 10:38–42). Remember when Martha invites Jesus into her home? And wherever He went, crowds followed. I imagine Martha frantically ran around her home, getting food and water for all the guests. She served those who needed help, cleaned up messes, and probably fluffed pillows so all could be comfortable. Meanwhile Mary lounged on the floor at Jesus's feet, soaking up His every single word. Martha complained to Jesus about her sister not helping, and Jesus gently reminded her that Mary had chosen the good way.

Celebrating the birth of Jesus should be a peaceful experience. He is the Prince of Peace and He longs for us to rest in Him, not be busy because of Him. So this Christmas I challenge you to choose the good way—Mary's example of soaking in the words of Jesus. Celebrate His birth with a heart desiring to know Him. His yoke is easy and His burden is light. Don't have another Martha Christmas—this year have a very "Mary" Christmas. —JEANNIE BLACKMER

FAITH STEP: *Pick a project you planned to do today and don't do it. Instead, prayerfully read Matthew 11:28–30 and experience rest for your soul.*

THURSDAY, DECEMBER 2

And he said to me, "It is done! I am the Alpha and the Omega,
the beginning and the end. To the thirsty I will give from the spring
of the water of life without payment." Revelation 21:6 (ESV)

ONE OF OUR MINISTRY COUPLES lives in a Romanian village. I took a team of volunteers to work alongside them recently. When we arrived, they asked us to do manual labor in and around the new building that was nearly ready to open as a church and ministry center.

I raked leaves on a soccer field where community kids and teenagers gather to play. As I worked, I noticed the locals walking on a road adjacent to the field. The occasional man or woman strolled onto the church property. At first, I paid no attention to what they were doing. But suddenly it dawned on me that they were all carrying empty bottles and buckets. Why? They were coming to draw water from a well.

Apparently, most of the villagers have no access to clean drinking water. My friends realized that they could meet the community's basic need by drilling a well on the church property and making water available at no cost. "Come," they said. "Take as much as you need." Providing this service has built trust between them and people who otherwise would have rejected them for following Christ.

Clean, free water quenches the community's thirst. It's vital for life. But more importantly, it's the tool that draws them to Jesus, the Living Water. They're discovering that He's the only answer to quenching their spiritual thirst—and at no cost. —GRACE FOX

FAITH STEP: *Drink a glass of water. Thank Jesus for quenching your spiritual thirst and ask Him to help the Romanian villagers and others suffering the same plight to understand that He is the water of life.*

FRIDAY, DECEMBER 3

In this the love of God was made manifest among us, that God sent his only Son into the world, so that we might live through him. In this is love, not that we have loved God but that he loved us and sent his Son to be the propitiation for our sins. 1 John 4:9–10 (ESV)

MY HUSBAND AND I RETURNED from our small-group Bible study one Sunday night. "I'm upset with myself right now," I said as I got ready for bed. "I meant to be a good listener and instead I talked about myself. I meant to affirm the goodness of Christ in my conversations, but instead I complained about hardships. I was selfish and grouchy. I really don't like myself."

"That's okay," my husband answered. "I like you enough for the both of us."

Not only did Ted make me laugh and cheer me up, he made me realize the tremendous gift of being liked when I can't find good qualities in myself. Throughout our forty years of marriage, Ted has modeled the generous love of Jesus to me a million times.

When we aren't able to love ourselves and when we can't muster acceptance of ourselves, much less anyone else, Jesus invites us to live through Him. We don't lean on our own perfection or even our own attempt to try harder. We stop covering our ears and allow our hearts to hear the truth. Jesus loves us enough for the both of us.

We are dearly loved by our Savior, too precious to be the victim of self-disdain. So next time we fail, instead of pummeling ourselves with self-loathing, let's run to Jesus and ask Him to turn us around and live in us and manifest His love in us. —SHARON HINCK

FAITH STEP: *Go ahead and look in the mirror. See how precious you are, and thank Jesus for loving you so much.*

SATURDAY, DECEMBER 4

*Behold, there was a man in Jerusalem whose name was Simeon,
and this man was just and devout, waiting for the Consolation of Israel,
and the Holy Spirit was upon him. And it had been revealed to him
by the Holy Spirit that he would not see death before he had seen
the Lord's Christ. Luke 2:25–26 (NKJV)*

I BELIEVE SIMEON EXPERIENCED INDESCRIBABLE joy as he awaited the
Messiah's arrival. He trusted the Holy Spirit's revelation. It was just a
matter of time. The thrill of at last seeing—and holding—baby Jesus
offered this prophet hope. And once he had, he could die at peace.

Like Simeon, I've known similar desires and possess a rising hope.
I haven't touched Jesus, He's touched me.

At a recent doctor's appointment, my husband underwent time-
consuming tests. I sat in the waiting room, praying for positive
results. As minutes dragged by, I read a magazine, then fiddled with
my phone. After a while I'd run out of things to do and had no choice
but to admit it was out of my hands. Like other situations in my life,
from reaching out to someone in friendship, to stretching forward in
my work, the next move belongs to somebody else. And that someone is Jesus. He's the Author of my life. When times are hard, He's
with me. He'll never leave me or forsake me (Hebrews 13:5). And the
closer He draws me to Him, the greater my satisfaction.

Deep within, quiet anticipation stirs as unshakable joy takes
root. I know the thoughts He thinks toward me, thoughts of peace
and not of evil, thoughts to give me a future and a hope (Jeremiah
29:11). And like Simeon, I'm willing to wait. —HEIDI GAUL

FAITH STEP: *Are you experiencing trials beyond your control? Acknowledge
your powerlessness, take a seat in Jesus's prayer room and prepare for the joy
found in absolute trust.*

SECOND SUNDAY OF ADVENT, DECEMBER 5

For God so loved the world that he gave his one and only Son, that whoever believes in him shall not perish but have eternal life. John 3:16 (NIV)

JACK, OUR OLDEST, IS GETTING ready to go off to college. I remember watching Jack get in line for his first day of kindergarten as if it were yesterday. Dressed in a blue cardigan and tie for chapel, he followed his teacher toward the classroom. Jack looked at me and grinned. I smiled while furiously blinking back tears. There he was. My very heart walking away from me into his amazing future.

Fast-forward to this past week. Jack is staying in California until he leaves for school, while the rest of us move across the country. I went into Jack's room the night before we moved. He was on the floor in a sleeping bag, his bed already loaded for the move. I lay down next to him and began to cry. He patted my back, and I told him, "I love you. I am so proud of you. I am going to miss you like crazy." He grinned at me and said, "I know, Mom. I love you too." Once again, my heart is walking away from me.

What must it have been like for our heavenly Father to send Jesus, His beloved Son, to earth? His very heart leaving the brightness of heaven for earth's darkest reaches. Jesus left His Father for one reason alone: for His love of us. His love is so great, so sacrificial, and so all-encompassing, that the magnitude of it is still echoing throughout all of eternity. Our hearts are tended by the One who is love incarnate. In this Advent season, recognize His love for you. —SUSANNA FOTH AUGHTMON

FAITH STEP: *Turn off the lights and sit in the dark, knowing the brightness of Jesus's love surrounds you this Advent season.*

MONDAY, DECEMBER 6

She gave birth to her first-born son. She dressed him in baby clothes and laid him on a bed of hay, because there was no room for them in the inn. Luke 2:7 (CEV)

ONE OF THE REASONS THE Jewish people didn't accept Jesus as a future king was that He came into the world too simply for their taste. Think about it: Jesus was born to a teenager in a small town on Israel's West Bank; He wasn't attended to by a midwife; and He was birthed into a horse trough. Later, when He became a man and tried to preach in His home synagogue, the townsfolk interrupted, saying, "Is this not the carpenter, the Son of Mary...?" and we're told that "they were offended at Him." (Mark 6:3, NKJV). He didn't have the pedigree they wanted in a Messiah.

Yet, our Lord's humble presentation should affect us deeply. Often, we are awed by the pomp and circumstance of visiting pastors, priests, and bishops—someone carries their Bible and wipes their brow with a hanky as they preach (confession: I always check out the first lady's outfit and shoes!). But Jesus was a simple guy. The prophet Isaiah said, "He has no form or comeliness; And when we see Him, There is no beauty that we should desire Him" (Isaiah 53:2, NKJV). Jesus rode a donkey, ate with known sinners and lodged with outcasts. My husband and I have the privilege of attending a church that welcomes the homeless and provides care and counseling. I am thankful for the reminder that Jesus loved me in the middle of my mess, too, just as He loves the homeless. I want to make more room in my life for the people the world considers unlovely—just as Jesus did. —PAMELA TOUSSAINT HOWARD

FAITH STEP: *Take time this Christmas season to show kindness to someone who you would normally bypass or avoid. Look for Jesus's beauty in them.*

TUESDAY, DECEMBER 7

Then God said, "Yes, but your wife Sarah will bear you a son, and you will call him Isaac. I will establish my covenant with him as an everlasting covenant for his descendants after him. Genesis 17:19 (NIV)

THIS IS ONE OF THE earliest prophecies of Jesus. I chose it because it mentions Isaac (which means "laughter"), who is just like my youngest son named Isaac, who brings much laughter. Earlier in this verse, the very thought of Abraham and his postmenopausal wife, Sarah, having a baby made them both laugh. Yet through this very unlikely scenario, God foreshadowed another seemingly far-fetched situation that produced Jesus as the promised everlasting covenant for Isaac's descendants: God's people, the Israelites.

Hundreds of years later, Paul wrote in Romans 9:7–8 that the adopted Gentile children of the promise—*you and me*—are now regarded as Isaac's descendants, aka God's people. In Christ, we are truly God's sons and daughters with a spiritual lineage dating back to Isaac. We're every bit the children of God, just as Isaac was a child of Abraham and Sarah, and Jesus Himself was a child of Mary and Joseph.

My women's Bible group recently studied Paul's letter to the Ephesians. In it, Paul repeatedly prays that we understand the "glorious riches" of our spiritual inheritance through the promised Messiah, Jesus, which was first foreshadowed to a faithful old couple more than twenty-five hundred years ago. —ISABELLA YOSUICO

FAITH STEP: *Ponder your glorious spiritual inheritance by praying Ephesians 1:15–20; 3:14–21 for yourself.*

WEDNESDAY, DECEMBER 8

Do not conform to the pattern of this world, but be transformed by the renewing of your mind. Then you will be able to test and approve what God's will is—his good, pleasing and perfect will. Romans 12:2 (NIV)

THE HOLIDAY DINNER WAS A total fiasco and I was red-faced with disappointment and embarrassment. There were a series of fumbles preparing the meal, despite my hard work and planning. The fresh trout I baked was awful. The potatoes were burnt. The shellfish appetizer was a mess. The veggies were overcooked. To top it off, the house was smoky from an oven grease splatter. I'm usually a confident and adept cook, but this time everything was unraveling.

This was years ago, when I was very briefly engaged to a man I'd been dating on and off for a while. I had finally and reluctantly accepted his marriage proposal. I had all sorts of misgivings, but I was pushing thirty and a few friends had gotten married. I was feeling pressured. We'd just gotten engaged, and I hosted a holiday dinner for my fiancé and my family. I wanted everything to be perfect, but the evening was a disaster. Nothing flowed.

Later, after I broke off the engagement and later married my husband, my sister-in-law and I were recalling that awful evening. "It wasn't flowing because it wasn't meant to be," she said.

I've found that when I'm anxious, confused, or clumsy, it reveals something that needs loving attention, which fruitless, stress-filled laboring will not quiet. Instead, pausing to talk to Jesus and waiting on His reply can lead to serene confidence, good fruit, and an undeniable flow that tells you you're right where He wants you.
—ISABELLA YOSUICO

FAITH STEP: *Do you feel deep unrest about a decision or situation? Rather than fret, take it to Jesus and leave it there.*

THURSDAY, DECEMBER 9

Because Joseph her husband was faithful to the law, and yet did not want to expose her to public disgrace, he had in mind to divorce her quietly.
Matthew 1:19 (NIV)

IT'S HARD TO IMAGINE JOSEPH'S shock and disappointment when he learned that Mary was pregnant. In their culture, Joseph and Mary were as good as already married to each other. Now it seemed that Mary had been unfaithful to Joseph—that she had sinned against God and her betrothed. Many men would have let their hurt and anger dictate their response, wanting to be vindicated for the way they'd been treated. But Joseph reacted in a different way: he wanted to spare Mary the humiliation of being publicly exposed. So, he decided he would divorce her quietly.

Things are not always what they seem on the surface. The reality was that God was doing something never done before. Joseph didn't fully understand that plan, but he responded in a compassionate, selfless way to the situation. And God honored him. He revealed His plan to Joseph and gave him specific instructions: Mary's baby would fulfill the prophecy in Isaiah 7:14 about the Messiah's virgin birth. As Mary's husband, Joseph would be entrusted with the role of protecting and nurturing the Savior of the world.

The little we see of Joseph in Scriptures shows us how to respond to a sudden turn of events that we don't understand. Like him, we can respond to people with compassion, trusting God to reveal anything we need to know and to show us what role He wants us to play. Because when God seems to be turning our plans upside down, it just might be that He's doing something never done before in our lives. —DIANNE NEAL MATTHEWS

FAITH STEP: *The next time you're surprised by a situation that disappoints you, ask Jesus for the grace to respond selflessly and to trust Him for guidance.*

FRIDAY, DECEMBER 10

After Jesus was born in Bethlehem in Judea, during the time of King Herod, Magi from the east came to Jerusalem and asked, "Where is the one who has been born king of the Jews? We saw his star when it rose and have come to worship him."... When they saw the star, they were overjoyed.
Matthew 2:1–2, 10 (NIV)

LAST NIGHT, I COULDN'T SLEEP. Thoughts swirled in my mind like a tornado, fractured and chaotic. I rose, walked to the porch and settled into a rocker, waiting for Jesus's peace to calm me. In the darkness, tree limbs swayed to a melody only they could hear. Silence blanketed the night, and I took a deep breath of the chilled air. My eyes drifted upward to the stars.

The longer I stared at the sky, the more stars I saw—each one seeming to sparkle just for me. As I reveled in their distant beauty, childlike awe welled inside me at the sight of God's vast universe. Did the wise men experience the same wonder? How could they have focused on the allure of just one star in a sea of twinkling light? Because of what it represented to them—a path to the King.

It's been thousands of years since those men made that long journey in search of the Christ child. It couldn't have been easy, yet they continued their trek until they found Him and honored Him with gifts. During Christmastime, I can become overwhelmed by a sea of glittering distractions that lead me away from Jesus. I want to keep my eyes on the true Star of the season—baby Jesus—and honor Him. —HEIDI GAUL

FAITH STEP: *The next time the night skies are clear, bundle up and spend some time outside looking at the stars. As you take in the stellar show, give thanks to the One who created it.*

SATURDAY, DECEMBER 11

But you, O Bethlehem Ephrathah, are only a small village among all the people of Judah. Yet a ruler of Israel, whose origins are in the distant past, will come from you on my behalf. Micah 5:2 (NLT)

WE WERE LIVING IN A large southern city when my husband started a job in the Midwest. By the time our two little boys and I joined him, he had rented a house in a small rural town (called a village in that area). The place had one stop light, one grocery store, one restaurant, and a Dairy Queen. At first his choice surprised me, but I soon discovered a community filled with friendly people, vibrant church congregations, and excellent schools. A forest preserve offered wonderful opportunities to enjoy nature. Anything else we needed could be reached by a short drive down the interstate.

Bethlehem may have seemed like an insignificant village in the world's eyes, but God had big plans in store. This location held special worth because it would be the birthplace of the Savior of the world. At the right time, Jesus was born and the light of His glory shone in the sky in the form of a star. This light drew shepherds and Magi to Him.

In the world's eyes, we may seem insignificant or unimportant. We may even feel that way about ourselves sometimes. But we have great worth because the One who was born in Bethlehem also lives inside us. If we live in close fellowship with Him, when the time is right His glory will shine from us and be seen by anyone we're interacting with. How can we feel insignificant when Jesus wants to use us to draw people to Himself? —DIANNE NEAL MATTHEWS

FAITH STEP: *The next time you feel unimportant, thank Jesus for living inside you. Ask Him to help you shine His light for everyone around you to see.*

THIRD SUNDAY OF ADVENT, DECEMBER 12

You will go out in joy and be led forth in peace; the mountains and hills will burst into song before you, and all the trees of the field will clap their hands. Isaiah 55:12 (NIV)

WHEN SCOTT AND I GOT the news by text from our realtor that our offer had been accepted on our new home, I had to bust out a few nineties dance moves. Since college, the Running Man has been my dance of choice. Flinging back my head, I pumped my arms, proceeding with a jig of jubilation. Scott started laughing. His laughter wasn't just because of my superior dance skills or the fact that I could keep up the dance for only about seventy-two seconds. It was brought on by his sheer, unadulterated joy. We had been surprised, once again, by the goodness of Jesus—upended by His amazingness. He blessed our socks off. It is what He does.

When Mary learned that she was going to miraculously give birth to the Son of the Living God, she broke out into a hymn of praise about the Lord's goodness. When her cousin Elizabeth, who was living out her own pregnancy miracle, greeted Mary, John the Baptist broke out into his own dance of joy ... in utero. They were all caught off guard by the promise and presence of Jesus. The Savior. Emmanuel. God with us. Jesus is too wonderful to understand. His ways are too marvelous to behold. He delights in surprising us with His mercy, grace, and love. In the most out of the way places and in the most impossible circumstances, Jesus is always waiting to break into our lives with His goodness. In this Advent season, embrace His joy. —SUSANNA FOTH AUGHTMON

FAITH STEP: *Consider how Jesus surprises you regularly with His goodness. Do a jig of joy in your living room and let that joy fill you up.*

MONDAY, DECEMBER 13

Therefore, if anyone is in Christ, the new creation has come:
The old has gone, the new is here! 2 Corinthians 5:17 (NIV)

THE NUMBER ONE REQUEST ON my Christmas list last year was a new printer. The old one was slow, noisy, and had lost its scanning function. I told my husband, "Even if a printer is all you get me, I'll be fine with that."

I was elated when I found what looked like the printer of my dreams at a Black Friday sale. But when we tried to hook it up, nothing worked. My computer wouldn't recognize it. The driver download repeatedly failed, no matter what new tricks we tried. Because it was a holiday weekend, I couldn't call tech support for three days. I decided to pack up my new printer and take it back for a refund.

As it turned out, the sound of that old printer wasn't half as annoying as I'd once imagined. And we had an old scanner in the basement I could use if needed. I was happy to go back to my old ways.

Jesus told the people of His day that they needed new wineskins, rather than putting new wine in old skins, which would cause the skins to break. It was His way of saying that just as with me and my printer, we tend to be more comfortable with our old way of doing things. Sometimes it seems like too much trouble to change and learn something new.

Knowing this tendency, Jesus offers us entire new lives. We don't have to change ourselves. When we invite Him to take over, He transforms us from the inside out, making us new creations. His spirit in us is all we need to live victorious lives—no tech support required. —JEANETTE LEVELLIE

FAITH STEP: *Contact an old friend you haven't talked to in a long time and catch up with her. Tell her how much you value her.*

TUESDAY, DECEMBER 14

On coming to the house, they saw the child with his mother Mary, and they bowed down and worshiped him. Then they opened their treasures and presented him with gifts of gold, frankincense and myrrh. Matthew 2:11 (NIV)

CHRISTMAS IS ALMOST HERE. MANY of us are spending time shopping for gifts for loved ones. Some are baking, some are volunteering, and some are decorating. That's what I'm doing this week. As my husband and I set up our white porcelain nativity set, my hand rests on one of the wise men. He's traveled a long way and is tired, but he's kneeling before the infant King, a look of deep reverence on his face. He's holding an urn, stretching his arms toward Jesus. The other wise men seem expectant, eager as children to present Him with their treasures. In his bed of straw, Jesus is napping. I sigh as I rearrange a few of the animals and push the wise men closer. This is peace.

Soon we'll begin our family traditions. Baking day is important. As all of us crowd the kitchen, scooping flour and adding extracts, laughter draws us closer. Then we'll handstamp our wrapping paper and tags, stealing an opportunity to slow down and be creative. We'll attend the Christmas Eve candlelight service and share a German apple puff pancake on Christmas morning.

But this year, I want to give Jesus something. Something precious and irreplaceable, something worth more than gold, frankincense, and myrrh. Something beyond tithing and even volunteering. I'm anticipating how much this gift will please Him. Because I plan to give Him *everything* this season. All my hopes, dreams, talents, and trust. All my love. All of me. Every single bit. Just like He did for me. —HEIDI GAUL

FAITH STEP: *You can give everything to Jesus. What have you held back? Give Him every bit of you. That's exactly what He wants!*

WEDNESDAY, DECEMBER 15

Do not lay up for yourselves treasures on earth, where moth and rust destroy and where thieves break in and steal; but lay up for yourselves treasures in heaven... Matthew 6:19–20 (NKJV)

THIS TIME OF YEAR, WE can be very distracted by presents, trips, and preparations. But this Christmas, I want to be focused on that most important gift—Jesus—and the treasure He is to me. I was lost in my sin, but He saw me. And through the prayers of my mom and her Bible study group, I accepted His offer of salvation during my last year in college. That is a treasure in my heart that no moth or economic downturn can destroy!

My friend Melinda and I, along with our moms, were on a Christmas Eve outing one year in midtown Manhattan. (Anyone who loves the city must experience Christmas in the Big Apple at least once). We walked the snowy streets after a holiday concert and spotted a woman near the subway entrance who was literally wearing a large black plastic garbage bag, the kind used for leaves. Her arms and legs were bare. It was cold! Compassion welled up in us, and we shared Jesus's love with her. Then each of us took off an article of our outer clothing and gave it to her. I remember vividly how Melinda took off her late father's wool sweater—a treasure to her—and gave it to this stranger. I wrapped my winter scarf around her. Our moms gave gloves and a hat, if my memory serves me correctly. We met that woman's physical needs that cold day, but we hope her memory of us is that we gave her Jesus, the best treasure of all. —PAMELA TOUSSAINT HOWARD

FAITH STEP: *Pray about who you can share Jesus with this Christmas, and do it. Don't worry about the outcome, just share your treasure.*

THURSDAY, DECEMBER 16

Look! The virgin will conceive a child! She will give birth to a son and will call him Immanuel (which means "God is with us"). Isaiah 7:14 (NLT)

MY HUSBAND AND I USUALLY spend part of our Christmas road trip in the town where our sons live, and our daughter's family goes to visit my son-in-law's family. We used to stay at a hotel and meet them at a restaurant for a couple of hours, but two years ago, we decided to rent a house instead of a hotel room. This gave us plenty of space, and I was able to cook for my family. We all agreed it was a better option.

Last year, I found a rental house that looked perfect online. But after driving one thousand miles over two days, we arrived to find that the cleaning crew had not come—and wouldn't be coming. I spent the evening pulling sheets off stained mattresses, washing dirty towels, and cleaning bathrooms. The next day, I bought some household items along with groceries, did prep work for our Christmas meal, and more cleaning. Late that night, I settled down to sleep on the couch since my husband had been sick in bed since the day after we arrived. Suddenly, the doorbell rang. It was a man holding giant packages of toilet tissue, which we didn't need. The next day, as I cleaned up after dinner, the garbage disposal cracked and gushed out water.

The older I get, the more I realize I can't make Christmas perfect for my family. But that's okay. The baby in the manger was called Immanuel because God had come down to earth in human form. If we know Jesus as our Savior, He is still with us, now and forever. And that's enough to make any imperfect holiday perfectly wonderful. —DIANNE NEAL MATTHEWS

FAITH STEP: *Each time you feel stressed about holiday details, take a deep breath and meditate on what "Immanuel, God with us," means to you.*

FRIDAY, DECEMBER 17

I began to weep loudly because no one was found worthy to open the scroll or to look into it. Revelation 5:4 (ESV)

ONE TIME, MY HUSBAND, BILL, buried our son-in-law's gift in a waterproof box at the bottom of a frozen pond. Another time, he filled a fifty-gallon barrel with the spray-foam insulation that hardens almost instantly. Caleb's gift card was in the middle of the hardened foam. Who knew the spray-foam would melt a plastic gift card? That idea didn't turn out as funny as it sounded in the design phase. Caleb became very creative trying to outdo his father-in-law with impossible-to-reach presents—good-natured pranks.

When meditating on the deep joy of Jesus that is offered to us, I thought about how much fun those two men have as they try to out-prank each other. But fun isn't joy. We use them interchangeably too often.

This week, I read with new understanding the scene in Revelation 5:4 that opens with grievous sorrow. John had a vision of heaven, and he saw the Father with a scroll in His hand, sealed with seven seals. But when the question "Who is worthy to open the scroll and break its seals?" resounded throughout the crowd, the answer was no one (v. 2, ESV). No one living or dead, in heaven or on earth. No one was found worthy to unlock the secrets contained in the scrolls. No one... except Jesus, the Lamb of God.

The crushing sorrow over not having access to what the scrolls contained turned to exuberant joy several verses later at the discovery that there *is* One who is worthy. Jesus the Lamb! That's a powerful message that changes everything for us. —CYNTHIA RUCHTI

FAITH STEP: *Read Revelation 5. If you're grieving, trust Jesus to turn your sorrow into joy.*

SATURDAY, DECEMBER 18

*Joseph also went up from the town of Nazareth in Galilee to Judea,
to Bethlehem. . . . He went there to register with Mary, who was pledged
to be married to him and was expecting a child. Luke 2:4—5 (NIV)*

WHEN MY BOYS WERE BORN, we lived in the country, nearly an hour
from the hospital. Since my first son, Pierce, was overdue by two
weeks, we schlepped to the hospital for a sonogram to see how he
was doing. Discovering he was frank breech—folded in two like
a book—the doctor sent me back home to get my bags, instructing me to return right away for a C-section. With my first-time
mom jitters and an overripe belly, that round-trip journey on a cold
December day was quite a haul. My husband and I prayed *a lot.*

Later, I hoped to deliver my next son, Isaac, the old-fashioned
way. It was late one night in April. My husband and Pierce were
asleep. I was restless in the way pregnant women can be, awake and
cleaning and folding laundry. My water broke. Uncertain, I busied
myself for a good hour before calling a friend to sit with Pierce
while my husband drove me to the hospital. By then the contrac-
tions had started. I finally understood Eve's curse!

All this driving on the eve of my babies' arrival was trying.

Mary rode some ninety miles from Nazareth to Bethlehem. On
a donkey. For a week. In the desert. Without bucket seats or heat.

What was that like? Did Mary whine as I would? Did Joseph ask
himself what he'd gotten himself into? Or, did the Spirit of the baby
inside Mary give them the grace to carry on? I believe so.

Jesus gives us the grace for our journey, however arduous.
—ISABELLA YOSUICO

FAITH STEP: *Whatever you're facing, Jesus has grace for your journey.*

FOURTH SUNDAY OF ADVENT, DECEMBER 19

Do not be anxious about anything, but in every situation, by prayer and petition, with thanksgiving, present your requests to God. And the peace of God, which transcends all understanding, will guard your hearts and your minds in Christ Jesus. Philippians 4:6–7 (NIV)

MY UNCLE JOHN USED TO have a saying that he would ask my cousins and me every time we got antsy in church. As we wiggled, he would whisper, eyes twinkling, "Are you nervous in the service?" We usually were. It was really hard to sit still and pay attention when we had other things on our minds. I still get "nervous in the service." Just yesterday, I got antsy when things didn't go the way I thought they should. I get stressed about bills, raising kids, sticky relationships, and my friends getting cancer. Life often feels too big for me to handle. Jesus looks at my fretful mind and whispers, "Sue, are you nervous in the service?"

Jesus is inviting me and you to a place of peace. He is asking us to trust Him completely with our every concern and desire. He is the Prince of Peace. He reigns over our hearts. Nerves, worries, anxiety, and fear are not found in His kingdom. He asks us to simply talk to Him about our concerns. He wants us to share our thoughts with Him. The good, the bad, and the ugly. And He says if we will turn over our cares to Him with a thankful heart, then He will blow our minds with His unfathomable peace. That peace will hold our hearts and minds in a place of safety. In this Advent season, let the peace of Jesus invade your life. —SUSANNA FOTH AUGHTMON

FAITH STEP: *Share your burdens with a close friend. Ask them to join you in prayer and invite the peace of Jesus into your present situation.*

MONDAY, DECEMBER 20

Today in the town of David a Savior has been born to you; he is the Messiah, the Lord. This will be a sign to you: You will find a baby wrapped in cloths and lying in a manger. Luke 2:11–12 (NIV)

EVERY YEAR MY FAMILY GATHERS at my parents' home in Colorado the week between Christmas and New Year's Day. Living out of state, I rarely get time with my parents. Phone calls and text messages can't compare with seeing them face to face. The anticipation of being together is almost more than I can handle. On the plane, I count the moments until I am on the ground. Once we land, I can hardly wait for my dad to come pick us up. My mom is waiting on the porch when we drive up to the house. We run up the stairs into her arms, laughing—excited to be together.

I know that my siblings feel the same way I do. These are the people that have loved us since birth. They know us and love us no matter what. Our parents have grounded us in the foundation of their love. We feel it each time we are together. Being in their presence is sheer joy. That is what Christmas is all about. Our heavenly Father couldn't stand being separated from the people that He loved most... His kids. Jesus solved that problem. The Son of God came to earth to crush sin, bring freedom, and restore relationship. He is eagerly anticipating the day that He sees us face to face. His long-lost family. He loves us no matter what. He will grab us in His arms, squeeze us tight and say, "Welcome home!" —SUSANNA FOTH AUGHTMON

FAITH STEP: *Jesus knows you and loves you completely. Reread Luke 2:11–12. Recognize that Jesus came to earth two thousand years ago, so that one day He would be able to see you face to face.*

TUESDAY, DECEMBER 21

I no longer call you servants, because a servant does not know his master's business. Instead, I have called you friends, for everything that I learned from my Father I have made known to you. John 15:15 (NIV)

I RECENTLY READ A SMALL book about the Swedish word *hygge* (pronounced hoo-gah), which means "cozy." Christmas traditions are hygge. Warm blankets and crackling fires are hygge. Flickering beeswax candles are hygge. But the most hygge thing of all is spending time with a close friend. I share a hygge relationship, built over decades of shared joy and struggles, with my cousin Beth. We understand each other. We pray for each other. We give each other a great amount of grace in the face of our weaknesses. We stand up for each other. After years of being in each other's lives, our hearts are knit together. I can go to Beth at any time and find empathy, hope, and some belly laughs. She gets me. She loves me. And she knows that she will receive the same love from me.

Close friendship is what we are created for. When Jesus came to this world, He didn't just come to bring salvation. He came to show us what real friendship is, laying down His very life for us. He came to engage us, laugh with us, and heal us. He delights in creating a path of joy for us. He gives us unimaginable grace and offers us refuge in His love. He intertwines His heart with ours, inviting us into an intimate relationship with Him. He gets us. He loves us. He calls us friends. He restores our souls. That is more than hygge (cozy). That is life-giving. —SUSANNA FOTH AUGHTMON

FAITH STEP: *Spend time with a close friend. Enjoy the fun you have in each other's presence. Thank Jesus for your friend and the gift of friendship that He offers you.*

WEDNESDAY, DECEMBER 22

Suddenly a great company of the heavenly host appeared with the angel, praising God and saying, "Glory to God in the highest heaven, and on earth peace to those on whom his favor rests." Luke 2:13–14 (NIV)

MY FAMILY LOVES WATCHING TALENT shows on television. My favorite contestants are the singers. I am captivated by their hope as they sing their hearts out. The other night, a choir from South Africa was performing. The judges had forewarned them that no choir had ever placed in the finals. A hush fell on the crowd. Then the choir began to sing. They swayed with every note, moving in jubilation to the music. Their joy filled the auditorium. When they finished, the crowd went crazy. The choir responded back to the applause, shouting, jumping, and ululating. Joy unspeakable. This is why the singers were born. The whole world had witnessed it.

The night that Jesus was born, a different kind of choir performed. There were no judges. The audience was a group of humble shepherds. There was no applause. There may have been some fainting. Someone probably cried. A vast multitude of angels cracked the heavens open with their joy, singing, "Glory to God in the highest!" It was the performance of a lifetime. The King of kings had come to earth. Men were going to be set free from sin. Death would be conquered, and love would abound. They sang their hearts out. This is what they were made for, and it is what we are made for too—praising Jesus, announcing His goodness, telling of His love. Whether you are tone-deaf or a mezzo-soprano, you were made to revel in the joy of who Jesus is, announcing His love to the world.
—SUSANNA FOTH AUGHTMON

FAITH STEP: *Gather a group of friends to go caroling at a nearby nursing home. Share the love of Jesus and the glorious Hope of Heaven with each resident.*

THURSDAY, DECEMBER 23

Every good and perfect gift is from above, coming down from the Father of the heavenly lights, who does not change like shifting shadows. James 1:17 (NIV)

CHRISTMAS STOCKINGS HAVE ALWAYS BEEN a big deal on my side of the family. *Who doesn't love a big sock full of tiny treasures to dig into on Christmas morning?* One of my favorite stories about my mom's childhood was her overnight trip from Portland, Oregon, to Modesto, California, after church on Christmas Eve. Driving through the night to reach their grandparents' house, she and her four siblings woke up Christmas morning to find treat-filled stockings hung in each of the car windows. Wonder and laughter abounded. It was a golden moment.

I have continued the tradition with my boys, filling their stockings with chocolate, fun gadgets, and silly socks. I love hearing their laughter when they pull out their gifts. This year as I fill their stockings, I will be looking to find special treats for each one: drawing pencils for Will, remote control gadgets for Addie, and good fiction for Jack. I want to see that look of joy on their faces as they empty their stockings—the look that shows they feel known and loved. Jesus is the best Giver of gifts. He knows us inside and out. He knows what we need, what we long for, and the things that will fulfill our greatest hearts' desires. In the Psalms, it says He satisfies our desires with good things so that our youth is renewed like the eagle's (Psalms 103:5, NIV). Good gifts are restorative. He pours His goodness out upon us, supplying our every need. In the presence of His love, wonder and laughter abound. —SUSANNA FOTH AUGHTMON

FAITH STEP: *Invite family and friends to fill stockings with special treats. In the spirit of Jesus, deliver them to a homeless shelter, showing those staying there that they are known and loved.*

CHRISTMAS EVE, FRIDAY, DECEMBER 24

While they were there, the time came for the baby to be born, and she gave birth to her firstborn, a son. She wrapped him in cloths and placed him in a manger, because there was no guest room available for them. Luke 2:6–7 (NIV)

THE OTHER MORNING, I WENT down into the garage where my three teenage boys play video games. The floor was littered with soda cans and empty popcorn bags. Napkins and old socks peeked out from under the couch cushions where they sit. When I looked behind the couch, I needed a moment. The volume of trash crammed in between it and the wall was breathtaking. I thought, *I need go no farther*. I called to them, "Boys! Come clean up!" The clutter was disheartening. I didn't want to get my hands dirty. I wanted the boys to clean up their own mess.

Jesus took the opposite approach when He came to earth on that holy Christmas night so long ago. Instead of picking a pristine palace or a comfortable home to make His appearance, He chose a smelly stable. Surrounded by animals and nestled in a bed of hay, the Son of God made Himself known. He also made His heart known. He is not afraid of our mess. In fact, He knows that He is the only One Who can clean up our hearts, minds, and situations. Try though we might, we always come up short when it comes to cleaning ourselves up. But Jesus—Emmanuel, God with us—is here, and He's willing and able to create order out of chaos, wrapping us in His righteousness and cleansing us from all sin.
—SUSANNA FOTH AUGHTMON

FAITH STEP: *Today as you tidy your house, recognize how Jesus has entered the mess of your life willingly and know He is not put off by it. His heart is for you. He has come to make you whole.*

CHRISTMAS DAY, SATURDAY, DECEMBER 25

For unto us a child is born, unto us a son is given: and the government shall be upon his shoulder: and his name shall be called Wonderful, Counsellor, The mighty God, The everlasting Father, The Prince of Peace. Isaiah 9:6 (KJV)

WHEN MY THIRTEEN-YEAR-OLD SON, ADDISON, was two, he was enthralled with the Christmas lights that decked out the houses in our neighborhood. Each time he would see a beautifully lit home, he would call out with joy, "Kiss-mas!" The lights symbolized all the beauty of the season for Addie. He would ask, hopefully, as we pulled up to our unlit house, "Kiss-mas come my house?" Sadly, for Addie, he had to make do with indoor lights.

But Addison has kept his sense of wonder when it comes to Christmas. I asked him the other morning, "Why do you like Christmas so much?" He said, "I like it because of the feeling. Everyone is happy." There is a sense of goodwill in the air. There is a sense of anticipation that some delightful gift or experience is around every corner. The feeling that we experience each Christmas is an echo of the miraculous birth that happened that first Christmas. Anything is possible with Jesus. It is an acknowledgment of that goodness right now—that Jesus is still making Himself known today. It is a foreshadow of the eternal joy that we will have in His presence when we finally see Him face to face. Christmas is a celebration for every human when we recognize that Jesus came to earth to be with us and we will never be alone again. Christmas has come to your house and mine. —SUSANNA FOTH AUGHTMON

FAITH STEP: *Speak out Jesus's powerful names, saying, "You are wonderful. You are my Counselor. You are my mighty God. You are my everlasting Father. You are my Prince of Peace." Praise Him for His presence in your life this Christmas.*

SUNDAY, DECEMBER 26

For I am the LORD your God who takes hold of your right hand and says to you, Do not fear; I will help you. Do not be afraid, you worm Jacob, little Israel, do not fear, for I myself will help you," declares the LORD, your Redeemer, the Holy One of Israel. Isaiah 41:13–14 (NIV)

I PULLED THE CHRISTMAS PRESENT out of a shiny gift bag and unfolded the yellow T-shirt so I could read the message emblazoned on the front: "The only thing we have to fear is fear itself…and spiders." Below the words, a tiny cartoon spider hovered.

We all laughed at the appropriate gift from my mom. She knows bugs make me very jumpy. A few days later, I wore the shirt. Late in the day, I startled, brushing frantically at my chest. My eyes had caught a glimpse of a spider, and I'd forgotten it was a cartoon. Even the image of the spider stirred fear.

With so many frightening dangers in this world, spiders may not seem very important. However, the things that make me nervous—large or small—remind me of how much I need Jesus to stand up for me. He is our Redeemer. He stands between us and the source of fear. Even if I coax myself to be brave, my own efforts often fall short. But when I hear Jesus declare, "I Myself will help you," I can breathe again.

Is there anything stirring fear in you today? Are you worried about a relationship? Concerned about a problem at work? Anxious about changes in your health? Jesus sees how tiny you feel in the face of your need. He promises to hold your hand and personally help you.
—SHARON HINCK

FAITH STEP: *Lift your hand. Picture Jesus taking your hand and speaking directly to you: "Do not fear, for I Myself will help you."*

MONDAY, DECEMBER 27

"A virgin will have a baby boy, and he will be called Immanuel,"
which means "God is with us." Matthew 1:23 (CEV)

MY SON HARPER IS SIXTEEN years old as I write this. The first years
of his life it was easy to be close to him. Life was slow; I wasn't
working full-time, and he and I would go on walks, sit on the porch
swing and tell stories, and chase lizards all we wanted. I cried when
he went to kindergarten, but he was still my little boy. We captured
crawdads, went on picnics, and watched bulldozers. Weekends were
for playing and snuggling.

As time passed, he gained two younger sisters, and I started working full-time. He got interested in football, four-wheelers, and hunting. He learned to beat me in chess and read his own books and make
fishing poles and longbows. He surpassed me in his ability to play
the guitar. He got a dog he took everywhere with him. To be a part
of his world, I needed to get more creative. So I helped him build a
deer stand. I hiked into the woods in the wee hours of the morning to
watch him hunt. Right now, I'm gearing up for every football game,
memorizing plays so we can talk about them after the game.

I'm a girl who loves literature, writing, and traveling. I play the
piano, bake bread, and watch Game of Thrones. It's not that I love
football or hunting or even eating wild game. But I love Harper.
And to know him I have to be with him—wherever he is.

Jesus feels the same way about us, times infinity. That's why He
came down from heaven to be with us. God became a baby, grew
up and walked among us to know us intimately. Because He loves
us. —GWEN FORD FAULKENBERRY

FAITH STEP: *Today spend quality time with Jesus, and also with a friend or*
family member.

TUESDAY, DECEMBER 28

I have come that they may have life, and have it to the full. John 10:10 (NIV)

LAST YEAR MY FRIEND MARY Ellen decided to host a "Swell Life" party. She gathered our close-knit community together to celebrate the blessings of the past year. We spent the day biking, riding paddleboards and doing other fun activities. Then we met in the evening and shared dinner. After dinner, we gathered around her pool, and she handed us each a white tea candle to place on a floating flower. After lighting our candles and thinking about one thing we were thankful for that year, we each placed our candle on the water. I thought about how Jesus came to give us abundant life, and I was overwhelmed with gratitude for the many blessings I had experienced in the past year, including gratefulness for this community of people God has put in my life.

We stood around the pool, holding hands, watching the glimmering, floating candles meander around and mix together. On my right was my husband, Zane, who had survived intense hip-replacement surgery. He has a bleeding disorder, so it was a complicated procedure. On my left was my friend who was in the midst of battling a rapidly spreading cancer. Across from me stood a young, smiling, recently engaged couple. I don't know what everyone else was thinking because we all had different experiences, some heart-wrenching and some joy-filled, yet we stood together and gave thanks.

After a few minutes of silence, another friend prayed out loud to conclude our time. Music started playing, we released our hands, and I spent the evening celebrating the swell, abundant life Jesus gives to those who love Him. —JEANNIE BLACKMER

FAITH STEP: *Gather your family or friends this week for your own simple "Swell Life" party and have everyone share how Jesus has helped them live their life to the full.*

WEDNESDAY, DECEMBER 29

*His head and hair were white like wool, as white as snow,
and His eyes like a flame of fire. Revelation 1:14 (NKJV)*

I'M AN ENGLISH PROFESSOR, AND sometimes I just have to pause and take in the literary genius of the Bible, such as when I read the description of Jesus, the Son of Man, in Revelation 1. There's so much that's amazing, but if we just read that one verse—14—we see a snapshot of the whole package that He is: the Lion and the Lamb, and how we can't have one without the other.

John wrote that the Son of Man's "head and hair were white like wool, white as snow." Such comparisons are packed with layers of meaning. Wool—which comes from a lamb—keeps us warm. It wraps around us, blocking out the cold. And snow represents purity. Children whoop with joy at the sight. Snow comes to us softly in winter when everything is gray and dead, and it covers the barrenness. It smooths over any rough edges. It lends beauty and light to an otherwise dark, dull landscape.

Juxtapose that imagery with eyes that are "like a flame of fire." These are the bright gold eyes of the Lion. They see everything. Fire is fierce, and it refines, burning away every unclean thing. It lights the world and heats it and gives life. It cannot be hidden or contained.

Jesus defies any neat classification. He's whatever we need, whenever we need Him. He embodies truths that appear contradictory—the Lion and the Lamb; the man and the God for all seasons.
—GWEN FORD FAULKENBERRY

FAITH STEP: *Pick an attribute of Jesus from today's devotion that challenges or inspires you to think of Him in a more expansive way. Meditate on that attribute today. What does it tell you about God?*

THURSDAY, DECEMBER 30

Surely I am with you always, to the very end of the age. Matthew 28:20 (NIV)

AT THE END OF A long hallway, my bedroom is also my prayer place. Several days ago while I was praying, I heard pitiful crying coming from the living room. We'd had our new kitten, Wally, only a few days. Kevin and I had cuddled, coddled, and carried him around most of that time. When I heard his pathetic wails, I realized he thought I'd left him alone in our huge house. Opening the door of the bedroom, I called his name. On his stubby little legs, he came galloping down the hall and into my outstretched arms.

"Wally," I cooed, "I never left you alone. I was here all the time—you just couldn't see me."

How many times have I behaved exactly like Wally? When my daughter's husband abandoned her, I laid awake at night and worried about her kids. When I had conflicts with my boss, I looked for a new job. When health issues forced me to give up coffee, I became depressed. In every one of these crises, I acted as if Jesus had abandoned me. Instead of asking Him for help, I tried to manage life by my own wits (which is never a wise idea).

Despite my doubts and immaturity, Jesus got me through every crisis. Afterward, I was calm enough to hear His voice: *I'm here, Jeanette—I've been here the whole time. I would never, never leave you alone.*

Someday Wally will grow up. He'll realize I can be trusted to take care of him. May I also grow up, trusting Jesus even when I can't see Him. —JEANETTE LEVELLIE

FAITH STEP: *Find a photo of yourself. Now paste a picture of Jesus beside you in the photo as a reminder that He will never leave you alone.*

New Year's Eve, Friday, December 31

In the same way, after supper he took the cup, saying, "This is the new covenant in my blood, which is poured out for you." Luke 22:20 (NIV)

GETTING NEW THINGS—A NEW DRESS, a new piece of furniture, new car, new cellphone, new linens—is wonderful! I'm a big thrift shopper and welcome hand-me-downs, but I really enjoy new stuff. New things feel fresh, unsullied, exciting—with all the caché of being the latest and greatest. New is especially satisfying when I'm replacing something really old and icky and outdated.

Jesus is all about new. Among other things, *He* is the new covenant that does away with the old covenant and death penalty once and for all (Hebrews 8:13; 9:15). This is a breathtaking promise for those who believe. In Christ, we are also new creations—the old man is gone for good (2 Corinthians 5:17). Elsewhere in Scripture, Jesus's totally free, unconditional, and permanent newness is foretold. We're promised new beginnings, new hearts, new life, new strength. We're also told His mercies are new every morning.

This side of heaven, new things cost money. Sometimes a lot of money. However, all the newness Jesus offers us every day is completely free. For us, that is. But it cost our Savior His lifeblood, which He poured out for us willingly so that we could enjoy new life at no cost. —ISABELLA YOSUICO

FAITH STEP: *Are you holding onto something old and icky—some old sin or shame? Resolve to replace it with the pristine newness you have in Jesus! Discard an old item and replace it with something brand new to remind you of the newness available in Jesus.*

ABOUT THE AUTHORS

SUSANNA FOTH AUGHTMON is an author and humor writer in Idaho. She is the mother of three fantastic teenage boys, Jack, Will, and Addison. Susanna is also wife to Scott, a pastor and writer, who makes her laugh every day. Susanna's books include *Hope Sings* and *Queen of the Universe*. She loves to use Scripture and personal stories as a way of embracing God's grace and truth every day. Susanna often connects with her readers and fellow Christ followers through her blog, *Confessions of a Tired Supergirl*, her Facebook page, and speaking engagements.

JEANNIE BLACKMER is an author who lives in Boulder, Colorado. Her most recent books include *Talking to Jesus: A Fresh Perspective on Prayer* and *MomSense: A Common-Sense Guide to Confident Mothering*. She's been a freelance writer for more than thirty years and has worked in the publishing industry with a variety of authors on more than twenty-five books. She's also written numerous articles for magazines and blogs. She's passionate about using written words to encourage women in their relationships with Jesus. She loves chocolate (probably too much), scuba diving, beekeeping, a good inspirational story, and being outside as much as possible. She and her husband, Zane, have three adult sons. Find out more about Jeannie on her website at www.jeannieblackmer.com.

PAT BUTLER DYSON writes from her Gulf Coast hometown of Beaumont, Texas. A former English and special-education teacher, Pat is a freelance writer who has written for Guideposts publications for twenty-four years. She shares life with Jeff, her husband of thirty-eight years, who hammers away at the family-hardware stores and teaches business classes at Lamar

University. Parents of five children, Pat and Jeff recently welcomed two new grandbabies, Jameson and Blake, born a month apart. That makes *six* grandchildren, and all live in Beaumont! For the past ten years, Pat has found fulfillment volunteering at OASIS, a respite program for people with Alzheimer's or other cognitive or physical frailties. In the event that she's not writing, volunteering, or babysitting, Pat can be found reading, riding her bike, baking cookies, or scrunching sand between her toes on Galveston beach. She is delighted to be able to share slices of her life in *Mornings with Jesus*, and on prayerideas.org.

GWEN FORD FAULKENBERRY is an Ozark hillbilly. *Really*. That's the mascot of her hometown in the Arkansas mountains where she lives, teaches, writes, runs, plays music, bakes bread, and makes mischief of one kind or another. She's becoming quite a famous author. But you can call her Grace, Harper, Adelaide, and Stella's mom. Or Coach Faulkenberry's wife. That's what she's best known for. And she likes that just fine.

GRACE FOX writes at her little desk on the 48-foot sailboat she calls home. She and her husband, Gene, live in a marina on the Fraser River in Vancouver, British Columbia. They'll celebrate their thirty-ninth wedding anniversary in February. Grace loves connecting with people from other cultures. She trains church leaders in Asia and the Middle East, and she and Gene lead annual short-term mission teams to Eastern Europe. The author of nine books, Grace is also a devotional blogger and member of the writing team for First 5, the Bible study app produced by Proverbs 31 Ministries. She enjoys speaking at international women's events, walking, hosting marina neighbors and other guests on her boat-home, and spending time with her family—three grown kids and nine grandchildren. Connect with her at www.gracefox.com and www.fb.com/gracefox.author. Learn more about her work at www.gracefox.com/books.

HEIDI GAUL and her husband share a historic home with their furry family in Oregon's beautiful Willamette Valley. Heidi loves good food, good friends, and good books. When she's not busy with those passions, you'll probably find her hiking, gardening, or planning her next trip. Winner of the 2015 Cascade Award for devotionals, her work can be found in Guideposts' *Every Day with Jesus* and past years of *Mornings with Jesus*, and *Short and Sweet Takes the Fifth, plus many* devotionals for *The Upper Room*. Ten *Chicken Soup for the Soul* anthologies carry her stories. She enjoys leading workshops, mentoring fellow wordsmiths at writers' conferences and speaking to groups about discerning God's direction for our lives. Represented by Jim Hart of Hartline Literary Agency, her current project is *Broken Dreams and Detours: When God's Will Doesn't Match Your Plans*. She'd love to hear from you. Connect with her at www.HeidiGaul.com and www.Facebook.com/HeidiGaulAuthor.

SHARON HINCK has been a youth worker, a choreographer, a church organist, a speaker, and a teacher for writing conferences. Recently, she served as an adjunct professor for an MFA program in creative writing. One day she'll figure out what to be when she grows up. Meanwhile she treasures her roles as a wife, mom, grandmother, daughter, and friend. In addition to contributing to *Mornings with Jesus* for many years and doing freelance editing, she is busy writing novels, including a new fantasy series The Dancing Realms.

JEANETTE LEVELLIE of Paris, Illinois, has had a year of happy changes: her daughter and grandkids moved nearby, she adopted the ornery but lovable kitten Wally, and she's writing for Guideposts. Her goal in life is to introduce a million people to Jesus. Apart from that, she'd like to invent a house that never needs cleaning and surround herself with trees. Jeanette lived most of her life in California and spent her freshman year of high school on the tiny island of Saipan, near Guam. As a teenager, she aspired to sing opera and took three years of formal voice training. When God

ABOUT THE AUTHORS | 369

brought Pastor Kevin into Jeanette's life, her dreams enlarged. As a former history teacher and newspaper columnist, Jeanette is the author of five books and hundreds of articles, stories, and greeting cards. A popular humor and inspirational speaker, she offers her unique blend of laughter and encouragement to audiences of every flavor and size. When Jeanette isn't preparing messages or writing, she enjoys gardening, watching black-and-white movies with Kevin, and discovering new restaurants. She is the mother of two, grandma of three, and servant of three (cats). Find her splashes of hope and humor at www.jeanettelevellie.com.

 DIANNE NEAL MATTHEWS has enjoyed the privilege of sharing her faith journey with *Mornings with Jesus* readers since the 2013 edition. She is the author of four daily devotional books, including *The One Year Women of the Bible* and *Designed for Devotion: A 365-Day Journey from Genesis to Revelation* (a Selah Award winner). Dianne recently collaborated with Ron L. Deal on the book *Daily Encouragement for the Smart Stepfamily*. She has also published hundreds of articles, guest blog posts, newspaper features, stories for compilations, and one poem. She and her husband of forty-six years currently live in southwest Louisiana and have three children and four grandchildren. She loves to connect with readers through her Facebook author page or website www.DianneNealMatthews.com.

 CYNTHIA RUCHTI started her career in a chemistry lab, wrote and produced a scripted radio broadcast (slice of life scenes and devotional thoughts) for Christian radio, has written close to three dozen books, and serves as a literary agent, helping other people get their stories out to a reading world. In every endeavor, she's done the only thing she knows to do—say yes to Jesus. His quests are always unexpected, but the adventure is never a disappointment. Her books have garnered many industry awards, but her greatest joy is connecting with readers who have been touched, moved, or inspired by the words she's been given to share. The *Mornings with Jesus* readers are a true treasure for her, providing welcomed responses, and the gift of their prayers. Cynthia and her husband live in the heart of Wisconsin, close to their three children and six grandchildren. You can connect with Cynthia at cynthiaruchti.com or hemmedinhope.com.

PAMELA TOUSSAINT HOWARD is a native New Yorker who has lived and worked in Atlanta for ten years. After graduating from Fordham University with a degree in communications, Pamela followed in her dad's journalistic footsteps and became a women's magazine editor, then a trade newspaper reporter, and has now written or coauthored seven books by major publishers. Pamela also held the position of media spokesperson with the American Red Cross of Greater New York, and she served as an instructor trainer with the organization in Atlanta, Georgia. Pamela and her husband, Andrew, enjoy traveling, exercising together, and ministering to people in their neighborhood.

ISABELLA YOSUICO loves encouraging others with her everyday and epic life experiences, even while she's preaching to herself. Firmly in the "grace camp," Isabella is a recovering perfectionist who hopes that she and readers will forever grow in the experience of Christ's love, fullness, grace, peace, and utter sufficiency. She also longs for women to be their authentic selves, confident they're different by divine design. Isabella has been contributing to *Mornings with Jesus* since 2018. Her Bible study, *Embracing Life: Letting God Determine Your Destiny*, is aimed at helping women navigate challenging life events. With a master's in public relations and management, Isabella is also a "mompreneur" and longtime communications consultant. She lives life fully with husband, Ray, and sons, Pierce (the jock) and Isaac (the minister/musician), on Florida's Suncoast. Isabella enjoys having fun, including travel, cooking, writing, reading, running, arts and culture, random adventures, deep conversation, the beach, music and singing. Connect with Isabella at www.isabellayosuico.com, Instagram, Twitter, and Facebook.

Scripture Reference Index

Topical Index

A NOTE FROM THE EDITORS

WE HOPE YOU ENJOYED *Mornings with Jesus 2021*, published by the Books and Inspirational Media Division of Guideposts, a nonprofit organization that touches millions of lives every day through products and services that inspire, encourage, help you grow in your faith, and celebrate God's love.

Thank you for making a difference with your purchase of this book, which helps fund our many outreach programs to military personnel, prisons, hospitals, nursing homes, and educational institutions.

We also create many useful and uplifting online resources. Visit Guideposts.org to read true stories of hope and inspiration, access OurPrayer network, sign up for free newsletters, download free e-books, join our Facebook community, and follow our stimulating blogs.

You may purchase the 2022 edition of *Mornings with Jesus* anytime after July 2021. To order, visit Guideposts.org/Shop, call (1-800) 932-2145, or write to Guideposts, PO Box 5815, Harlan, Iowa 51593.

CPSIA information can be obtained
at www.ICGtesting.com
Printed in the USA
LVHW030700091220
673626LV00009B/77